P9-CME-596

GOODBYE, MY HAVANA

GOODBYE, MY HAVANA

THE LIFE AND TIMES OF A GRINGA IN REVOLUTIONARY CUBA

ANNA VELTFORT

REDWOOD PRESS
STANFORD, CALIFORNIA

STANFORD UNIVERSITY PRESS
Stanford, California

Goodbye, My Havana was originally published in Spanish in 2017 under the title *Adiós mi Habana* © 2017, Editorial Verbum.

Printed in Korea

Library of Congress Cataloging-in-Publication Data is available upon request.

ISBN 978-1-5036-1049-1 (paper)
ISBN 978-1-5036-1078-1 (electronic)

Designed by Anna Veltfort and Kevin Barrett Kane

TO STACY,

for her love, her wisdom and joy

TO SOPHIA,

our most sublime creation

CONTENTS

GOODBYE, MY HAVANA

CHAPTER 1

Havana Bay

HAVANA BAY
FEBRUARY 28, 1962—WE ENTERED HAVANA BAY AT DAWN & GLIDED PAST THE LIGHTHOUSE OF EL MORRO CASTLE. THE ONLY SOUND WAS THE SOFT SLAP-SLAP OF THE BAY'S WARM WATERS.

FOR A WEEK, THE FIVE OF US—ME (CONNIE), MY MOTHER LENORE & HER HUSBAND TED WITH THEIR KIDS NIKKI & KEVIN—HAD LIVED ON THE "FUNDADOR," A CUBAN CARGO SHIP, EN ROUTE TO HAVANA. BEFORE BOARDING THE SHIP IN VERACRUZ, WE'D SPENT FIVE ANXIOUS MONTHS IN MEXICO WAITING FOR OUR VISAS & FOR TED'S PROMISED INVITATION FROM THE CUBAN GOVERNMENT FOR HIM TO LIVE & WORK IN CUBA WITH HIS FAMILY.

FUNDADOR

THE SHIP DOCKED AT SIERRA MAESTRA TERMINAL & WE WAITED FOR SEVERAL HOURS FOR PERMISSION TO DISEMBARK. BUREAUCRATIC CHAOS CHOKED THE FLOW OF ALL OFFICIAL BUSINESS, BUT THE WEATHER WAS VERY PLEASANT. THIS WAS STILL HAVANA'S COOL SEASON & THE SKY WAS POSTCARD-PERFECT BLUE. WE WATCHED THE SCENE ON THE DOCK, WHICH WAS BUSY WITH ACTIVITY.
¡AY, MAMI RICA! ¡QUE BUENA TÚ ESTÁS!
BUT WHY ARE THOSE MEN HOLDING THEIR PENISES & STARING AT ME?
¡PSSSS!!!! ¡PSSSS!!!! ¡PSSSS!!!!

¡PSSSS!!!!
¡PSSSS!!!!
¡PSSSS!!!!
¡OYE RUBIA, MÁMAMELA!
THIS WAS THE SECOND TIME THAT MY MOTHER & I HAD STARTED LIFE ANEW IN A FOREIGN COUNTRY. TEN YEARS EARLIER, LENORE—THEN A SINGLE MOTHER—HAD DECIDED TO LEAVE HER NATIVE GERMANY & THE RUINS OF WORLD WAR II TO SEEK A NEW LIFE IN AMERICA. AS SHE LATER TOLD ME, HER LOVER AT THE TIME HAD REFUSED TO DIVORCE HIS WIFE & "GERMANY WASN'T BIG ENOUGH FOR THE BOTH OF US..."

TO AMERICA ON THE "S.S. ITALIA"

ITALIA

THE "ITALIA" WAS A PASSENGER SHIP WITH 1ST, 2ND, & 3RD CLASS ACCOMMODATIONS. WE WERE IN 3RD & SHARED A CABIN WITH TWO STRANGERS. I HAD BOARDED SCARED TO DEATH OF FALLING INTO THE OCEAN & DROWNING.

LENORE HAD SCRIMPED & SAVED FOR TWO YEARS & WADED THROUGH THE NECESSARY PAPERWORK. IN SEPTEMBER 1952, WE LEFT EVERYTHING I KNEW BEHIND. GROSSMAMA ANNA & GROSSPAPA JOSUÉ MET US IN HAMBURG TO SAY GOODBYE.

AFTER ABOUT TEN MINUTES ON THE SHIP, I WAS OFF & RUNNING WITH MY NEW ALLIES, ANOTHER GERMAN GIRL & HER LARGE SHAGGY DOG. I GOT INTO TERRIBLE TROUBLE FOR RUNNING OFF & DISAPPEARING.

BARF!

SEASICKNESS DEFEATED THE GROWNUPS, SO MY NEW FRIEND & I WERE FREE TO ROAM.

1ST CLASS ONLY
SHH... BE QUIET.

WE IMMEDIATELY DISOBEYED THE RULE THAT 3RD CLASS PASSENGERS HAD TO STAY IN THEIR SEGREGATED PART OF THE SHIP. WE CREPT PAST THE OFFICER GUARDS & EXPLORED THIS MYSTERIOUS CITY ON THE SEA.

LOOK AT THAT!
EW! DISGUSTING!

WE LEARNED ALL ABOUT THE SHIPBOARD BATHROOMS, MALE & FEMALE; THE BALLROOMS; THE BARBERSHOP & THE INFERNAL, DEAFENING ENGINE ROOM BELOW.

NEW YORK

WHERE ARE THE COLORED PEOPLE???

THE ONLY THING I HAD LOOKED FORWARD TO—THE RED, BLUE & GREEN PEOPLE THAT I IMAGINED & THAT THE "*AMI*" SOLDIERS HAD TOLD US ABOUT— WERE NOWHERE TO BE SEEN.

HURRY UP AND GET THAT LOOK OFF YOUR FACE!
ERIKA!
LENORECHEN!

WE CLEARED IMMIGRATION & CUSTOMS & THEN WERE MET BY ERIKA, A YOUNGER SISTER OF FRANCISKA, LENORE'S CHILDHOOD FRIEND. HER FAMILY HAD ESCAPED NAZI GERMANY JUST IN TIME. ERIKA & HER HUSBAND HAD SETTLED FOR NOW IN NEW YORK, BEFORE MOVING TO ISRAEL.

AFTER MAKING ARRANGEMENTS, MY MOTHER & I LEFT FOR ARLINGTON, VIRGINIA, TO STAY AT THE HOME OF MY MOTHER'S FRIENDS, THE WINSLOWS, AN AMERICAN COUPLE WHO'D BEEN STATIONED IN DARMSTADT BY THE STATE DEPARTMENT TO RUN A DE-NAZIFICATION PROGRAM. THEY HAD INVITED US TO STAY IN THEIR FINE HOUSE WHILE LENORE PLANNED HER NEXT MOVE. HERE I DISCOVERED A HEAVENLY AMERICAN SUBSTANCE—PEANUT BUTTER!

MMMM!!!
SKIPPY
WHAT'S THE MATTER WITH YOU, YOU STUPID CHILD?
TRA-LA-LA!

ONE EVENING SOMETHING DEEPLY DISTURBING HAPPENED. I WAS TOLD I MUST SING & BEG DOOR-TO-DOOR FROM PERFECT STRANGERS, WHILE WEARING FEATHERS ON MY HEAD. TO DISOBEY WAS NOT AN OPTION. I'D NEVER HEARD OF HALLOWEEN & ALMOST DIED OF EMBARRASSMENT.

TED VELTFORT, LENORE'S NEW BOYFRIEND
WE SETTLED IN CALIFORNIA & TWO YEARS AFTER ARRIVING IN AMERICA, LENORE BEGAN SEEING TED, HER NEW AMERICAN BOYFRIEND. HE QUICKLY DISCOVERED THAT LENORE WAS CLUELESS IN THE KITCHEN, SO HE BOUGHT HER A COOKBOOK & SET OUT TO EDUCATE HER IN MORE WAYS THAN ONE...
I'VE BROUGHT YOU SOMETHING. NO ONE CAN LIVE WITHOUT A RADIO!
HERE'S DINNER!
OH, BY THE WAY... I HAVE SOMETHING TO TELL YOU— I'M A COMMUNIST.
QUATSCH! I'LL KNOCK THAT RUBBISH OUT OF HIS HEAD.
A FEW MONTHS LATER...
ACH, CORNELIA, GUESS WHAT WE DID TODAY?!
TED & I GOT MARRIED THIS MORNING! ISN'T IT WONDERFUL? HA! HA!!
OH NO! DOES THAT MEAN THIS ONE'LL NEVER LEAVE?

LENORE IGNORED MY LACK OF ENTHUSIASM— WE CERTAINLY NEVER TALKED ABOUT IT— & HAPPILY FORGED AHEAD WITH HER NEW LIFE. TED WAS ALMOST PENNILESS, SO THERE WAS NO HONEYMOON. HE EKED OUT A LIVING FIXING RADIOS IN HIS GARAGE, HAVING BEEN BLACKLISTED AS A POLITICAL LEFTIST & REJECTED BY ALL THE ELECTRONICS FIRMS THAT MIGHT OTHERWISE HAVE EMPLOYED HIM.

AFTER TED & LENORE GOT MARRIED, TED FINALLY GOT A REAL JOB. HE DECIDED THEY NEEDED A BIGGER PLACE TO LIVE—NOT IN THE VALLEY, WHICH WAS TOO CROWDED—BUT SOMEWHERE IN THE HILLS, AS HE'D LIVED BEFORE MARRYING LENORE. THEY SCRAPED TOGETHER THE MONEY TO RENT A TWO-STORY HOUSE IN THE LOS ALTOS HILLS...

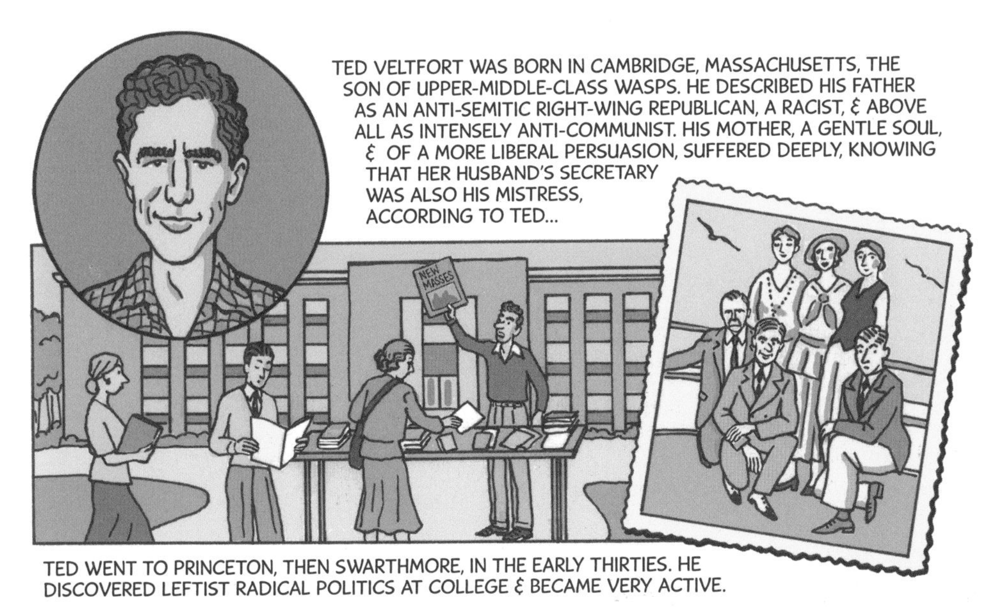

TED VELTFORT WAS BORN IN CAMBRIDGE, MASSACHUSETTS, THE SON OF UPPER-MIDDLE-CLASS WASPS. HE DESCRIBED HIS FATHER AS AN ANTI-SEMITIC RIGHT-WING REPUBLICAN, A RACIST, & ABOVE ALL AS INTENSELY ANTI-COMMUNIST. HIS MOTHER, A GENTLE SOUL, & OF A MORE LIBERAL PERSUASION, SUFFERED DEEPLY, KNOWING THAT HER HUSBAND'S SECRETARY WAS ALSO HIS MISTRESS, ACCORDING TO TED...
NEW MASSES
TED WENT TO PRINCETON, THEN SWARTHMORE, IN THE EARLY THIRTIES. HE DISCOVERED LEFTIST RADICAL POLITICS AT COLLEGE & BECAME VERY ACTIVE.

AT PRINCETON, STUDENTS WERE EXPECTED TO ATTEND RELIGIOUS SERVICES. A NUMBER OF AGNOSTICS & OTHERS FORMED AN ALTERNATIVE STUDY GROUP & DISCUSSED ISSUES OF THE DAY, ESPECIALLY POLITICS. ONE OF THEIR ADVISORS WAS ALBERT EINSTEIN.

DAILY WORKER
They Murdered Hundreds in Guernica
FASCIST BOMBERS
IN 1936, WHEN HE WAS 21, THE SPANISH CIVIL WAR BROKE OUT. FRANCO & HIS GENERALS ATTACKED THE SPANISH REPUBLIC.

SAVE SPAIN
SUPPORT THE INTERNATIONAL BRIGADES
YOUNG COMMUNIST LEAGUE

ESPAGNE

TED WAS AMONG THE 3,000 OR SO YOUNG AMERICANS WHO VOLUNTEERED IN RESPONSE TO THE REPUBLIC'S CRY FOR HELP. THE USA & THE REST OF EUROPE ABANDONED SPAIN. THE MAIN COUNTRY TO STEP UP WAS THE SOVIET UNION. HE MADE HIS WAY TO FRANCE & WALKED OVER THE MOUNTAINS TO SPAIN, WHERE HE SOON BECAME AN AMBULANCE DRIVER ON THE FRONT LINES.

HE SAW ACTION ON THE ARAGON FRONT & AT THE DOOMED BATTLE OF TERUEL.
THE COMMUNISTS ARE THE ONLY ONES WHO KNOW HOW TO GET THINGS DONE!
TED DEVELOPED AN IRONCLAD LOYALTY TO & ADMIRATION FOR THE SOVIET GOVERNMENT & THE SPANISH COMMUNISTS. HE LOATHED THE ANARCHISTS & THE LIBERALS.

LA PASIONARIA
THE REPUBLICANS WERE DEFEATED, FASCISM TRIUMPHED, & SURVIVORS FROM THE INTERNATIONAL BRIGADES WERE SENT HOME AS HEROES BY A GRATEFUL BUT SOON-TO-BE-DEFEATED REPUBLICAN GOVERNMENT IN THE FALL OF 1938...

HE RETURNED TO THE USA, ONE OF THOSE FORTUNATE TO BE ALIVE. HE WENT BACK TO COLLEGE, WHERE HE BECAME ACTIVE IN A COMMUNIST YOUTH GROUP. WHEN WWII BROKE OUT, HE WAS DRAFTED & SERVED IN THE SIGNAL CORPS AS A RADIO TECHNICIAN. BUT HE NEVER SERVED ABROAD, TAINTED AS AN UNTRUSTWORTHY "PREMATURE ANTI-FASCIST."

U.S. ARMY SIGNAL CORP.

HE MARRIED HELENE RANK—WHO WAS JEWISH—& THIS WAS THE LAST STRAW FOR HIS FATHER & STEPMOTHER. TED'S MOTHER HAD DIED SHORTLY AFTER FILING FOR DIVORCE. TED BECAME AN OUTCAST FROM HIS FAMILY, A RIFT THAT NEVER HEALED.

HELENE, THE DAUGHTER OF SIGMUND FREUD'S COLLABORATOR OTTO RANK, WAS A CHILD PSYCHOLOGIST. SHE & TED HAD TWO DAUGHTERS, DANYA & SUZY, BUT IN 1949 HELENE DIVORCED HIM. TED MOVED INTO A SHACK IN THE WOODS. HERE HE FIXED RADIOS OUT OF HIS GARAGE. COLD WAR HYSTERIA WAS IN FULL SWING & NO ONE WOULD HIRE A RED.

WE'LL HUNT DOWN EVERY LAST ONE!
THE RED MENACE
SUNDAY NEWS
10¢
FINAL
N. KOREA REDS DECLARE WAR
Invade South by Land an
ROSENBERGS DIE
PICTORIAL
Pair Executed for Atom Spying
I HAVE A LIST OF HUNDREDS OF COMMUNISTS!

TED FINALLY FOUND WORK AS AN ELECTRONICS ENGINEER, BUT THAT WAS SHORT-LIVED BECAUSE THE FIRM GOT A MILITARY CONTRACT WHICH REQUIRED SECURITY CLEARANCE FOR ALL EMPLOYEES. HE CHANGED JOBS OFTEN, JUST ONE JUMP AHEAD OF THE INVESTIGATORS. WE MOVED FROM HOUSE TO HOUSE.

CORNELIA, COME DOWNSTAIRS & MEET OUR VISITORS, YOUR NEW SISTERS!
YOU SHOULD CALL HIM DADDY, CORNELIA.
I DON'T HAVE TO!
BEHAVE YOURSELF! I DON'T LIKE YOUR ATTITUDE!
CHEERIOS

NO BACK TALK! I'M PAYING THE BILLS, & SHE'D BETTER OBEY!
TO SCHOOL IN THE 4TH GRADE

ANOTHER JOB, ANOTHER MOVE. BUT WE HAD TO LEAVE THE HILLY WOODS. TO TED'S DISGUST, WE MOVED RIGHT INTO A CITY—THIS TIME BERKELEY—IN THE FLATLANDS OF VIRGINIA STREET. OUR HOUSE WAS ACROSS THE STREET FROM MY NEXT SCHOOL. BEFORE STARTING, I VOWED TO FREE MYSELF OF MY GERMAN NAME & FIND AN ACCEPTABLY AMERICAN ONE. I WON THAT BATTLE.

I'M SICK OF BEING CALLED CORNY CORNCOB. I'M CHANGING MY NAME TO CONNIE.
2008
PLEASE DON'T CALL ME CORNELIA AGAIN.

RIGHT ABOUT THEN, LENORE DISCOVERED SHE WAS PREGNANT.

OH MY GOD, TEDDY! THE DIAPHRAGM DIDN'T WORK!
THE DOCTOR'S CONFIRMED IT!
SHIT! I JUST SPENT SO MUCH MONEY ON THE CHEVY! WE CAN'T AFFORD A BABY!

NIKKI WAS A SERIOUS & COMPLICATED BABY. I ADORED HER PASSIONATELY. SHE NEEDED A SPECIAL LEG BRACE THAT FORCED HER TO WALK LIKE A TURTLE. SHE BECAME THE CENTER OF OUR HOME LIFE, BUT THERE WAS ALSO PLENTY OF TENSION—OVER MONEY, POLITICS, TED'S DRINKING & ME.

HA! THE CHILD LOOKS JUST LIKE WINSTON CHURCHILL.

LENORE FILED THE PAPERS TO BECOME AN AMERICAN CITIZEN, BUT SOON THE FBI BEGAN INVESTIGATING. MCCARTHYISM WAS ALIVE & WELL. TED WAS SUSPECT—NOT ONLY FOR JOINING THE ABRAHAM LINCOLN BRIGADE IN SPAIN BUT AS A MEMBER OF THE COMMUNIST PARTY IN THE THIRTIES AND FORTIES—SO HE DREW THE HEAT OF HOOVER'S AGENTS. I BEGAN TO TAKE NOTICE OF THE POLITICAL TURBULENCE THAT PREOCCUPIED TED & NOW LENORE AS WELL.

IS THEODORE VELTFORT HOME? WE'D LIKE TO SPEAK WITH HIM.

REMEMBER—NEVER ANSWER ANY QUESTIONS!

NIGHTS & WEEKENDS, I BABYSAT MY DARLING NIKKI WHILE TED & LENORE WENT TO POLITICAL MEETINGS OR TO SOCIALIZE WITH FRIENDS—OR HAD THEIR LOUD, SCREAMING FIGHTS.

THAT WAS A VICIOUS THING TO SAY! UNFORGIVABLE!

EL CERRITO & BABY KEVIN

LENORE'S BIRTH CONTROL SLIPPED AGAIN, & UNEXPECTANTLY ANOTHER BABY WAS ON THE WAY. KEVIN ARRIVED IN THE SPRING OF '58, JUST IN TIME TO START LIFE IN A NEW HOUSE. TED & LENORE DECIDED THEY COULD MANAGE BUYING A HOME, IN THE HILLS OF EL CERRITO, ACROSS FROM SAN FRANCISCO IN THE NORTHERN EAST BAY. TED WAS MAKING GOOD MONEY NOW, WORKING FOR WILLIAM SHOCKLEY, A CO-INVENTOR OF THE TRANSISTOR, NOBEL PRIZE WINNER & NOTORIOUS RACIST.

M-M-M..!
OUR FAVORITE FOOD—THE BLACKBERRIES THAT GREW AT THE BOTTOM OF THE HILL.

WAKE UP! WAKE UP!
LITTLE NIKKI BEGAN TO HAVE AWFUL NIGHTMARES WITH FEVERS. LENORE WOULD SHAKE HER VIOLENTLY TO TRY TO SNAP HER OUT OF IT.

SIGH. SHE'S SUCH A DIFFICULT CHILD. SHE'S THE INTELLIGENT ONE, NOT BEAUTIFUL LIKE OUR KEVIN.

OH, GOD! SHE'S BURNING UP!
ONCE HER FEVER WAS SO HIGH, THAT TED & LENORE PUT HER INTO THE TUB FILLED WITH ICE. SHE SCREAMED DELIRIOUSLY, BUT I COULDN'T DO A THING...

I BECAME NIKKI'S PROTECTOR. SHE LEARNED TO SNEAK INTO MY BED WHEN HER NIGHTMARES WOKE HER IN THE MIDDLE OF THE NIGHT.

Z-Z-Z!!!

GET AWAY FROM ME, YOU AWFUL WITCH!!! I HATE YOU!!! I HATE YOU!!! I HATE YOU!!!

BUT I COULDN'T PROTECT HER FROM THE WITCH IN HER NIGHTMARES. SHE HATED THE WITCH, & WAS TERRIFIED OF HER.

SOON I STARTED HAVING A RECURRING DREAM OF MY OWN ABOUT THAT WITCH, FOR MAYBE A YEAR.
LATE AT NIGHT, I MOWED HER DOWN, RAN HER OVER... AGAIN & AGAIN...

TED GAVE LENORE COMMUNIST PARTY PAMPHLETS & BOOKS TO READ. HE DREW HER INTO A COMMUNITY UNDER SIEGE. MANY WERE EX-PARTY MEMBERS WHO HAD QUIT AFTER KHRUSHCHEV'S 1953 SPEECH WITH REVELATIONS OF STALIN'S CRIMES & NOW WERE LABELED "FELLOW TRAVELERS."

ALL RIGHT EVERYBODY! IT'S TIME TO ORGANIZE! WE'RE GOING TO CREATE A SERIES OF FUNDRAISERS & DEFEND THE POWELLS!
LET'S HAVE AN AUCTION! THAT'LL RAISE POTS OF MONEY!

TWO WOMEN IN THIS CIRCLE IMPRESSED ME DEEPLY: MARGE FRANTZ & DECCA TRUEHAFT. MARGE SPEARHEADED THE DEFENSE FOR JOHN & SYLVIA POWELL, TWO JOURNALISTS ACCUSED BY THE EISENHOWER GOVERNMENT OF TREASON & SEDITION. THEY WERE INDICTED IN 1956. MARGE & HER FAMILY WERE OUR NEIGHBORS & ALSO MY BEST BABYSITTING CLIENTS.

Powell Trial Opens---
Reds in Magazine Charged
By Elmont Waite
John W. Powell, his wife Sylvia and Julian Schuman "conspired to publish false statements" to aid Red armies and hamper American forces in Ko-
ALL RIGHT DARLING, YOU CAN WRITE THESE LABELS NOW.
HERE'S THE PRICE LIST FOR EACH ITEM ON THE TABLE.
TELL ME ABOUT YOUR SISTER UNITY...
TELL ME ABOUT SPAIN WHEN YOU RAN AWAY TO THE SPANISH CIVIL WAR!
MARGE & DECCA LET ME PARTICIPATE IN THE PREPARATIONS FOR THE AUCTION. I DRANK IN THEIR CONVERSATIONS, THRILLED TO BE INSIDE THEIR MAGIC CIRCLE.

THE POWELLS WERE AN AMERICAN COUPLE WHO FOR MANY YEARS HAD WORKED & LIVED IN CHINA, WHERE THEY PUBLISHED AN ENGLISH LANGUAGE JOURNAL, "THE CHINA MONTHLY REVIEW." THERE THEY'D ACCUSED THE AMERICAN GOVERNMENT OF GERM WARFARE DURING THE KOREAN WAR.

UPON THEIR RETURN TO THE STATES IN 1950, THE GOVERNMENT HOUNDED THEM MERCILESSLY. THEY FACED TRIAL IN '59 & WERE CONSTANTLY IN THE PAPERS. THEY WERE THREATENED WITH DECADES BEHIND BARS & AT FIRST HAD NO POLITICAL FRIENDS, NO SUPPORT. THE ATMOSPHERE WAS REMINISCENT OF THE ROSENBERG TRIAL.

DECCA TRUEHAFT, A.K.A. JESSICA MITFORD, WAS ONE OF MARGE'S CLOSEST FRIENDS. SHE PLAYED A BIG ROLE IN SOLIDARITY EVENTS. ONE OF THE FAMOUS BRITISH MITFORD SISTERS, SHE WAS THE FAMILY COMMUNIST, WHILE TWO OF HER SISTERS WERE NOTORIOUS FASCISTS. DIANA HAD BEEN MARRIED, IN THE BERLIN HOME OF JOSEPH GOEBBELS, TO THE HEAD OF THE BRITISH UNION OF FASCISTS, OSWALD MOSLEY. ANOTHER SISTER, UNITY, HAD BEEN A PERSONAL FRIEND OF ADOLF HITLER.

TED BEGAN TO FOCUS ON SOMETHING ELSE IN THE NEWS. TWO OF HIS PARTY FRIENDS FROM THE BAY AREA WERE LIVING & WORKING IN CUBA, WHERE A REVOLUTIONARY MOVEMENT HAD JUST COME TO POWER ON JANUARY 1, 1959. THEY URGED TED TO JOIN THEM.

TED, YOU'D LOVE IT HERE. WE CAN HELP YOU GET INVITED.
LENORECHEN— I'VE GOT NEWS FOR YOU! I WANT TO MOVE TO CUBA! LIONEL & J.P. ARE THERE ALREADY!
OH, TEDDY, YOU'RE CRAZY! I LOVE LIVING HERE. THIS IS MY COUNTRY NOW!
TED'S LATEST JOB INVOLVED WORKING ON A CONTRACT FOR COMMUNICATIONS SYSTEMS FOR THE MILITARY & GOVERNMENT ELITE IN A POST-NUCLEAR USA. HE DESPAIRED & HATED HIS JOB.

WHILE TED'S ATTENTION TURNED TO CUBA, MINE TURNED TO SOCIAL JUSTICE & THE CIVIL RIGHTS MOVEMENT UNDERWAY IN THE SOUTH. MY SUNDAY SCHOOL TEACHER, MRS. RIBERA (I BRIEFLY REBELLED & JOINED THE UNITARIAN CHURCH) WAS A PASSIONATE SUPPORTER OF THE LUNCH-COUNTER SIT-INS IN GREENSBORO & OF THE STUDENTS IN LITTLE ROCK CONFRONTING SEGREGATION. WITH HER INFLUENCE & THE MUSIC OF PAUL ROBESON, PETE SEEGER & OTHERS AT TED & LENORE'S POLITICAL EVENTS, I BECAME CONSUMED BY THE DESIRE TO FIGHT INJUSTICE, TOO.

MRS. RIBERA, WHAT CAN I DO? MY PARENTS WON'T LET ME GO TO THE SOUTH. I'M ONLY 14.
JOIN THE NAACP! THEY ACCEPT WHITE PEOPLE. YOU CAN PICKET AT WOOLWORTH'S DEPT. STORE.
WOOLWORTH CO.
JIM CROW MUST GO!
...SO I DID JOIN, THE ONLY WHITE KID IN A GROUP OF YOUNG ADULT BLACKS. WE PICKETED WOOLWORTH'S IN THE EAST BAY. MY HOME ECONOMICS TEACHER SAW ME & GAVE ME A D IN HER CLASS.

THE BAY OF PIGS INVASION
APRIL 17, 1961—COUNTERREVOLUTIONARY FORCES INVADE CUBA! WE HUNKERED DOWN IN FRONT OF OUR TV FOR FOUR DAYS UNTIL THE CUBAN REVOLUTIONARY GOVERNMENT HAD PREVAILED, DEFEATING THE INVADERS.
DIRTY FASCIST BASTARDS!
ANTI-CASTRO UNITS LAND IN CUBA; REPORT FIGHTING AT BEACHHEAD; RUSK SAYS U. S. WON'T INTERVENE
TUESDAY, APRIL 18, 1961
A Flood of Revolution Reports
Castro Says He'll Win; Rebels Claim Advance
Biggest Landings 'Still To Come'---Key Battle Expected Within Hours
Castro Jets Attack Rebels
Exiles Cite Losses; Bomb Raid Reported
¡LA LUCHA CONTINÚA!
I'M GOING TO CUBA! IF YOU WANT TO STAY WITH ME, YOU'LL HAVE TO COME ALONG!
WHAT ABOUT THE CHILDREN?
THE REVOLUTION WILL TAKE CARE OF THEM!
IF WE'RE GOING TO CUBA, YOU'LL HAVE TO ADOPT CONNIE FIRST!
Castro Claims Rebels Wiped Out, War Ended
Kennedy Calls In Top
LENORE AND HER MOTHER EXCHANGED ANGRY, ANXIOUS LETTERS.
"...There is no other course for Ted. This is what he must do at this point. He is frustrated and unhappy, and if I were to try to stop him from going, I would ruin our marriage. I am not very courageous or adventurous at all. I am most inclined to have a home for a lifetime, a quiet life after all the upheavals and changes I have experienced in my life. But my place is with my husband who supports us all, and I can't make him work at something he hates, just so I can have a comfortable and carefree life... Please don't discuss or tell anyone our plans, please. It can really hurt us seriously. Burn this letter..."

THE HUAC PROTESTS AT SAN FRANCISCO CITY HALL

MARGE FRANTZ'S HUSBAND LAURENT WAS A LABOR LAWYER WHO'D BEEN SUMMONED TO TESTIFY IN COURT BEFORE THE HUAC, THE HOUSE UN-AMERICAN ACTIVITIES COMMITTEE. FOR THREE DAYS IN 1960—MAY 12, 13, 14—MARGE HELPED ORGANIZE THE PICKET LINE AT SAN FRANCISCO CITY HALL. THE HAUAC HAD BEEN PERSECUTING LEFTISTS IN EVERY PROFESSION, ALL OVER THE COUNTRY. TO THE COMMITTEE'S SURPRISE, THEY WERE MET WITH INTENSE PUBLIC OPPOSITION. MARGE URGED ME TO GO.

San Francisco Chronicle

THE VOICE OF THE WEST

BATTLE OF CITY HALL

400 Cops Fight Student Crowd

MAY 12
DEFEND THE BILL OF RIGHTS
FREE SPEECH
PROTECT OUR TEACHERS FROM INTIMIDATION
PRESERVE FREEDOM ABOLISH HUAC
FREE SPEECH PROTECT OUR LIBERTY

THE NEXT DAY, ALL HELL BROKE LOOSE WHEN THE POLICE ATTACKED THE PROTESTERS.

MAY 13

MAY 14

DID THEY WASH YOU DOWN THE STAIRS, BILLY BOY, BILLY BOY? DID THEY WASH YOU DOWN THE STAIRS, CHARMING BILLY?

YES THEY WASHED ME DOWN THE STAIRS, AND THEY REARRANGED MY HAIR WITH A CLUB IN THE CITY HALL ROTUNDA!

PROTECT CIVIL LIBERTIES ABOLISH HUAC

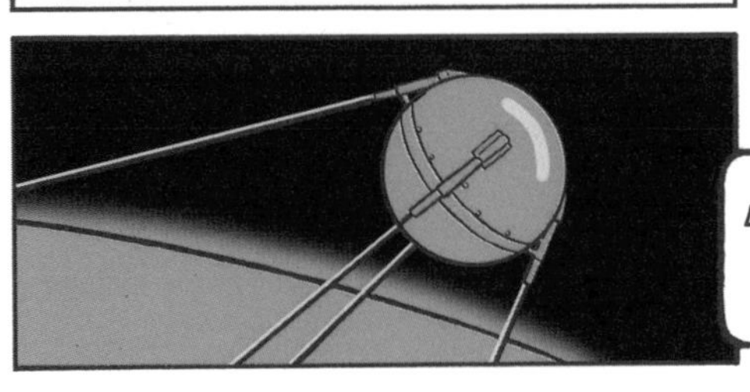

MEANWHILE, EVER SINCE THE USSR'S LAUNCH OF THE FIRST SATELLITE IN '57, AMERICANS WERE FEVERISHLY COMPETING WITH THE SOVIETS.

Man Enters Space

Soviet Officer Orbits Globe In 5-Ton Ship

Maximum Height Reached Reported As 188 Miles

'So Close, Yet So Far,' Sighs Cape ... Hoped

VON BRAUN'S REACTION

To Keep Up, U.S. Must Run Like

I WAS 15 NOW, & THRILLED TO PLAY A PART. BUT IT WAS TO BE MY LAST PARTICIPATION IN THE RADICAL POLITICS OF THE 1960S IN THE USA. IN THE SUMMER OF 1961, WE LEFT OUR LIFE IN CALIFORNIA & EMBARKED ON ANOTHER ONE, ON ANOTHER PLANET, FAR, FAR AWAY...

MEXICO

WHAT DO I DO IF HE'S NOT THERE..?
LENORE SENT ME TO GERMANY TO SAY GOODBYE TO HER MOTHER & BROTHER. I WAS TO JOIN LENORE & FAMILY IN MEXICO CITY TO WAIT FOR OUR VISAS TO CUBA. SHE SENT ME A POSTCARD PROMISING THAT TED WOULD PICK ME UP AT THE AIRPORT. TED, LENORE & THE TWO CHILDREN WOULD DRIVE FROM CALIFORNIA TO JALAPA IN THE STATE OF VERACRUZ. I HOPED THEY'D MAKE IT IN TIME.

TED DID SHOW UP & THE NEXT DAY HE DROVE US TO JALAPA IN THE MOUNTAINS TO MEET UP WITH THE OTHERS.

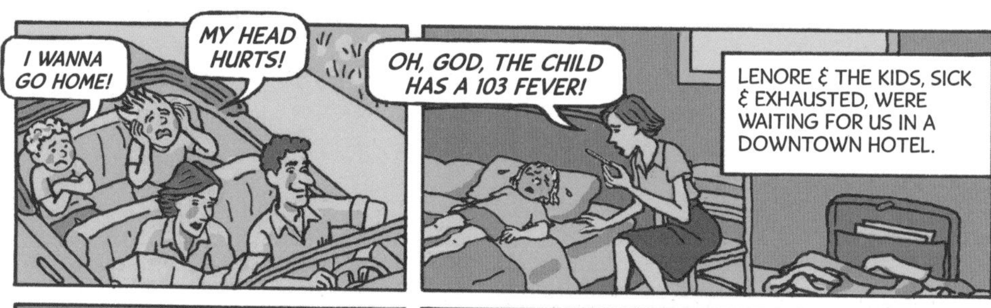
I WANNA GO HOME!
MY HEAD HURTS!
OH, GOD, THE CHILD HAS A 103 FEVER!
LENORE & THE KIDS, SICK & EXHAUSTED, WERE WAITING FOR US IN A DOWNTOWN HOTEL.

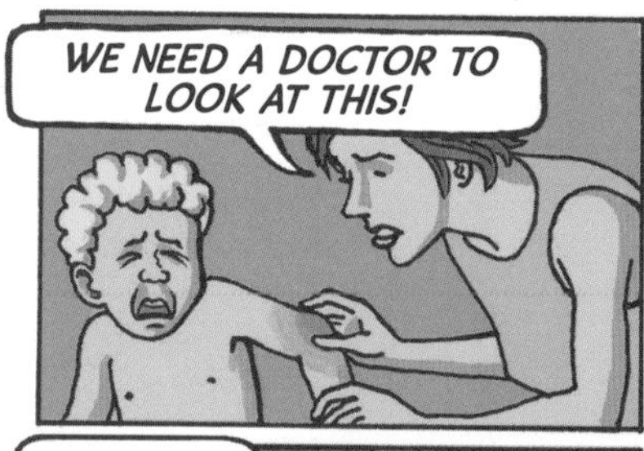
WE NEED A DOCTOR TO LOOK AT THIS!

I MISSED YOU SO MUCH!

EVERY DAY STARTED WITH A RUN TO THE BAKERY FOR SWEET ROLLS & FRUIT BOUGHT FROM AN INDIAN WOMAN ON THE CORNER. WE ATE IN OUR TWO DARK HOTEL ROOMS.

I CALLED THE CUBAN CONSULATE IN VERACRUZ. THEY'VE NO NEWS AT ALL.
IT'S BEEN THREE WEEKS, *HOW LONG CAN THOSE DAMN VISAS TAKE?*
WE HAD SUPPER EVERY NIGHT IN A STUDENT DIVE & GOT SICK OFTEN.
WE'LL BE BACK LATE. MAKE SURE THEY'RE IN BED BY 8 PM.
AT NIGHT LENORE & TED EXPLORED THE TOWN & WENT TO CONCERTS.

LUCKILY FOR US, AN AMERICAN FAMILY, OLD FRIENDS OF TED'S, WITH A BOY A BIT OLDER THAN NIKKI, LIVED IN JALAPA & LENT US THEIR APARTMENT FOR A MONTH. SURELY WE'D BE OUT OF THERE LONG BEFORE THEIR RETURN... ALAS, WE WOUND UP WAITING FOR FIVE INCREASINGLY DESPERATE MONTHS, THE LAST ONES IN PRETTY SEEDY HOTELS.

NIKKI SHOULD BE IN SCHOOL. I'M GOING TO ENROLL HER IN PAUL'S SCHOOL.
SHE CAN GO WITH HIM.
NIKKI KNEW NOT A WORD OF SPANISH...
¡MI HIJA NIKKI!
¡AY, MIRA QUE GÜERITA MAS LINDA!
...HER NEW TEACHER NOT A WORD OF ENGLISH.

I NEED TO MAKE PEE PEE!
THE FIRST DAY ENDED BADLY.
NO SABEMOS QUE PROBLEMA TIENE...
ACH! YOU STUPID CHILD!
MOMMY, MY PANTIES!
THE TEACHER BROUGHT HER "HOME."

THE TEACHERS DECIDED TO SEGREGATE PAUL & NIKKI AT LUNCHTIME FROM THE LOCAL KIDS & MADE THEM EAT EVERYDAY BY THEMSELVES IN ONE OF THE EMPTY CLASSROOMS.

¡GRINGOS DE MIERDA!
¡QUE FEOS SON!
¡ESTÚPIDOS! ¡NO SABEN HABLAR!

MANY YEARS LATER PAUL TOLD ME IT WAS THE MOST HUMILIATING EXPERIENCE OF HIS CHILDHOOD.

TO HAVANA ON THE "FUNDADOR"

WE WERE OFF TO SEA AT LAST! CONVENIENTLY FOR US, THE FIRST MATE HAD DEFECTED IN TAMPICO, SO WE HAD A CABIN, THE SIZE OF A LARGE ELEVATOR CAR, FOR THE FIVE OF US TO SHARE. THE TRIP SHOULD HAVE TAKEN NO MORE THAN FOUR DAYS, BUT THAT'S NOT WHAT HAPPENED.

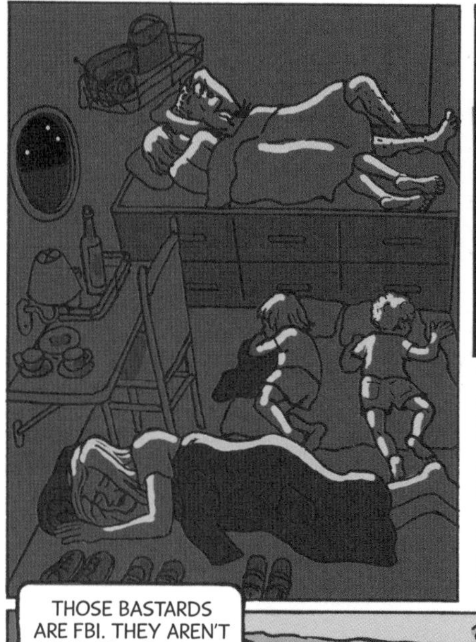

WITH MUCH RELIEF, WE SCRAMBLED ABOARD. BUT OUR SHIP DIDN'T HEAD STRAIGHT FOR CUBA. THE CAPTAIN HAD RECEIVED AN ORDER TO HEAD FOR TAMPICO, MEXICO, INSTEAD, TO PICK UP ADDITIONAL CARGO. THAT NIGHT WE TURNED NORTH & SAILED UP THE COAST.

ON OUR SECOND DAY IN THE PORT OF TAMPICO, A COUPLE OF MEN IN SUITS ARRIVED & INVITED US TO DISEMBARK FOR DRINKS & DINNER.

THOSE BASTARDS ARE FBI. THEY AREN'T ALLOWED TO BOARD.
WE'RE NOT GETTING OFF THIS SHIP UNTIL HAVANA!
MOMMY I'M BORED!
I'M HOT!

WE STAYED PUT & TENSIONS ROSE. MEANWHILE, ON THE SEASIDE OF THE SHIP, MEXICAN WOMEN WOULD APPROACH IN SMALL BOATS, OFFERING THEMSELVES OR THEIR CHILDREN TO THE SAILORS.

LOOK! IT'S A GRINGO BABY!
YOU CAN HAVE IT FOR ONLY $80!

THE SHIP HAD A CREW OF 20 MEN. WE INTERACTED MAINLY WITH THE OFFICERS & SHARED THEIR MESS ROOM FOR ALL OUR MEALS. THEY WERE KIND & FRIENDLY, CURIOUS ABOUT THEIR ODD PASSENGERS. THE NIGHTS IN OUR CABIN WERE HELL, BUT THE DAYS ON DECK WERE MORE SERENE.

WHAT DID YOU DO BEFORE YOU BECAME AN INSTRUCTOR?
I FOUGHT IN THE REBEL ARMY & BEFORE THAT—A FACTORY WORKER. *¡SOY REVOLUCIONARIO!*
COMPAÑE
O DE ESTUDIOS
2pm-4pm
Patria o Muerte!

MIGUEL WAS THE POLITICAL COMMISSAR, *"EL INSTRUCTOR REVOLUCIONARIO."* EVERY SHIP IN THE CUBAN MERCHANT MARINE HAD ONE ON BOARD. HE WAS EARNEST, EAGER & POLITE.

LOOK! I CAN SEE THE LIGHTS!

A THIN SHORELINE GRADUALLY CAME INTO VIEW IN THE EARLY DAWN. WE TRAVELED OVER THE WARM, BLACK, SILENT WATER ALONG THE COAST, VISIBLE FIRST AS A GRAY SMUDGE ON THE HORIZON, THEN WITH RECOGNIZABLE SHAPES & TWINKLY LIGHTS.

NOW IN HAVANA, WE FINALLY DISEMBARKED & SAID GOODBYE TO OUR CREW & HOSTS. WE WERE MET BY OLD FRIENDS OF TED'S FROM CALIFORNIA WHO LIVED & WORKED THERE AS FOREIGN TECHNICIANS. ALSO AT THE DOCK WERE TWO FRIENDLY MEN WHO RUSHED UP & INVITED US INTO THEIR CAR & A TAXI. ONE WAS A CUBAN & THE OTHER WAS ROBERT WALDER, AN AMERICAN EX-PAT WHO TURNED OUT TO BE TED'S NEW BOSS, THE HEAD OF THE DEPARTAMENTO DE TECNOLOGÍA INDUSTRIAL DE JUCEPLAN.

ADUANA
TED! LENORE! YOU MADE IT!
WELCOME, COMRADE TED!
GET IN THE CARS. WE'LL TAKE YOU TO J.P.'S HOUSE & WE'LL FIGURE OUT WHERE YOU'LL SLEEP TONIGHT!
TAXI
YOU DON'T KNOW WHERE WE'LL LIVE?
WHY WON'T THEY LET US TAKE OUR CAR OFF THE SHIP?
MAÑANA! YOU'LL GET USED TO IT. EVERYTHING TAKES LONGER HERE.
MY, THIS IS A FANCY PART OF TOWN!
YEAH. THIS IS MIRAMAR. LOTS OF EMBASSIES HERE. THESE MANSIONS WERE HOMES OF THE VERY RICH BEFORE THE REVOLUTION TOOK OVER.
MOMMY, I'M THIRSTY!
MOMMY, I'M HOT! WHERE ARE WE GOING NOW?

WE ARRIVED AT J.P. MORRAY'S APARTMENT. J.P., AN ECONOMIST & HIS WIFE, WERE HOSTING A SMALL, JOLLY PARTY OF OLD COMMUNIST FRIENDS OF TED'S: JOE NORTH, A WRITER FOR "THE DAILY WORLD," THE COMMUNIST U.S. PAPER & MR. RABINOWITZ, THE AMERICAN LAWYER WHO REPRESENTED CUBA'S INTERESTS IN THE U.S.

WELCOME TO THE REVOLUTION!!!
YOU'RE GOING TO LOVE IT HERE!
LOOK AT THIS GREAT APARTMENT! YOU'LL GET ONE ASSIGNED TO YOU, TOO, IN NO TIME!

habana libre
FINALLY, AFTER OUR MEAL, THEY DROVE US TO OUR TEMPORARY HOME, THE HOTEL VEDADO, A COUPLE OF BLOCKS FROM LA RAMPA. THIS WAS THE MAIN DRAG OF DOWNTOWN HAVANA, IN THE SHADOW OF THE HOTEL HABANA LIBRE, A FORMER HILTON HOTEL UNTIL IT WAS NATIONALIZED.
HOTEL VEDADO
TAXI
EW! THIS IS DISGUSTING! I WON'T EAT IT!
BEHAVE YOURSELF, YOU STUPID CHILD. THAT'S WHAT THERE IS.
EXCUSE ME, I'D LIKE TO BUY SOME-THING TO EAT.
SORRY, *COMPAÑERA,* WE'RE OUT OF EVERYTHING BUT COFFEE & YOU HAVE TO MAKE A LINE OVER THERE FOR THAT.
THERE WERE NO SNACKS TO BE HAD, ALMOST NO FOOD TO BUY ANYWHERE. WE ATE STRICTLY WHAT WAS PUT ON OUR PLATES THREE TIMES A DAY IN THE HOTEL & WERE PRIVILEGED TO HAVE THAT, COMPARED TO THE LITTLE THAT CUBANS HAD TO EAT. LUCKY ME... I LOST 30 POUNDS IN FIVE MONTHS WITHOUT EVEN TRYING!
THE RATIONING SYSTEM WAS INITIATED ON MARCH 12—TWO WEEKS AFTER OUR ARRIVAL.
№ 772635
NUCLEO
C
CONTROL DE VENTAS PARA
PRODUCTOS ALIMENTICIOS
ESTA LIBRETA NO CONSTITUYE
UN DOCUMENTO DE IDENTIFICACION

PARTIDO SOCIALISTA POPULAR OFICINAS NACIONAL Y PROVINCIAL
The Communist Old Guard
Joaquín Ordoqui
Edith García Buchaca
Aníbal Escalante
HOY
TED STARTED HIS NEW JOB AS AN ELECTRONICS ENGINEER WITH JUCEPLAN (LA JUNTA CENTRAL DE PLANIFICACIÓN), WHICH HAD THE LOFTY MISSION OF MAPPING THE ECONOMIC & INDUSTRIAL DIRECTION OF THE NEW REVOLUTIONARY GOVERNMENT, UNDER THE MINISTRY OF INDUSTRIES. THE MINISTER AT THE TIME WAS COMANDANTE CHE GUEVARA, IN ONE OF HIS MANY INCARNATIONS.
TED WAS PLACED IN A SMALL DEPARTMENT CALLED ELECTRONICS & ELECTRICITY. HIS MISSION WAS TO EVALUATE THE NEED FOR PARTS THROUGHOUT VARIOUS MINISTRIES & FACTORIES. THOSE NEEDED WERE USUALLY SOVIET, CHINESE, CZECH, HUNGARIAN, OR SOMETIMES ANCIENT U.S. PARTS. HE WAS TASKED WITH PROCURING THEM FOR DISTRIBUTION BY HIS DEPARTMENT. HE TRAVELED EXTENSIVELY TO FIND THESE PARTS & GOT TO HOBNOB WITH DIPLOMATIC MOVERS & SHAKERS FROM ALL THE SOCIALIST COUNTRIES.
13 de marzo de 1962
LA LUCHA CONTRA EL SECTARISMO
TOVARICH! WE NEED MOTOR CONTROL SWITCHES FOR THE BASEBALL FACTORY. ANY HELP YOU CAN GIVE US WOULD BE MUCH APPRECIATED.
LENORE SOON FOUND WORK TEACHING ENGLISH & THEN GERMAN AT THE MINISTRY OF FOREIGN AFFAIRS, INFURIATING MANY OF HER POWERFUL STUDENTS BY CALLING THEM LAZY & LACKING IN THEIR HOMEWORK...
THE KIDS WERE LEFT WITH ROSITA, A BABYSITTER, WHO APPARENTLY SPOKE NOT A WORD OF ENGLISH. NIKKI & KEVIN WERE TERRIFIED TO BE LEFT ALONE WITH HER, AS LENORE BEMUSEDLY WROTE IN ONE OF HER LETTERS TO HER MOTHER.
Directorio Estudiantil Revolucionario
TOMORROW I EXPECT YOU ALL TO BE ON TIME!
MOMMY, DON'T LEAVE US WITH HER!!!
M-26-7
osé Antonio Echeverría
EL APORTE DEL DIRECTORIO REVOLUCIONARIO EN LA LUCHA CONTRA LA TIRANIA
(EL ATAQUE A PALACIO, Y EL ESCAMBRAY)
MARIO G. DEL CUETO

ONE GLASS OF OYSTERS, PLEASE.
OSTIONES
WHAT *ARE* THESE?
TURTLE MEMBERS...
WHAT FOR??
VIRILITY.

THE INSTITUTO PRE-UNIVERSITARIO DEL VEDADO

AFTER A WEEK IN CUBA, LENORE ANNOUNCED THAT IT WAS TIME FOR ME TO GO TO SCHOOL. SHE TOOK ME TO THE NEAREST HIGH SCHOOL, A 15-MINUTE WALK FROM OUR HOTEL, THE INSTITUTO PRE-UNIVERSITARIO DEL VEDADO "SAUL DELGADO," A FEW BLOCKS FROM LA RAMPA.

UNIVERSITARIO DEL VEDADO SAUL DELGADO

I BEGAN SCHOOL OVER A MONTH INTO THE SEMESTER, ARMED WITH ONLY MY JUNIOR HIGH SPANISH FROM CALIFORNIA. BUT I'D FACED SCHOOL IN A FOREIGN COUNTRY BEFORE, SO I DIDN'T PANIC. DESPITE HAVING TO REPEAT 10TH GRADE, THE HIGHEST GRADE OFFERED THAT YEAR, I WASN'T THE OLDEST STUDENT. SCHOOLS HAD BEEN SHUT DOWN DURING 1961 SO THAT THE STUDENTS COULD PARTICIPATE AS TEACHERS IN A COUNTRY-WIDE LITERACY CAMPAIGN.

OH, MY GOD... THERE'S NO BOOK. I HAVE TO TAKE NOTES & DON'T UNDERSTAND A THING. THEY TALK SO DAMN FAST...
H_2SO_4

¡PSS PSS PSS!

MY CLASSMATES, ALL 16 TO 19 YEARS OLD, WERE CURIOUS ABOUT *LA AMERICANA*. THEY WERE FRIENDLY, APOLITICAL & WANTED ME TO TELL THEM ABOUT MOVIE STARS IN THE USA.

CAN I COPY YOUR NOTES? I CAN'T UNDERSTAND HER.
SURE, ***SIN PROBLEMA***, WE'LL HELP YOU.

SWINE!

MARITZA & RAMONA BECAME MY PROTECTORS. THEY WATCHED OVER ME & BECAME MY FRIENDS.

ESPAÑOL
Matemática
Quimica 1

COME ON, REPEAT AFTER ME, *¡MARICÓN!*

EVERY NIGHT I STUDIED UNTIL LATE, TRANSLATING MY COPIED NOTES INTO ENGLISH, LEARNING THE LESSONS & STUDYING FOR EXAMS. MY SPANISH LIT. CLASS DID HAVE A TEXTBOOK. IT WAS EXCRUCIATING. IT WAS SINK OR SWIM.

¡NO JODAN! LEAVE HER ALONE.

MAY DAY, 1962
PLAZA DE LA REVOLUCIÓN
IN OUR COUNTRY CAPITALIST EXPLOITATION HAS CEASED & A PROFOUND SOCIAL REVOLUTION IS TAKING PLACE!
I DECIDED TO GO WITH MY FRIENDS MARITZA & RAMONA TO THE GIGANTIC MAY DAY RALLY. I DIDN'T WANT TO GO WITH THE YOUNG COMMUNIST CADRES, NOR WITH MY FAMILY. WE WANTED TO BE FREE & ON OUR OWN.
TED & LENORE WERE INVITED GUESTS ON LA TRIBUNA, ONE TIER DOWN FROM FIDEL'S PINNACLE. UP THERE WERE EL CHE, DORTICÓS, CELIA SÁNCHEZ, ALL THE GOVERNMENT LUMINARIES, PRESIDING OVER THE MILLION OR SO CITIZENS BELOW.
LOOK! THERE'S CHE!
GO ON— SAY HELLO TO HIM!
WELL, WHAT'S YOUR NAME, LITTLE GIRL?
THIS IS AMAZING!
I THINK IT'S SHIT...
BUT WHY? YOU'RE NOT A REVOLUTIONARY?
NO. MY FATHER WAS A POLICEMAN BEFORE... HE TOLD ME THINGS...
ARTILLERIA

SACRIFICE IS NOT FAILURE! SACRIFICE IS TRIUMPH! SACRIFICE IS VICTORY!
LONG LIVE THE PROLETARIAN REVOLUTION! LONG LIVE THE WORKING CLASS! FATHERLAND OR DEATH!
301

COME ON, LET'S GET OUT OF HERE. I'M HOT.
LET'S GO TO MY HOUSE.
OK... SURE.
NOT ME. I'M GOING HOME. SEE YOU LATER.

THE REST OF THE CITY WAS SHUT DOWN. RESTAURANTS WERE CLOSED; THE HOTEL VEDADO HAD ONLY A SKELETON CREW ON DUTY. MAY DAY WAS LIKE THE FOURTH OF JULY, BUT WITH TANKS & BRIGADES OF MARCHING WORKERS, SOLDIERS & MILITIA.

WE WALKED ALL THE WAY TO MARITZA'S TINY TWO-ROOM GROUND-FLOOR APARTMENT ON A DUSTY LITTLE STREET BEHIND THE TELEPHONE COMPANY. SHE LIVED THERE WITH HER MOTHER, A SEAMSTRESS & HER BROTHER NENO.
HEY, EVERYBODY, THIS IS CONNIE, *LA AMERICANA,* I TOLD YOU ABOUT.
COME IN! WELCOME! NENO, BRING THE AMERICANA A CAFECITO!
¡ESTÁS EN TU CASA!

THAT DAY WAS THE FIRST OF MANY THAT I SPENT AT MARITZA'S HOUSE. I WAS QUICKLY ADOPTED & INTEGRATED INTO DAILY LIFE. I FOUND OUT THAT REALITY FOR POOR CUBANS WAS QUITE DIFFERENT FROM THE RARIFIED WORLD OF THE FOREIGN *TÉCNICOS* & DIPLOMATS.

UM... WHERE'S THE BATHROOM?
HERE'S THE BUCKET. I'LL SHOW YOU WHERE TO GET WATER.
USE THIS NEWSPAPER TO CLEAN YOURSELF.

"MODERN TIMES"
I SOON REALIZED SOMETHING STRANGE WAS HAPPENING. MARITZA AVOIDED BEING ALONE WITH ME & I FELT AN UNSPOKEN EXCITEMENT, AN ODD ELECTRICITY IN THE AIR WHENEVER WE WERE TOGETHER... ONE DAY IN MAY I INSISTED ON GOING TO THE MOVIES WITH HER RIGHT AFTER SCHOOL. "MODERN TIMES" WITH CHARLIE CHAPLIN WAS PLAYING AT RADIO CENTRO & I WANTED TO SEE IT WITH HER. I HAD NO CLUE ABOUT WHAT WAS GOING ON BUT I WANTED TO FIND OUT.
RADIOCENTRO
CMQ
TIEMPOS MODERNOS CHARLES CHAPLIN
TIEMPOS MODERNOS
I KNOW YOU ARE GOING TO LIKE THIS...
ABOUT HALF WAY THROUGH THE MOVIE, MARITZA SLOWLY TOOK MY HAND IN HERS & WITHOUT A WORD, OR LOOKING MY WAY, PERFORMED MAGIC ON IT, SLOWLY STROKING MY PALM & FINGERS...
PETRIFIED, EXHILARATED, I DIDN'T MOVE A MUSCLE. WE WATCHED THE MOVIE THREE FULL TIMES IN A ROW THIS WAY.
WHEN WE FINALLY LEFT, I KNEW... YET HAD NO NAME FOR THIS, NO CLUE, NO HISTORY, NO REFERENCES AT ALL. I JUST REALIZED THAT THIS WAS IT & THERE WAS NO TURNING BACK.

MARITZA KNEW EXACTLY WHAT SHE WAS DOING. THREE YEARS OLDER THAN ME, MARITZA & HAD BEEN IN A PREVIOUS RELATIONSHIP. SHE GUIDED ME INTO THE DANGEROUS WATERS OF LESBIAN LIFE IN HAVANA. WE FOUND WAYS TO BE ALONE, AT MY HOTEL OR AT HER APARTMENT WHEN OUR FAMILIES WERE OUT.

SO THAT'S WHY YOU WOULDN'T EVER BE ALONE WITH ME BEFORE?
I WAS SURE YOU'D BE ANGRY IF YOU KNEW HOW I FELT. I THOUGHT I COULDN'T HIDE IT THEN.
WHY SHOULD I BE ANGRY?
IT'S VERY BAD HERE FOR *INVERTIDAS*. YOU NEED TO KEEP THIS SECRET.
IF PEOPLE SEE US TOGETHER A LOT, THEY'RE GONNA START TO TALK.
YOU HAVE TO DENY EVERYTHING. REMEMBER THAT.
WATCH OUT FOR FULANO & MENGANO, THEY'RE THE CLASS SNITCHES.
IT DIDN'T TAKE LONG FOR FEAR & PARANOIA TO SET IN.
EVEN LENORE STARTED TO NOTICE.
WHY DO YOU SPEND SO MUCH TIME WITH MARITZA? YOU HAVE NOTHING IN COMMON WITH HER... SHE'S SO... LOWER CLASS...
LEAVE ME ALONE! SHE'S MY FRIEND!
DISASTER STRUCK WHEN LENORE CAME HOME ONE DAY & CAUGHT US *INFLAGRANTE* IN MY ROOM.
THE WELL OF LONELINESS
SHE DIDN'T SAY A WORD. I JUST GOT GLOWERING LOOKS FROM TIME TO TIME. MYSTERIOUSLY, A STRANGE & RIDICULOUS BOOK APPEARED ON TED'S BOOKSHELF WHERE I OFTEN HELPED MYSELF TO OLD PAPERBACKS TO READ.

LUCKILY LENORE WAS SOON DISTRACTED BY THE MOVE INTO OUR NEW APARTMENT IN MIRAMAR. WE HAD BEEN ASSIGNED A REAL HOME, & A VERY SUMPTUOUS ONE AT THAT, INTO A 1950S BUILDING WITH DUPLEX APARTMENTS. EACH HAD A WIDE BALCONY, SERVANTS' QUARTERS & THREE BEDROOMS. THE BUILDING HAD BELONGED TO AN OLD SPANISH LABORER WHO BOUGHT IT WITH HIS LIFE SAVINGS, TO RETIRE ON AS THE LANDLORD. WHEN THE REVOLUTION PASSED THE URBAN REFORM LAWS, HE LOST HIS BUILDING. NOW, AS THE GARDENER, HE LIVED IN A SHACK IN THE BACK WHERE HE RAISED RABBITS TO EAT.

TED & LENORE SOON DISCOVERED THE PLAYGROUND OF THE EASTERN EUROPEAN *TÉCNICOS* & OTHERS LIKE THEMSELVES, WHO HAD COME FROM CAPITALIST COUNTRIES TO WORK FOR THE REVOLUTION.
THE SEASIDE SIERRA MAESTRA HOTEL, A FEW BLOCKS FROM OUR BUILDING, HAD A FULL BAR, AN ENORMOUS SWIMMING POOL, LOUNGE CHAIRS & SOFT WHITE SAND. HERE THE GLITTERATI OF THE RESIDENT WHITE, INTERNATIONAL LEFT MINGLED UNDER THE SUN, AS THEY RELAXED WITH RUM & COLA CUBA LIBRES.
OH, MAURICE, TELL US ABOUT YOUR ADVENTURES & HOW CHE GOT YOU TO CUBA! EDITH PROMISED YOU WOULD!
MAURICE HALPERIN, A WELL-KNOWN EX-PAT AT THE TIME, WAS A FREQUENT MEMBER OF THEIR CIRCLE, UNTIL HE BECAME DISENCHANTED WITH THE REVOLUTION & LEFT. CHE HAD MET HIM IN MOSCOW & INVITED HIM TO LIVE & WORK IN HAVANA AS AN ECONOMIST AT THE UNIVERSITY.

LENORE UNPACKED HER TYPEWRITER & WROTE OFTEN TO HER MOTHER.

Dear Mama,
Cuba seems to be full of viruses— Kevin has had tonsilitis three times since we came here, Nikki a bad bronchitis, both children right now have worms, & I have a painful bladder infection. But we have no lack of the necessary medications. The children get penicillin, I am taking tetracycline, and the children also get good medications against the worms. Apparently all newcomers get sick here until they get used to the local atmosphere. Ted had only a small throat infection a few weeks ago.

NIKKI, NOW 7, HAD BEEN PLACED IN SCHOOL—THE "UNIVERSITY ANNEX SCHOOL," THAT CHE GUEVARA'S FIRST CHILD, HILDITA, ALSO ATTENDED. IN THE MORNING, SHE & HILDITA WOULD BE PICKED UP BY A SCHOOL MINIBUS & THEY RETURNED THE SAME WAY. NIKKI HATED THE SCHOOL...

¡AY, PERO QUE GRINGUITA MÁS LINDA TÚ ERES, TAN GORDITA Y CON OJOS TAN AZULES!!!

EVERY DAY TED CAME HOME AFTER WORK & WAS SERVED HIS AFTERNOON COCKTAILS & SNACKS. LENORE HIRED A SERVANT TO COOK & CLEAN IN THE MORNINGS WHILE SHE TAUGHT ENGLISH & GERMAN. BOTH WENT SWIMMING AT "THE CLUB" EVERY WEEKEND & AS OFTEN AS POSSIBLE DURING THE WEEK. THEIR SOCIAL LIFE WAS VERY LIVELY.

WE HAVE TO START SENDING REPORTS BACK TO OUR FRIENDS & COMRADES IN THE STATES. *THEY'RE BEING DUPED BY THE FASCIST PRESS!*

I'LL DICTATE IT TO YOU...

Dear Friends,

It seems very strange to listen to Miami on the radio and realize that the source of the fantastic stuff we hear is so close: the commercials, the Kennedy blah, the hate propaganda. Here it now seems incredible that we know people, good, fine people who could be duped by a Stevenson, and would even cast a vote for a creature like Kennedy.

Our Latin American friends are very excited these days, jumping on every item in the papers about guerrilla activity or crisis in their respective home countries, and exchanging latest news of their friends in the mountains or striking workers and students in the awakening continent. You can imagine what they thought of Kennedy's congratulations (premature, as usual) to his latest favorite butcher, the Venezuelan dictator, Betancourt. But we can point to a few notes for pride: the continuing and apparently growing peace demonstrations and struggles for Negro rights in the States.

You kids in the old country have a long way to go to catch up with the rest of the world!

SUNNY LITTLE KEVIN WENT TO A KINDERGARTEN NEARBY & AFTER SCHOOL ROAMED THE NEIGHBORHOOD. HE LOVED THE ATTENTION HE GOT AS AN *AMERICANITO* & LIKED TO DROP BY AT PEOPLE'S HOUSES TO VISIT. ONE DAY HE ROAMED SO FAR THAT THE POLICE PICKED HIM UP & EVENTUALLY BROUGHT HIM HOME. HE HAD A GREAT TIME.

¡HOLA! ¡SOY KEVIN!
SO... ARE YOU RUSSIAN?

NIKKI OFTEN GOT SICK WITH INTENSE FEVERS. SHE STILL HAD NIGHTMARES & OFTEN WALKED IN HER SLEEP. SHE & LENORE FOUGHT EVERY DAY. LENORE WAS USUALLY TENSE. LIFE WAS GOOD, BUT TED'S PAY DIDN'T COME THROUGH FOR MONTHS & SHE HAD TO BORROW FROM FRIENDS. SHE SHOPPED FOR FOOD AT THE *TÉCNICO* GROCERY AT THE SIERRA MAESTRA HOTEL, WHERE CUBANS WERE NOT ALLOWED & WHERE WE FOREIGNERS GOT SPECIAL, GENEROUS RATIONS.

I WON'T EAT THAT! I HATE IT!
WHY ARE YOU SO DIFFICULT? PUT THAT IN YOUR MOUTH RIGHT NOW!
I WON'T!
SMACK!
DO WHAT YOU'RE TOLD, YOU AWFUL CHILD!

LENORE HAD FREQUENT FITS OF RAGE—NOT ONLY AT NIKKI, BUT AT TED & ME AS WELL. FORTUNATELY, THERE WAS ALWAYS THE SIERRA MAESTRA CLUB, WHERE THEY SPENT MOST OF THEIR FREE TIME.

TED, YOU & LENORE SHOULD JOIN OUR ORGANIZATION, THE NORTEAMERICANOS AMIGOS DE CUBA.
BAH! THAT'S FULL OF TROTSKYITES!
OK, MAYBE A FEW, BUT WE NEED PEOPLE LIKE YOU TO SHUT THEM UP & HELP US BUILD A SOLIDARITY ORGANIZATION. ICAP* WANTS TO ORGANIZE ALL THE FOREIGNERS.
ALL RIGHT, WE'LL COME TO A MEETING, BUT I'M NOT PUTTING UP WITH ANY BULLSHIT.

LIONEL MARTIN & BOB PURDY WERE OLD COMMUNIST FRIENDS OF TED'S FROM BEFORE, SINCE CALIFORNIA.

* ICAP—INSTITUTO CUBANO DE AMISTAD CON LOS PUEBLOS, THE CUBAN INSTITUTE OF FRIENDSHIP AMONG PEOPLES.

LOS NORTEAMERICANOS AMIGOS DE CUBA

BACK IN APRIL OF THAT YEAR, WHEN FIDEL UNLEASHED HIS ATTACKS ON THE OLD GUARD COMMUNISTS, TED RATIONALIZED THIS IN HIS REPORTS BACK TO HIS FRIENDS IN THE NORTH.

THE NORTEAMERICANOS AMIGOS DE CUBA BECAME A NEW PLATFORM FOR TED TO VOICE HIS VIEWS & SHOW HIS COMMITMENT TO THE CUBAN REVOLUTION. ICAP PROVIDED THE VENUE.

Dear Friends,

The talk of the last couple of days has been on Fidel's speech on ORI and sectarism and the follow-up by Blas Roca and others. Although a few tried to see in Fidel's attack on Anibal Escalante a general attack on the old Communist leaders and even on Communism, a more general feeling is that ORI is strengthened and will soon develop into an effective mass Communist Party. This feeling has been strengthened by the recent acceptance by the former "Jovenes Rebeldes" of Fidel's suggestion to change their name to "Jovenes Communistas." The wonderful thing to see is the general acceptance and active support of Marxist-Leninist ideas, rather than those of a more revolutionary nationalism. I think that in his own way Kennedy deserves as much credit for this as Fidel. Incidentally, Lenore is translating Fidel's ORI speech on request from the Habana reporter of a well-known New York newspaper. If you get to read it you may see some of the reasons for this worship of a leader who tells everybody he has no use for leadership worship, that Cuban leaders including he himself, make mistakes and have to be needled from below.

COMPAÑEROS, WE MUST DENOUNCE THE YANKEE LIES ABOUT CUBA & DECLARE TO THE WORLD THERE ARE NO FOREIGN TROOPS ON CUBAN SOIL!

THE INTERNAL DIVISIONS OF THIS EX-PAT GROUP MIRRORED THE DIVISIONS OF THE OLD LEFT IN THE U.S. THERE WERE THE CP PEOPLE, ALL ALLIED WITH THE EX-COMMUNIST PARTY "FELLOW TRAVELERS," LIKE TED, WITH VARYING DEGREES OF STALINIST SYMPATHIES (MOST OF TED & LENORE'S FRIENDS CAME FROM THIS FACTION). THERE WERE THE "HATED TROTSKYITES," REPRESENTED BY THREE WOMEN WRITTEN OFF BY TED & LENORE'S FACTION AS THE "THREE WITCHES" & THERE WERE ALSO SOME UNAFFILIATED FREE SPIRITS.

TODAY WE ARE GOING TO VOTE ON OUR NEW LEADERS. PLEASE RAISE YOUR HANDS TO VOTE FOR TED AS PRESIDENT! THANK YOU!
DIRTY STALINIST!
CONNIE! I'M GLAD TO SEE YOU HERE!
BOB, THEY DRAGGED ME HERE. I'D RATHER BE WITH MY FRIENDS.

THE MAOISTS WOULD COME IN A LATER WAVE OF *AMERICANOS* HOSTILE TO ALL THE OTHERS. THERE WERE A FEW OLD LEFTIES LIKE AGNES, MARRIED TO A CUBAN UNION MAN IN THE STATES, WHO HAD BROUGHT HER HERE WHEN THE REVOLUTION CAME TO POWER.

AUGUST 24, 1962— WE GOT THE NEWS THAT THE SIERRA MAESTRA HOTEL HAD BEEN ATTACKED THE NIGHT BEFORE BY GUNFIRE FROM TWO SHIPS ANCHORED ABOUT A KILOMETER OFF THE COAST.
COME ON, KEVIN! WE'RE NOT AFRAID OF THEM. LET'S GO & INSPECT THE HOTEL.
OH, MY GOD! DID YOU HEAR THE SHOTS?
ONE OF THE BULLETS CAME RIGHT INTO A RUSSIAN APARTMENT & JUST MISSED A LITTLE GIRL!
LOOK! THERE ARE THE BULLET HOLES! THE BASTARDS! ¡NO PASARÁN!
MOMMY, ARE THE YANKEES COMING TO KILL US?
JUAN MARINELLO, THE CURRENT RECTOR OF THE UNIVERSITY & A FAMOUS OLD COMMUNIST WHO LIVED IN THE BUILDING, WAS HOLDING A PRESS CONFERENCE IN THE LOBBY OF THE SIERRA MAESTRA HOTEL.
COME HERE, LITTLE BOY. WHERE ARE YOU FROM?
ALL THAT SUMMER, THE U.S. HAD FLOWN U-2 SPY PLANES OVER CUBA, ALARMED BY THE HEAVY VOLUME OF SOVIET SHIPPING BOUND FOR CUBA. THEN, IN EARLY SEPTEMBER, IT HAPPENED: THE USSR SENT BALLISTIC MISSILES TO CUBA.
ПОЛТАВА

THE OCTOBER MISSILE CRISIS

EVERY DAY IN SEPTEMBER WE SAW WARSHIPS ON THE HORIZON & WORRIED THAT ANOTHER INVASION WAS ABOUT TO BEGIN, LIKE THE YEAR BEFORE, AT PLAYA GIRÓN, FOR AMERICANS, THE BAY OF PIGS.

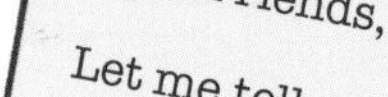

Dear Friends,

Let me tell you about the "police state" we are supposedly living in. We recently met a very nice young Cuban policeman (who speaks fluent English) who told us a lot about how the police work here. Because of the terrible memories the people have of the many arbitrary and unlawful actions of the Batista police, the new police act under the strictest orders to respect people's privacy and freedom in a way that cannot be matched by American police. For instance, they suspected anti-revolutionary, illegal broadcasts were transmitted abroad from a particular house but had no proof, and consequently could not go in and search the place. The house is still under surveillence, but not searched. Handcuffs have been abolished, in order not to hurt the dignity even of criminals. In general, police are very little in evidence; traffic police are very polite, and there are never any abuses.

LENORE NOW WAS ALSO A FOREIGN CORRESPONDENT FOR AN OBSCURE WEST GERMAN NEWSPAPER, "DAS ANDERE DEUTSCHLAND."

AT MY SCHOOL, LIFE WENT ON AS USUAL. CLASSES WEREN'T SUSPENDED. WE STUDIED, OBLIVIOUS TO THE LOOMING NUCLEAR ABYSS, WHILE MILITIA UNITS ERECTED SANDBAG BARRIERS & ANTI-AIRCRAFT STATIONS ALONG THE SEA FRONT.

MEANWHILE, ON OCTOBER 11, ON THE EVE OF THE NUCLEAR CONFRONTATION BETWEEN THE UNITED STATES & CUBA, LIFE GOT RADICALLY WORSE FOR A CERTAIN PART OF THE HAVANA POPULATION. ICAP DID NOT OFFER ANY PRESS RELEASES OF THIS EVENT.

THE NIGHT OF THE THREE PS
PROSTITUTAS, PROXENETAS Y PÁJAROS—PROSTITUTES, PIMPS & QUEERS
¡SUÉLTAME! ¡CON QUÉ DERECHO?!!
SMACK!
¡MARICONES DE MIERDA!
BAM!
¡AQUÍ TODO EL MUNDO VA PRESO!
THIS WAS THE FIRST MAJOR POLICE CRACKDOWN BY THE GOVERNMENT IN THE SIXTIES, TARGETING MOSTLY YOUNG PEOPLE DEEMED PERVERTS & DEVIANTS. THESE WERE PEOPLE PERCEIVED AS MALE HOMOSEXUALS, AS WELL AS PROSTITUTES & PIMPS. THE REVOLUTION WAS BY & FOR THOSE WHO CONFORMED TO THE MACHO IDEAL. QUEERS WERE JUST ANOTHER KIND OF COUNTERREVOLUTIONARY.

OCTOBER 14— AN AMERICAN U-2 SPY PLANE TOOK PHOTOS OF THE INSTALLATION OF SOVIET LAUNCHING SITES FOR NUCLEAR MISSILES & ALL HELL BROKE LOOSE.

TED WAS DELIGHTED THAT THE MISSILES WERE NOW IN CUBA & PARTICIPATED IN PRESS CONFERENCES & RADIO BROADCASTS AIMED AT THE UNITED STATES.
YOU CAN'T IMAGINE THE RELIEF WE ALL FELT ON RECEIVING THE NEWS OF THE SOVIET STATEMENT THAT THE RUSSIANS WOULD SEND ARMS TO CUBA. FOR TWO WEEKS PREVIOUS WE FELT THAT THE PROBABILITIES OF A LARGE-SCALE INVASION WERE VERY GREAT.
MUERTE
EN EL AIRE
RADIO HABANA CUBA
THESE WORDS WERE A REASSURING HINT OF THE WORLD-SHAKING ANNOUNCEMENT OF SOVIET POLICY THAT FOLLOWED THE NEXT DAY. WITH A FEW FIRM WORDS, THE WHOLE MAXWELL TAYLOR POLICY OF "LIMITED WARFARE," OF NICE, EASY "BRUSHFIRE" WARS, TO SAVE THE VITAL INTERESTS OF U.S. CAPITALISM, BECAME AS OBSOLETE AS THE "MASSIVE RETALIATION" OF JOHN FOSTER DULLES.
THE IMPLICATIONS OF THE SOVIET STATEMENT ARE TREMENDOUS, NOT JUST FOR CUBA— WHICH HAS NOW BEEN MADE AS SAFE AS ANY SPOT ON THE GLOBE— BUT FOR THE WHOLE WORLD.

OCTOBER 22— PRESIDENT KENNEDY ANNOUNCED THE INSTALLATION OF THE MISSILES, DEMANDED THEIR REMOVAL & PROCLAIMED A NAVAL BLOCKADE.

OCTOBER 25— AMBASSADOR ADLAI STEVENSON SHOWED AERIAL PHOTOS TO THE UNITED NATIONS SECURITY COUNCIL.

36 MISSILES WERE DEPLOYED AT 6 DIFFERENT SITES. EACH MISSILE CONTAINED A NUCLEAR WARHEAD 70 TIMES MORE POWERFUL THAN THE HIROSHIMA BOMB.

UNITED ARAB REPUBLIC
UNITED KINGDOM
UNITED STATES
UNDER SECRETARY
FINAL
DAILY NEWS
NEW YORK'S PICTURE NEWSPAPER
5¢
WE BLOCKADE CUBA ARMS
JFK: Blast Reds If

FOR US ON THE GROUND IN HAVANA, THE ATMOSPHERE WAS AMAZINGLY UPBEAT. IN THE STATES OUR FRIENDS HAD NIGHTMARES ABOUT NUCLEAR ANNIHILATION; HERE EVERYBODY WAS BUSY SHOUTING "PATRIA O MUERTE!"
¡COMPAÑEROS, I AM YOUR BRIGADE LEADER! YOU MUST PRESENT YOURSELVES HERE EVERY MORNING AT 8 AM!
ICAP ORGANIZED WESTERN FOREIGNERS INTO AN INTERNATIONAL BRIGADE THAT I, AT 17, JOINED, ALONG WITH AROUND 100 LATIN AMERICAN RESIDENTS OF HAVANA.
TODAY'S LESSON: YOU'LL LEARN TO TAKE APART & CLEAN THIS SEMI-AUTOMATIC RIFLE.
¡1–2–3–4! ¡ABAJO LOS IMPERIALISTAS!
WE LEARNED HOW TO MARCH UP & DOWN IN THE PARKING LOT OF A BIG HOTEL & WENT FOR TARGET PRACTICE AT A NEARBY RIFLE RANGE. I WAS A PRETTY GOOD SHOT.
BAM!

ON NOVEMBER 1, 1962, NIKITA KHRUSHCHEV ORDERED THE REMOVAL OF THE MISSILES FROM CUBA & AFTER MORE NEGOTIATIONS, ON NOVEMBER 20, HE AGREED TO REMOVE SOVIET AIRPLANES STATIONED IN CUBA AS WELL. KENNEDY LIFTED THE BLOCKADE & THE CRISIS WAS OVER.
¡NIKITA MARIQUITA! ¡LO QUE SE DA NO SE QUITA!
¡BOLOS DE MIERDA!
HOY
The Washington Post
FINAL
Reds Agree to Scrap Bases in Cuba; U. S. Greets Move as Tension Eases; Thant, Aides Go to Havana Tuesday
THE REST OF THE WORLD MAY HAVE BEEN CELEBRATING THE END OF THIS BRUSH WITH THE NUCLEAR ANNIHILATION OF THE PLANET, BUT IN CUBA THERE WAS FRUSTRATION & ANGER.
LIFE WENT BACK TO "NORMAL" AGAIN. TED & LENORE WROTE MORE GLOWING REPORTS BACK TO THE STATES VIA RADIO PROGRAMS & NEWSLETTERS.

Dear Friends,

The government has given us two magnificent penthouses, one in the ICAP Hotel, the other in a big apartment building downtown, called Club de la Torre. Both were the most elegant and exclusive clubs in Havana with beautiful and luxurious rooms. The Club de la Torre has two restaurants, one for bachelors where they can get cheap and very good food. We have several times been there as guests of a bachelor (two of our American bachelor friends are just marrying Cuban girls – but there is always Joe North). The other restaurant is expensive but marvelous. This and the bar– a dream of a bar– are 30 stories above the city and the ocean, with glass all around, so you can have a magnificent view from every table. Naturally we have gone there quite frequently; there is always beer which one cannot always buy in stores, and one always runs into friends and acquaintances there; all the foreign diplomats go there, too, so there is always an interesting crowd.

DEAR FRIENDS,
... I NOTICED IN A RECENT MONTHLY REVIEW ONE ERROR APPEARED IN THEIR USUALLY QUITE CORRECT & CAREFUL COVERAGE OF CUBAN EVENTS. THEY MENTION SOMETHING ABOUT AN "ECONOMIC CRISIS" HAVING BEEN OVERCOME. I HAVE GONE OVER CONSIDERABLE ECONOMIC DATA AT JUCEPLAN & CAN FIND NO TRACE OF ECONOMIC DIFFICULTIES OF THIS SORT, NOR HAVE I SEEN ANY EVIDENCE OF THIS IN ANY OTHER WAY...
RADIO HABANA CUBA
IF ONLY OUR "LIBERAL" FRIENDS KNEW WHAT IT IS TO LIVE IN A COUNTRY WITH A LITTLE TOO MUCH LIBERTY FOR THE INDIVIDUAL!

TANG... WHAT IS THIS STUFF? ***MMMM! ORANGE POWDER!***
Tang

OH! LOOK WHAT ELSE I GOT. HMM... TING... SOME KIND OF SKIN CREAM...
PRE- UNIVERSITARIO DE VEDADO

SOMETIME IN DECEMBER, THE CUBAN GOVERNMENT BEGAN EXCHANGING BAY OF PIGS PRISONERS FOR FOOD & MEDICINES FROM THE AMERICAN GOVERNMENT. SOME OF THIS LARGESS TRICKLED DOWN TO MY HIGH SCHOOL & I RECEIVED A SMALL RATION.

IN MY SECOND YEAR OF HIGH SCHOOL, I STARTED HANGING OUT WITH SILVIA, A CLASSMATE, WHO TOOK IT UPON HERSELF TO SAVE ME FROM EVIL.
CONNIE, YOU'VE GOT TO BREAK OFF WITH MARITZA.
YOU'RE AN AMERICAN, YOU DON'T UNDERSTAND.
SHE'S ONE OF THOSE... A HOMOSEXUAL.
I DON'T KNOW WHAT YOU'RE TALKING ABOUT. SHE'S JUST A FRIEND.
SHE'S A BAD IN-FLUENCE & PEOPLE ARE TALKING ABOUT YOU...

I DEFIED SILVIA'S ADVICE & WENT OUT WITH MY *COMPROMISO*. ONCE A WEEK WE'D GO AFTER SCHOOL WITH A FEW FRIENDS TO THE CMQ TELEVISION STUDIOS AT L & 23RD STREET & WATCH A LIVE MUSIC SHOW—MY INTRODUCTION TO CUBAN CHARANGA.

ARAGON
ESTIMADOS TELEVIDENTES, ¡AQUÍ LA TIENEN! LA LEGENDARIA ORQUESTA ARAGÓN! ¡UN APLAUSO POR FAVOR!
...AHORA EN MI JARDÍN NO HAY UNA ROSA PARA TI ME LLAMAN EL JARDINERO DEL AMOR...
BUT THE CONSTANT FEAR BEGAN TO WEAR ME DOWN.
WATCH OUT! THAT'S ROLANDO FROM THE CDR*!
HE'S SEEN US TOGETHER TWICE THIS WEEK. DUCK!
* COMITÉ DE DEFENSA DE LA REVOLUCIÓN

SILVIA WORKED ON ME FOR MONTHS & FINALLY AT THE END OF OUR SECOND SCHOOL YEAR, I BROKE UP WITH MARITZA. SHE DROPPED OUT OF SCHOOL & I WAS LEFT NUMB, DETERMINED TO SOMEHOW GET BACK ON TRACK. MAYBE I'D FIND A BOYFRIEND IF NECESSARY...

I'M SORRY MARITZA. I CAN'T DO THIS ANYMORE.
I'M TIRED OF BEING AFRAID ALL THE TIME.

SOY CUBA
I AM CUBA

NEAR THE END OF THAT YEAR, THE NORTEAMERICANOS AMIGOS DE CUBA WERE OFFERED A UNIQUE OPPORTUNITY—ESPECIALLY THOSE OF US WHO WERE FEMALE, YOUNG, & COULD LOOK THE PART OF AMERICAN TOURISTS—TO PLAY DECADENT, RICH, PRE-1959 GRINGAS IN BATISTA'S HAVANA.

THE SOVIET MOVIE DIRECTOR MIKHAIL KALATOZOV WAS WORKING WITH ICAIC, THE CUBAN FILM INSTITUTE, TO PRODUCE A MOVIE. KALATOZOV REQUESTED EXTRAS FROM ICAP FOR A SCENE ON THE ROOFTOP OF THE CAPRI HOTEL.

HOTEL
Capri
SALON de CAPRI
ALL RIGHT, THANK YOU! NOW LET'S HAVE ANOTHER SET OF FOUR FEMALES AT THAT CORNER TABLE.
SHIT. I'M GETTING BORED... WE'VE BEEN DOING NOTHING FOR FIVE HOURS NOW.
WHEN DO WE GET TO GO HOME? I'M STARVING...

ALAS... IT WAS NOT TO BE. AFTER THREE OR FOUR DAYS OF STANDING AROUND, WE ENDED UP ON THE CUTTING ROOM FLOOR & NEVER MADE IT INTO THIS DELICIOUSLY EXTRAVAGANT, WEIRD & HISTORIC FILM.

THE NEW YEAR IN REVOLUTIONARY CUBA WAS THE SEASON FOR PATRIOTIC POLITICAL CELEBRATIONS. THE REBELS HAD MARCHED INTO HAVANA ON JANUARY 8, 1959, SO ON OR CLOSE TO DECEMBER 31, ICAP ORGANIZED AN EXTRAVAGANZA FOR THE FOREIGN *TÉCNICOS* & THEIR FAMILIES WHO BELONGED TO THE VARIOUS RESIDENT SOLIDARITY ORGANIZATIONS UNDER ICAP. THIS TOOK PLACE AT A FORMER COUNTRY CLUB FOR RICH, SOCIETY CUBANS.

I'M NOT GOING. TOO MANY PEOPLE WILL BE THERE.
NONSENSE. WE'RE TAKING THE CHILDREN & IT'S BETTER IF YOU COME.
YOU HAVE SUCH A BAD ATTITUDE!

WE ALL WENT. BUT AFTER SMOLDERING IN MY SEAT FOR A FEW MINUTES, WISHING TO BE WITH MY FRIENDS, I REALIZED SUDDENLY WHO WAS SITTING A FEW TABLES AWAY.

OH, MY GOD! THAT'S CHE GUEVARA!
HA! WILL I GET INTO TROUBLE IF... DO I DARE..?
THIS IS MY CHANCE, I'VE GOT TO DO IT!
COMANDANTE... I'D LIKE TO SAY HELLO...
BUT OF COURSE! TELL ME, COMPAÑERA, WHERE ARE YOU FROM?
THE UNITED STATES. I'M HERE WITH MY FAMILY. MY FATHER, TED VELTFORT, WORKS FOR JUCEPLAN.
AH YES, VELTFORT'S FAMILY. VERY GOOD. WELL, VERY NICE TO HAVE MET YOU.
HAPPY NEW YEAR, COMANDANTE. THANK YOU VERY MUCH!

MARXISM & THE BEATLES

IN MY LAST YEAR OF HIGH SCHOOL, 1963/64, WE WERE INSTRUCTED TO START THE YEAR WITH HOMEMADE SCHOOL UNIFORMS. EACH STUDENT WAS ISSUED A RATION CERTIFICATE TO BUY A CERTAIN AMOUNT OF GRAY GABERDINE CLOTH FOR SKIRTS OR TROUSERS.

WE HAVE TO MAKE TWO SKIRTS FOR OUR SCHOOL UNIFORM. *IT'S REQUIRED NOW!*

UGH! I LOOK FAT IN THIS!

THIS YEAR, FOR THE FIRST TIME, WE WERE FORMALLY INTRODUCED TO POLITICS & IDEOLOGY. UNTIL THEN, OUR CURRICULUM HAD BEEN A TYPICAL LATIN AMERICAN BACCALAUREATE: MATH, CHEMISTRY, PHYSICS, HISTORY, GEOGRAPHY, SPANISH LITERATURE, FRENCH, ENGLISH, SCIENCES & PHYSICAL EDUCATION. NOW OUR CLASSES INCLUDED A SEMESTER EACH OF DIALECTICAL MATERIALISM & HISTORICAL MATERIALISM, PLUS TWO OF POLITICAL SCIENCE. OUR TEXTS WERE SOVIET MANUALS TRANSLATED IN MOSCOW INTO SPANISH.

COMPAÑEROS, TODAY WE ARE GOING TO STUDY THE INEVITABLE LAWS THAT GOVERN THE DEVELOPMENT OF ALL SOCIAL REGIMES THROUGHOUT HISTORY.
REPUBLICA DE CUBA
MINISTERIO DE EDUCACION
MATERIALISMO HISTORICO
...PRIMITIVE COMMUNISM, SLAVERY, FEUDALISM, CAPITALISM & FINALLY SOCIALISM, THE FIRST PHASE OF SCIENTIFIC COMMUNISM—THE HIGHEST FORM OF HUMAN SOCIETY.
República de Cuba
Ministerio de Educación
Materialismo Dialéctico
"THE RELATIONS BETWEEN MAN AND THE MEANS OF PRODUCTION DETERMINE ALL OTHER RELATIONS IN SOCIETY. FOR EXAMPLE, IN CAPITALISM, THE BOURGEOISIE—OWNERS OF THE MEANS OF PRODUCTION—ENJOY THE FRUITS OF THE LABOR OF THE WORKERS, WHO, IN THEIR MAJORITY, LIVE IN ABJECT MISERY."

MEANWHILE, KRINKA—A CLASSMATE & THE DAUGHTER OF YUGOSLAV DIPLOMATS IN HAVANA—INVITED US TO HER FAMILY'S APARTMENT TO HEAR THE BEATLES! LITTLE DID WE KNOW THIS WOULD SOON BE CONSIDERED SUBVERSIVE.

EVERYONE'S INVITED TO MY BIRTHDAY PARTY! PLEASE COME!

YOU'VE GOT TO HEAR THIS—IT'S THE BEATLES!
"DO YOU WANT TO KNOW A SECRET?"
THE BEATLES!
twist and shout
THE BEATLES

BEA JOHNSON WAS A HIGH-RANKING MEMBER OF THE AMERICAN COMMUNIST PARTY, DEPORTED AS AN ALIEN TO EUROPE & NOW SENT BY THE PARTY TO FORGE TIES WITH THE CUBAN GOVERNMENT. SHE WAS DEEPLY DISTRESSED BY THE *NORTEAMERICANOS* ORGANIZATION BECAUSE OF THE MAOISTS, TROTSKYITES & OTHER HERETICS IN THEIR MIDST. SHE VISITED US OFTEN TO COMPLAIN ABOUT THEIR IDEOLOGICAL FAILINGS. HER DAUGHTER JOSIE & I BECAME FRIENDS.

JOSIE! YOU'VE GOT TO TEACH ME HOW TO DO THE TWIST! YOU SAID YOU KNEW HOW.
AT SCHOOL EVERYBODY EXPECTS ME TO KNOW THESE THINGS, SINCE I'M THE AMERICANA.
OH, SURE! I'LL COME OVER TOMORROW. I'VE GOT SOME GOOD RECORDS.
I'M GOING TO BE SEEING DR. VALLEJO, FIDEL'S ASSISTANT TODAY. I'LL SET HIM STRAIGHT ABOUT THESE PEOPLE...
HERE, YOU MOVE YOUR HIPS LIKE THIS!

LATER I ENLIGHTENED MY SCHOOLMATES. THE BEATLES & ROCK & ROLL WERE A FREQUENT TOPIC OF CONVERSATION, ESPECIALLY ON OUR FIRST DAY TRIPS TO DO AGRICULTURAL WORK.

I WANNA HOLD YOUR HAND!
UGH! IT'S SO HOT!
COME ON, COMPAÑEROS! FOR THE REVOLUTION!
HEY! THIS IS FUN! JUST LIKE CAMP!
WHEN THE FUCK ARE WE GOING HOME?

SOME OF MY CLASSMATES WERE LESS THAN ENTHUSIASTIC. I HAD A GREAT TIME.

THE "MARQUITOS TRIAL" & THE PURGE OF THE COMMUNIST OLD GUARD

IN MARCH 1964, MARCOS RODRÍGUEZ—A COMMUNIST ACTIVE IN THE BATISTA-ERA-UNDERGROUND—WAS TRIED, CONVICTED & EXECUTED FOR THE BETRAYAL OF FOUR SURVIVORS OF A FAILED ASSAULT ON BATISTA'S PRESIDENTIAL PALACE IN 1957. THEY WERE MURDERED IN THEIR HIDEOUT AT HUMBOLT STREET, NO 7, BY BATISTA'S POLICE. AFTER THE TRIUMPH OF THE REVOLUTION, MARQUITOS WAS PROTECTED BY OLD COMMUNIST FRIENDS IN HIGH POWER, WHO WERE NOW IMPLICATED IN THE MARQUITOS TRIAL & PURGED.

COME TO MY PLACE. I HAVE A RECORD PLAYER & WE'LL LISTEN TO CHAVELA VARGAS.

I BECAME INVOLVED WITH GUILLERMO, A YOUNG CHILEAN. HIS PARENTS, LEFTIST ACADEMICS, WORKED IN CUBA & HAD BROUGHT HIM & HIS SIBLINGS TO HAVANA. THEY LIVED IN MY NEIGHBORHOOD IN MIRAMAR. "WILLY" HAD THE MAID'S ROOM WITH AN INDEPENDENT ENTRANCE TO HIS LAIR.

"PONME LA MANO AQUÍ MACORINA...PONME LA MANO AQUÍ."
CHAVELA VARGAS
ANTONIO BRIBIESCA

WILLY WAS ABOUT AS OUT OF PLACE AS ONE COULD BE... APOLITICAL, A NIGHT BIRD WHO DRESSED IN BLACK, READ POETRY & LISTENED TO BOHEMIAN MUSIC. I FOUND HIM ENCHANTING.

LOOK! I HAVE A GIFT FOR YOU...
FOR THE NEXT WANKER...
FANTASTIC! YOU'RE SO INGENIOUS!

WILLY REALLY GOT HOW ANGRY THE STREET WANKERS MADE ME. AFTER ONE OF THEM EJACULATED ON MY SHOULDER ON A CROWDED BUS, WILLY CONSTRUCTED A WEAPON OUT OF A HYPODERMIC NEEDLE INSIDE A FOUNTAIN PEN. I NEVER GOT TO USE IT BEFORE LOSING IT, WHICH WAS PROBABLY ALL FOR THE BEST.

THE BETRAYAL

7

THE MASSACRE

THE TRIAL

ORDOQUI

BUCHA

THE ACCUSED

I DON'T REMEMBER IF WILLY HAD A JOB, OR IF HE WAS STILL A STUDENT. HE READ A LOT OF POETRY & PHILOSOPHY & BROODED LATE INTO THE HOT HAVANA NIGHTS. THEN ONE DAY HE DISAPPEARED...

CONNIE, IS WILLY WITH YOU?
HE HASN'T BEEN HOME FOR THREE DAYS!
NO! I'VE BEEN WORRIED...
WE HAVE TO CALL THE POLICE!
...AND ALL THE HOSPITALS!
I RUSHED OVER TO HIS PARENT'S APARTMENT & FELT USELESS... I'D NEVER BEEN THAT CLOSE WITH HIS FAMILY.
AFTER SEVERAL DAYS, WILLY WAS FOUND IN A HOTEL ROOM BY THE MAID WHO CAME IN TO CLEAN...
¡AY, DIÓS MÍO!
¡QUÉ ES ESTO?

WILLY WAS STILL ALIVE BUT JUST BARELY. THE MAID HAD FOUND HIM JUST IN TIME. HE'D CHECKED INTO A SEEDY DOWNTOWN HOTEL WITH A BOTTLE OF PILLS & HAD HOLED UP THERE FOR DAYS.

PLAYA
THEY TOOK HIM TO A HOSPITAL. AS SOON AS I HAD PERMISSION, I WENT TO VISIT HIM.
WHAT AM I GOING TO SAY TO HIM? WILL HE LET ME NEAR HIM?
YOUR HAIR LOOKS AWFUL WHAT HAVE YOU DONE TO IT?
???
THE WIND, WILLY... THE BUS WINDOWS WERE BROKEN...
I... WANTED TO SEE YOU...

WILLY STARED AT ME COLDLY & LET ME KNOW HE DIDN'T WANT TO SEE ME AGAIN. WE SAID GOODBYE. A COUPLE OF YEARS LATER I HEARD HE TRIED TO KILL HIMSELF AGAIN. THIS TIME HE SUCCEEDED.

ICAIC – THE CUBAN FILM INSTITUTE

IN CALIFORNIA, I HAD WANTED TO SOMEDAY GO TO ART SCHOOL, OR TO GO TO COLLEGE TO STUDY ZOOLOGY & THEN WORK WITH WILD ANIMALS. BEING IN CUBA SEEMED TO MAKE ALL THAT IMPOSSIBLE. CUBA HAD AN ART SCHOOL, BUT NOT AT COLLEGE LEVEL. LENORE—WHO NEVER HAD THE OPPORTUNITY TO GO TO COLLEGE HERSELF—WAS ADAMANT THAT I GO TO THE UNIVERSITY OF HAVANA AFTER HIGH SCHOOL. TED HAD MADE IT CLEAR THAT HE WAS NOT GOING TO SPEND ONE DIME ON MY EDUCATION SO HERE WAS MY CHANCE TO GET A FREE ONE.

I ALWAYS EXPECTED TO BE AN ARTIST, BUT THERE'S NO WAY HERE FOR ME. I MISS THAT SO MUCH. IN CALIFORNIA...
HEY! WHY DON'T YOU SIGN UP AT THE ICAIC FOR THE ANIMATION COURSE THEY ARE OFFERING?
IT'S AN EVENING CLASS. YOU COULD GO AFTER SCHOOL.
MY HIGH SCHOOL LITERATURE PROFESSOR HAD A BRILLIANT IDEA. HER BUBBLY ENTHUSIASM FOR THE REVOLUTION HAD A LOT TO DO WITH MY CHOICE OF STUDIES AT THE UNIVERSITY FOR THE FOLLOWING SCHOOL YEAR, WHERE SHE TAUGHT GREEK.

YOUR FIRST ASSIGNMENT IS TO BUILD AN ANIMATION TABLE, SINCE YOU WON'T BE ABLE TO BUY ONE.
YOUR CLASS PROJECT WILL BE TO DRAW A ONE-MINUTE FILM.

SO I SIGNED UP FOR JESUS DE ARMAS'S CLASS. HE WAS ONE OF THE FOUNDERS OF THE FABLED ANIMATION DEPARTMENT OF THE *INSTITUTO CUBANO DE ARTE E INDUSTRIA CINEMATOGRÁFICOS*... AN ARTIST BORN WITH 1 1/2 ARMS, HE BECAME ONE OF MY HEROES.

HMM... THIS IS GOOD. YOU COULD HAVE A FUTURE WITH US.
THERE'S AN OPENING. I MIGHT BE ABLE TO GET YOU IN.
BUT I'M STILL IN HIGH SCHOOL.

OH, MY MOTHER WOULD NEVER LET ME.
THIS IS YOUR CHANCE... TALK TO HER.
LET'S SEE NOW... WRITE A THREE-PAGE PROFILE OF CAMILO CIENFUEGOS.

I WAS RIGHT. LENORE NIXED THAT IDEA & I APPLIED TO COLLEGE AT HAVANA UNIVERSITY. ELENA CALDUCH ADVISED ME TO GO TO THE SCHOOL OF LETTERS & ART IN THE FACULTAD DE HUMANIDADES AND MAJOR IN HISTORY OF ART. AT LEAST I COULD STUDY ABOUT ART, IF NOT MAKE IT... SHE WAS MY ONLY ADVISOR. LENORE HAD NO CLUE & TED WASN'T CONCERNED.

LOOK! I'VE GOT A PRESENT FOR YOU. HE'LL BRING YOU GOOD LUCK & PROTECTION.
BE SURE TO CHANGE THE WATER EVERY DAY.

IN MY CLASS AT ICAIC, I HAD MADE FRIENDS WITH A FELLOW STUDENT—A YOUNG PAINTER NAMED MANUEL MENDIVE. HE LIVED IN A SUBURB CALLED LUYANÓ WITH HIS FAMILY & LOTS OF PLANTS & CREATURES. HE TOOK ME TO VISIT & INTRODUCED ME TO THE AFRO-CUBAN RELIGION SANTERÍA.

THE GAME OF JUST SUPPOSING IS THE SWEETEST GAME I KNOW. OUR DREAMS ARE MORE ROMANTIC THAN THE WORLD WE SEE...
...AND IF THE THINGS WE DREAM ABOUT DON'T HAPPEN TO BE SO, THAT'S JUST AN UNIMPORTANT TECHNICALITY.
WHEN JOSEPHINE BAKER CAME TO HAVANA & PERFORMED, MANUEL GOT US ORCHESTRA TICKETS IN THE THIRD ROW.
MENDIVE WENT ON TO BECOME A WELL-KNOWN PAINTER OF AFRO-CUBAN THEMES.

CHEMISTRY WAS THE TORMENT OF MY ACADEMIC LIFE. WE WERE REQUIRED TO TAKE SIX SEMESTERS, A YEAR OF INORGANIC AND TWO OF ORGANIC. I COULDN'T GRADUATE WITHOUT PASSING THEM ALL.

COME TO MY HOUSE TOMORROW. WE COULD STUDY FOR THAT TEST TOGETHER.
ALL RIGHT! WE'LL QUIZ EACH OTHER. I'LL BRING ALL MY NOTES.
THANKS. YOU'RE A REAL PAL FOR HELPING ME.

OMAR, SILVIA'S BOYFRIEND, WAS IN MY CHEMISTRY CLASS. WE BONDED OVER MEMORIZATION DRILLS OF CHEMICAL FORMULAS. WE BECAME STUDY BUDDIES AFTER SCHOOL & ONE DAY I INVITED HIM HOME FOR A LONGER SESSION. WE HAD LOTS OF MATERIAL TO COVER.

I'VE GOT A LITTLE SONG FOR YOU TO MEMORIZE SULPHURIC ACID.
"POOR OLD MRS. GONZÁLEZ, HER FACE WE SEE NO MORE. FOR WHAT SHE THOUGHT WAS H_2O WAS H_2SO_4!"
HA! HA! WE SHOULD PUT THEM ALL INTO SONG.
CORNELIA! COME SET THE TABLE!
¡COÑO! DOESN'T SHE SEE OMAR IS SITTING HERE?
UM, I'M NOT HUNGRY. I'LL EAT LATER... I DON'T WANT TO JUST LEAVE OMAR THERE. CAN'T WE INVITE HIM TO DINNER?
ABSOLUTELY NOT! THERE ISN'T ENOUGH. YOU NEED TO SIT DOWN IMMEDIATELY!
DEBATE WASN'T AN OPTION IN THIS FAMILY.
EAT YOUR VEGETABLES, CHILDREN!

GRADUATION!

COMPAÑERAS, HERE IS YOUR QUOTA CERTIFICATE FOR THE THREE METERS OF WHITE POPLIN CLOTH. EACH FEMALE GRADUATING GETS ONE.
MAKE SURE YOU GET YOUR DRESSES SEWN ON TIME. ***YOU HAVE THREE WEEKS 'TIL GRADUATION!***
HERE, I HAVE A FINE DRESS PATTERN FROM J.C. PENNEY'S THAT I BROUGHT FROM CALIFORNIA. YOU CAN MAKE IT WITH THAT. I'LL HELP YOU.
GREAT! AND THESE HIGH HEELS THAT JOSIE GAVE ME WILL BE PERFECT. NOW ALL I NEED IS TO IRON THIS DRESS.

I WORKED FEVERISHLY ON MY GRADUATION DRESS. BUYING ONE WAS OUT OF THE QUESTION & LENORE KNEW TED WOULD BE ANGRY IF SHE SPLURGED ON A SEAMSTRESS. LENORE'S PRIVATE STASH OF EXTRA CASH WAS ALWAYS LOW.

MY DRESS FELT SPLENDID & EVERYTHING WENT WELL. WE GRADUATED IN THE AUDITORIUM OF THE JEWISH COMMUNITY CENTER ON LINEA STREET & POSED FOR LOTS OF PICTURES. MY FAMILY DIDN'T GO, BUT THAT WAS OK. LENORE COULD BE SO EMBARRASSING. IT WAS REALLY A RELIEF.

UNIVERSIDAD DE LA HABANA

CHAPTER 2

The University of Havana

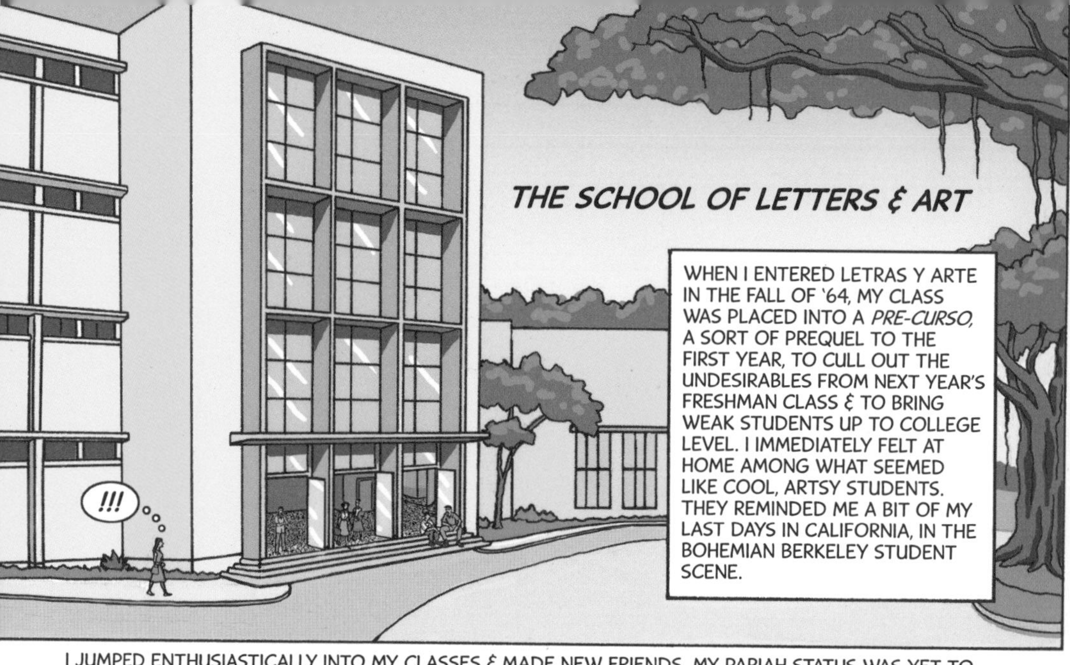
THE SCHOOL OF LETTERS & ART
WHEN I ENTERED LETRAS Y ARTE IN THE FALL OF '64, MY CLASS WAS PLACED INTO A *PRE-CURSO,* A SORT OF PREQUEL TO THE FIRST YEAR, TO CULL OUT THE UNDESIRABLES FROM NEXT YEAR'S FRESHMAN CLASS & TO BRING WEAK STUDENTS UP TO COLLEGE LEVEL. I IMMEDIATELY FELT AT HOME AMONG WHAT SEEMED LIKE COOL, ARTSY STUDENTS. THEY REMINDED ME A BIT OF MY LAST DAYS IN CALIFORNIA, IN THE BOHEMIAN BERKELEY STUDENT SCENE.
!!!

I JUMPED ENTHUSIASTICALLY INTO MY CLASSES & MADE NEW FRIENDS. MY PARIAH STATUS WAS YET TO COME SO I ENJOYED A CAREFREE SEMESTER.

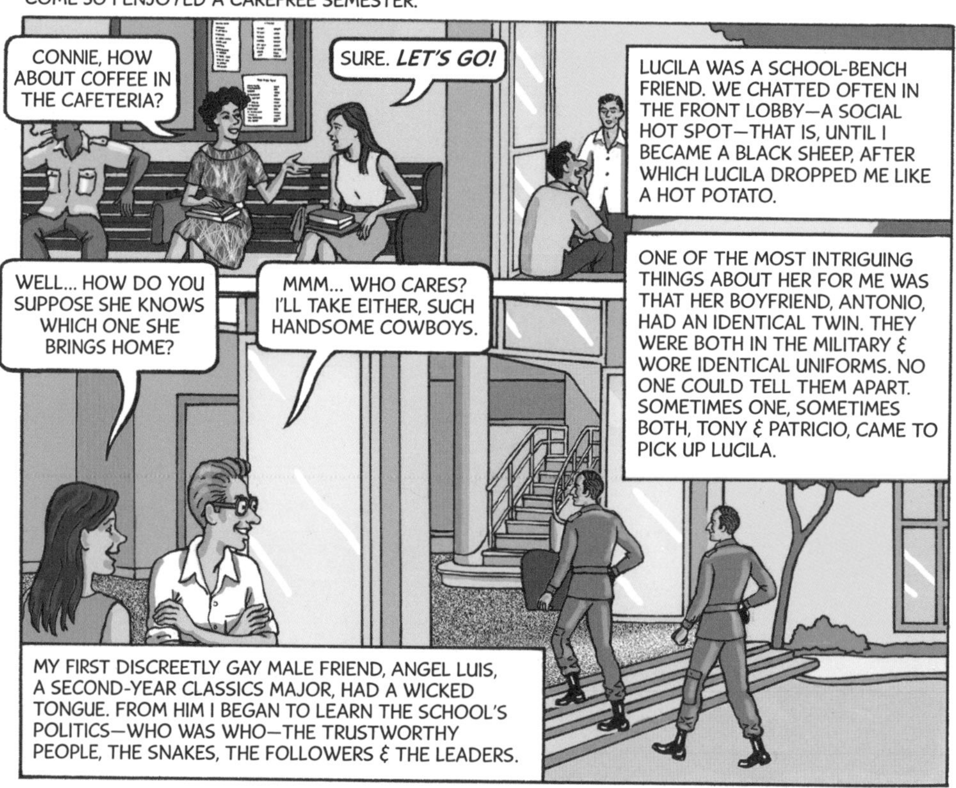
CONNIE, HOW ABOUT COFFEE IN THE CAFETERIA?
SURE. ***LET'S GO!***
LUCILA WAS A SCHOOL-BENCH FRIEND. WE CHATTED OFTEN IN THE FRONT LOBBY—A SOCIAL HOT SPOT—THAT IS, UNTIL I BECAME A BLACK SHEEP, AFTER WHICH LUCILA DROPPED ME LIKE A HOT POTATO.
ONE OF THE MOST INTRIGUING THINGS ABOUT HER FOR ME WAS THAT HER BOYFRIEND, ANTONIO, HAD AN IDENTICAL TWIN. THEY WERE BOTH IN THE MILITARY & WORE IDENTICAL UNIFORMS. NO ONE COULD TELL THEM APART. SOMETIMES ONE, SOMETIMES BOTH, TONY & PATRICIO, CAME TO PICK UP LUCILA.
WELL... HOW DO YOU SUPPOSE SHE KNOWS WHICH ONE SHE BRINGS HOME?
MMM... WHO CARES? I'LL TAKE EITHER, SUCH HANDSOME COWBOYS.
MY FIRST DISCREETLY GAY MALE FRIEND, ANGEL LUIS, A SECOND-YEAR CLASSICS MAJOR, HAD A WICKED TONGUE. FROM HIM I BEGAN TO LEARN THE SCHOOL'S POLITICS—WHO WAS WHO—THE TRUSTWORTHY PEOPLE, THE SNAKES, THE FOLLOWERS & THE LEADERS.

ABOUT 25 YEARS LATER, IN 1989, TONY, LUCILA'S NOW-DIVORCED HUSBAND, WAS EXECUTED, ALONG WITH THE MUCH-DECORATED DIVISION GENERAL ARNALDO OCHOA & TWO OTHER OFFICERS, AFTER ONE OF THE COUNTRY'S MOST SPECTACULAR & INFAMOUS SHOW TRIALS,

THE STREET PERVERTS WERE DRIVING ME CRAZY, SO I SET OUT TO FIND A WAY TO FIGHT BACK. I DISCOVERED JUDO & SENSEI ANDRÉS KOLYCHKINE AT THE UNIVERSITY GYM.

KOLYCHKINE, WHO'D EMIGRATED FROM BELGIUM IN THE LATE FORTIES & ESTABLISHED A JUDO SCHOOL IN HAVANA IN THE EARLY FIFTIES, WAS NOW TEACHING JUDO AT THE UNIVERSITY. I ADORED IT WHEN I LEARNED HOW TO FLING BIG GUYS OVER MY SHOULDER & DELIGHTED IN THE POLITE FEROCITY OF THE SPORT.

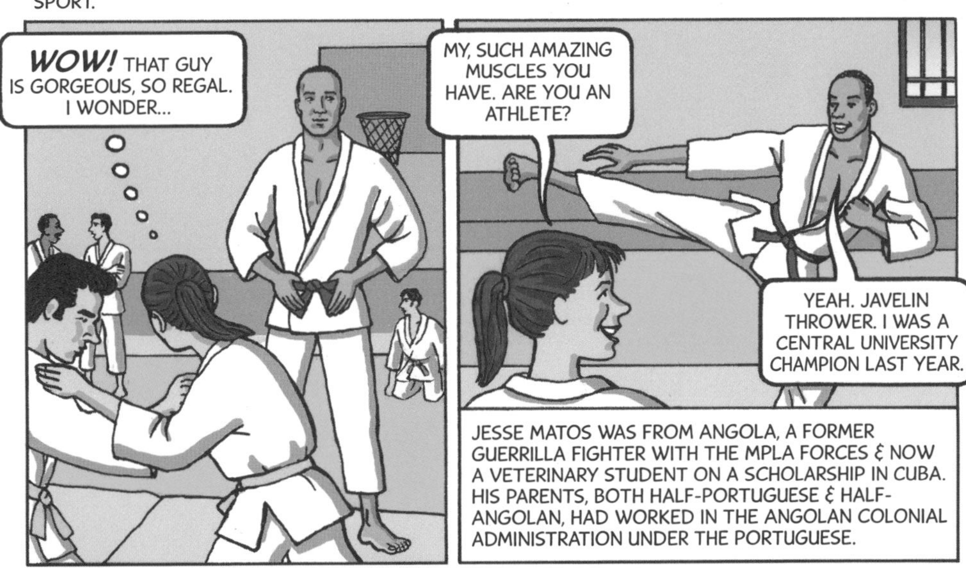
WOW! THAT GUY IS GORGEOUS, SO REGAL. I WONDER...
MY, SUCH AMAZING MUSCLES YOU HAVE. ARE YOU AN ATHLETE?
YEAH. JAVELIN THROWER. I WAS A CENTRAL UNIVERSITY CHAMPION LAST YEAR.
JESSE MATOS WAS FROM ANGOLA, A FORMER GUERRILLA FIGHTER WITH THE MPLA FORCES & NOW A VETERINARY STUDENT ON A SCHOLARSHIP IN CUBA. HIS PARENTS, BOTH HALF-PORTUGUESE & HALF-ANGOLAN, HAD WORKED IN THE ANGOLAN COLONIAL ADMINISTRATION UNDER THE PORTUGUESE.

WE WERE SOON GOING OUT. I BECAME KNOWN AS HIS GIRLFRIEND IN HIS AFRICAN STUDENT CIRCLE. I FELT SLIGHTLY GUILTY FOR HAVING PURSUED SOMEONE ESSENTIALLY FOR HIS PHYSIQUE (HE HAD NO SENSE OF HUMOR!) & BEFORE LONG I STARTED TO FEEL BORED & RESTLESS...

MEANWHILE, NOT LONG BEFORE, TED HAD A BRIEF CONVERSATION WITH CHE GUEVARA AT JUCEPLAN.

COMANDANTE GUEVARA, WHAT CAN BE DONE TO ACCELERATE THE DEVELOPMENT OF SEMICONDUCTORS IN CUBA?
DON'T YOU NEED A BACKGROUND IN PHYSICS BEFORE YOU CAN GO AHEAD WITH THE ENGINEERING ASPECT?
LET'S GET YOU INTO THE SCHOOL OF PHYSICS AT THE UNIVERSITY. THEN YOU CAN DEVELOP A PROGRAM THERE.

CHE GUEVARA WAS DETERMINED TO INDUSTRIALIZE THE CUBAN ECONOMY & ACTIVELY PROMOTED ATTRACTING FOREIGN SCIENTISTS, ENGINEERS & PROFESSORS. IN '61, SHORTLY AFTER THE TRIUMPH OF THE REVOLUTION, THE SCHOOL OF PHYSICS WAS CREATED & SOON FACULTY WERE RECRUITED FROM THE SOCIALIST CAMP & SEVERAL WESTERN COUNTRIES.

TED TAUGHT CLASSES IN SOLID STATE PHYSICS, TRAINED GRADUATE STUDENTS & BEGAN TO BUILD AN ELECTRONICS LAB TO DEVELOP & PRODUCE SEMICONDUCTORS IN CUBA.
IN OCTOBER 1964, WHILE I WAS STARTING COLLEGE LIFE, TED & HIS COLLEGUE DINA WEISMAN, AN ARGENTINIAN PHYSICIST, WENT ON A TRIP TO THE SOVIET UNION FOR ADVICE & MATERIAL SUPPORT FOR THEIR LAB & TEACHING PROGRAM.
LENORECHEN! I'M GOING TO LENINGRAD & MOSCOW! THE ACADEMY OF SCIENCE IS SENDING US!
OH! HOW WILL I MANAGE ALONE WITH THE CHILDREN? YOU HAVE TO BRING BACK LOTS OF SHAMPOO & HAIR DYE FOR ME.
THEY WERE WARMLY RECEIVED AT THE JOFFE SEMICONDUCTOR INSTITUTE IN LENINGRAD. THEY BROUGHT BACK MATERIALS & MADE PERSONAL CONNECTIONS THAT STRENGTHENED TIES BETWEEN SOVIET & CUBAN SCIENTIFIC RESEARCH AT THE UNIVERSITY FOR YEARS TO COME.
WHAT DO YOU NEED, COMRADE TEODORO?
EVERYTHING!
HERE! WE'LL GIVE YOU ALL THESE LAB MANUALS NOW & SHIP LOTS OF OUR EXTRA EQUIPMENT LATER.

NICKAROO! YOU GOT A POSTCARD FROM DADDY! LOOK!
OCT. 14— DEAR NIKKI
...THE PICTURE ON THE OTHER SIDE YOU MAY RECOGNIZE FROM THE COLOR OF THE GENTLEMAN'S BEARD. TO SEE WHAT HAPPENED TO HIM, WAIT FOR THE NEXT POSTCARD.
LOVE, DADDY
OCT. 17— DEAR NIKKI
WELL, AS YOU GUESSED, HE CAME TO NO GOOD END. I SEND POSTCARDS SO YOU WILL GET ALL THESE GORGEOUS STAMPS. BE SURE TO STEAM THEM OFF GENTLY, DON'T SOAK— THAT WILL RUIN THE POSTCARD PICTURE!
LOVE, DADDY
OHH!

TED RETURNED FROM THE USSR FILLED WITH PRAISE FOR ALL THINGS SOVIET, READY TO PROMOTE SOVIET RESEARCH METHODOLOGY AT HAVANA UNIVERSITY.

TED RESUMED HIS BUSY SOCIAL LIFE WITH LENORE & THE KIDS AT THE SIERRA MAESTRA HOTEL & THE RIO MAR APARTMENT COMPLEX. A FEW OF THE APARTMENTS WERE STILL INHABITED BY THE ORIGINAL CUBAN CONDO OWNERS, BUT MOST NOW HOUSED FOREIGN TECHNICIANS & THEIR FAMILIES.
CZECHS, BULGARIANS, EAST GERMANS, POLES & RUSSIANS, AS WELL AS LATIN AMERICANS, HAD THE POOLS, THE SAND, THE BAR & MOST IMPORTANTLY, THE SUPERMARKET AT THEIR EXCLUSIVE DISPOSAL. IT WAS FILLED WITH GOODS SOLD ONLY TO THEM, IN NATIONAL CURRENCY, IN CUBAN PESOS. SHORTAGES WERE RARE.
THESE WERE A FEW OF TED & LENORE'S ENGLISH-SPEAKING FRIENDS & ACQUAINTANCES. MANY HAD FLED OR BEEN EXPELLED FROM THE U.S. UNDER A CLOUD, REFUGEES OF THE COLD WAR.
JOE NORTH, *JOURNALIST,* "THE DAILY WORKER"
BOB PURDY *TOOL & DIE MAKER*
LIONEL MARTIN *JOURNALIST*
BARBARA MARTIN *TRANSLATOR*
MARTHA DODD *WRITER, DAUGHTER OF WILLIAM DODD, THE AMERICAN AMBASSADOR TO NAZI GERMANY, 1933-1937*
GEORGE BELFRAGE *FOUNDER, EDITOR & CO-OWNER OF THE NEWSPAPER* "THE NATIONAL GUARDIAN"
GEORGE EISEN *PHYSICIAN*

EDITH HALPERIN
MAURICE HALPERIN
PROFESSOR, LATIN AMERICAN SPECIALIST, FORMER OSS OFFICER
ESTELLE BRAVO
FILMMAKER
ANGELA MOUTSOS
TEACHER & TRANSLATOR
MARILYN
TRANSLATOR
ADA D.
TEACHER & TRANSLATOR
ED BOORSTEIN
ECONOMIST & WRITER
ANITA W.
TRANSLATOR
BELLA SCUPP
EDUCATOR

SCHOOL ELECTIONS

IN FEBRUARY OF '65, UNIVERSITY STUDENTS BEGAN CAMPAIGNING FOR THE STUDENT BODY GOVERNMENT. THE UJC HADN'T YET CONSOLIDATED ITS MONOPOLY ON POLITICAL EXPRESSION & A VARIETY OF PEOPLE ROSE TO SPEAK ABOUT THE CANDIDATES IN A SERIES OF SCHOOL ASSEMBLIES, WHICH I EAGERLY ATTENDED.

OHHH... LOOK AT HER. SHE'S SO WITTY & HIP!
... AND NOT FRÚ-FRÚ!
HOW DO I MEET HER?
ELECCIONES FEU
DAMAS Y CABALLEROS, VOTE FOR FULANO! WE NEED HIM FOR PRESIDENT. HE'S THE INTELLIGENT CHOICE!

ONE OF THE SPEAKERS—MONICA, A SECOND-YEAR STUDENT—WAS QUITE SERIOUS & ALSO VERY FUNNY. SHE CAUGHT MY ATTENTION & I WAS SMITTEN. MY RESOLVE TO KEEP LIFE SIMPLE & GO "STRAIGHT" IN MY ROMANTIC RELATIONS QUICKLY DISSOLVED. OVER THE NEXT FEW DAYS, I WATCHED HER FROM AFAR & PLOTTED MY APPROACH...

MAYBE THIS'LL DO IT... I'LL MAKE SOME POSTERS ABOUT THE ELECTION.
HEY, ANGEL LUIS, I'D LIKE TO GIVE THESE TO MONICA, CAN YOU HELP ME?
¡FANTÁSTICO! CAN YOU MAKE SOME MORE?

I KNEW I HAD TO SAY GOODBYE TO JESSE, MY ANGOLAN BOYFRIEND. HE TOOK IT HARD. I COULDN'T HAVE CHOSEN A WORSE TIME TO HEAD IN THIS DIRECTION...

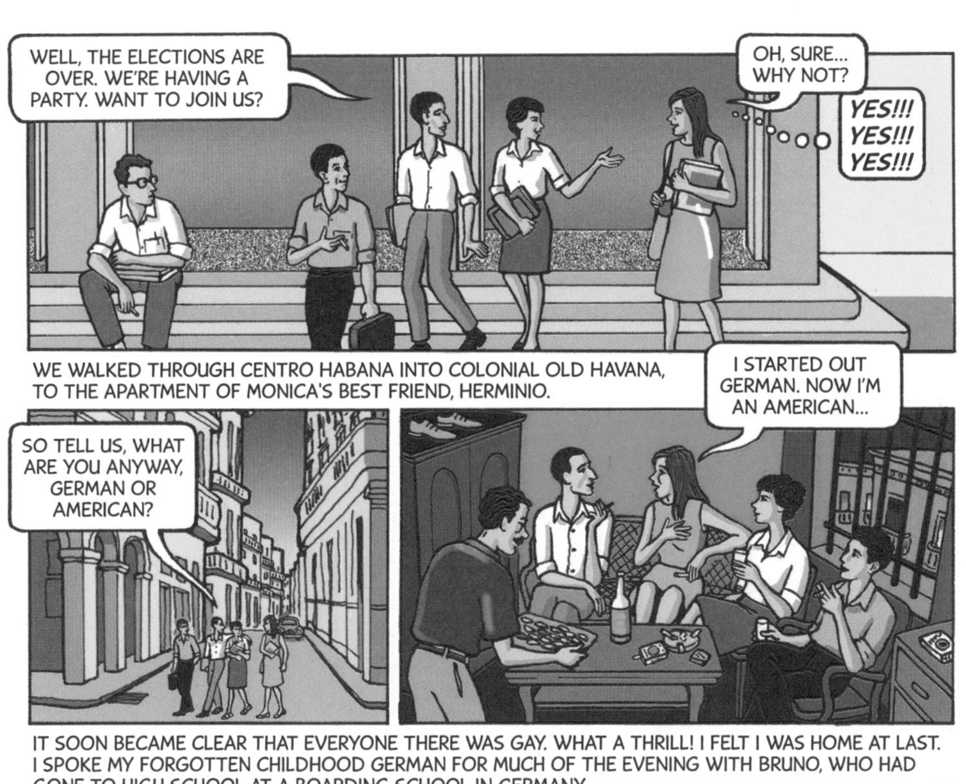
WELL, THE ELECTIONS ARE OVER. WE'RE HAVING A PARTY. WANT TO JOIN US?
OH, SURE... WHY NOT?
YES!!! YES!!! YES!!!
WE WALKED THROUGH CENTRO HABANA INTO COLONIAL OLD HAVANA, TO THE APARTMENT OF MONICA'S BEST FRIEND, HERMINIO.
SO TELL US, WHAT ARE YOU ANYWAY, GERMAN OR AMERICAN?
I STARTED OUT GERMAN. NOW I'M AN AMERICAN...
IT SOON BECAME CLEAR THAT EVERYONE THERE WAS GAY. WHAT A THRILL! I FELT I WAS HOME AT LAST. I SPOKE MY FORGOTTEN CHILDHOOD GERMAN FOR MUCH OF THE EVENING WITH BRUNO, WHO HAD GONE TO HIGH SCHOOL AT A BOARDING SCHOOL IN GERMANY.

ICH WUCHS IN DEUTSCHLAND AUF UND GING DORT IN DIE SCHULE. UND WO KOMMST DU HER?
DARMSTADT, DIE STADT WURDE WÄHREND DES KRIEGES SEHR ZERSTÖRT. MIENE MUTTER BRACHTE MICH NACH AMERIKA ALS ICH SIEBEN WAR.
YOU NEED TO GO HOME NOW, CONNIE. COME ON... I'LL TAKE YOU.
OH, YESH...
¡QUÉ FELIZ ESTOY!
SHHH! I'M HAPPY TOO, BUT SHUT UP NOW BEFORE SOMEONE DENOUNCES US.

YOU'RE DISGUSTING! WHERE HAVE YOU BEEN?
OHHH... MY HEAD'S KILLING ME. I'M GONNA THROW UP AGAIN!
QUE ME QUITEN LO BAILAO! FUCK HER.
ARRGGG!!!

I WAS SOON ADOPTED BY MONICA'S FRIENDS AS HER GIRLFRIEND. SHE WAS THE CENTRAL FIGURE IN A GROUP OF BRIGHT STUDENTS, TWO YEARS AHEAD OF ME. BRUNO & GUSTAVO WERE A COUPLE & CLOSE TO MONICA. MOST OF THE CORE GROUP WAS GAY, WITTY & ARTSY— NOT AT ALL IN THE MOLD OF "THE NEW MAN." THE OUTER CIRCLE WAS A MIX OF GAYS & BOHEMIAN STRAIGHT PEOPLE —STUDENTS FROM THE ARQUITECTURE SCHOOL, THE SCHOOL OF LETTERS, PAINTERS & WRITERS— SOME CONSIDERED THEMSELVES REVOLUTIONARIES, SOME DISCREETLY NOT. MANY WERE SEEN AS *"CONFLICTIVOS."*

WE WENT OUT DRINKING & LISTENED TO JAZZ, TO *"FILIN,"* TO THE GRAND DIVAS & MASTERS OF CUBAN CABARET MUSIC AT THE GATO TUERTO NIGHTCLUB & OTHER HIP VENUES. WE TALKED FOR HOURS ABOUT ART & LOVE & POLITICS & BEING TOGETHER.

WE ALL WENT TO SEE FOREIGN FILMS AT THE CINEMATECA AT 23RD & 12TH STREET, WHERE I FELL IN LOVE WITH SERGEI EISENSTEIN.

CICLO DE CINE SOVIETICO
IVAN EL TERRIBLE
ПОТЕМКИН

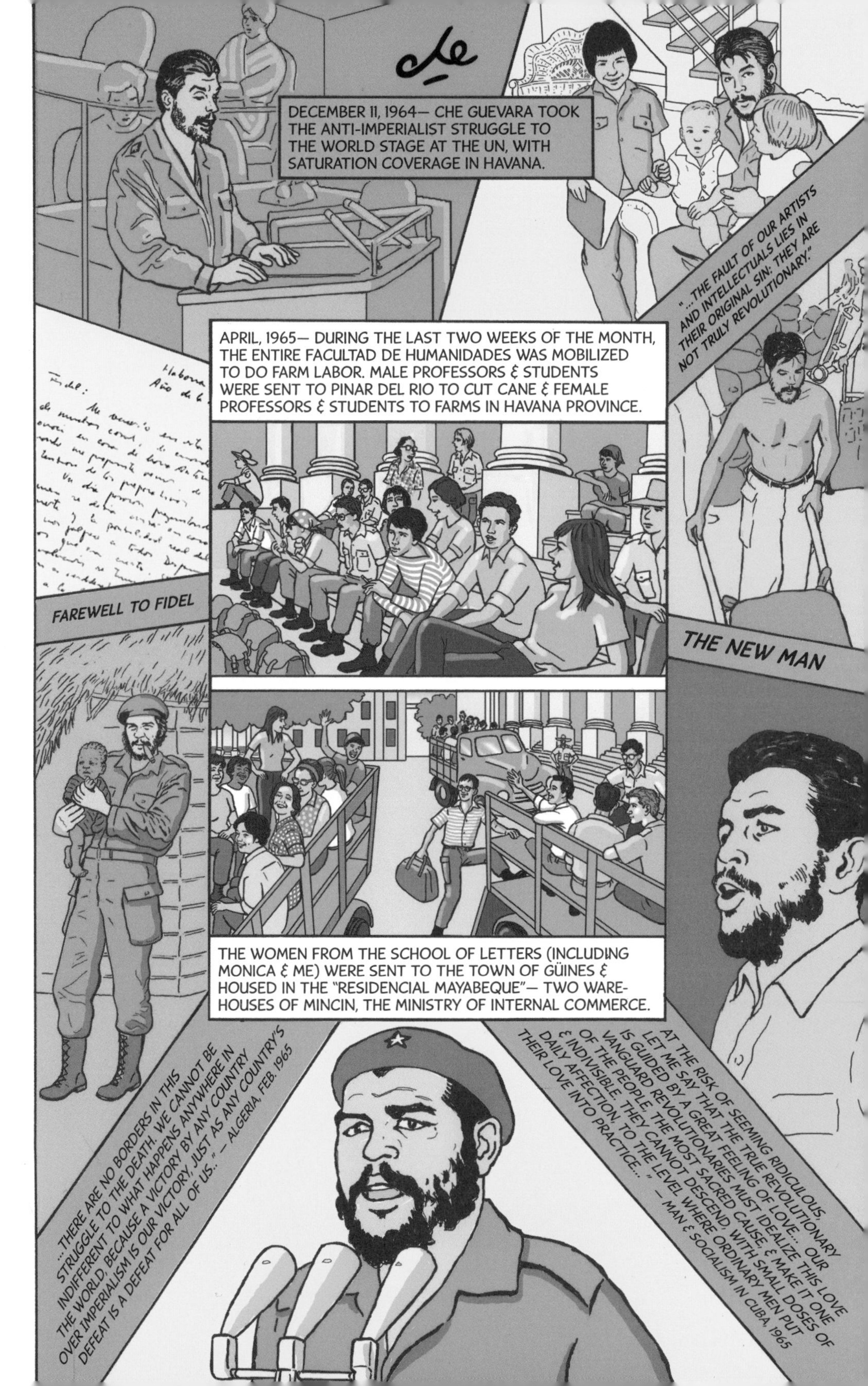

Che
DECEMBER 11, 1964— CHE GUEVARA TOOK THE ANTI-IMPERIALIST STRUGGLE TO THE WORLD STAGE AT THE UN, WITH SATURATION COVERAGE IN HAVANA.
"...THE FAULT OF OUR ARTISTS AND INTELLECTUALS LIES IN THEIR ORIGINAL SIN: THEY ARE NOT TRULY REVOLUTIONARY."
APRIL, 1965— DURING THE LAST TWO WEEKS OF THE MONTH, THE ENTIRE FACULTAD DE HUMANIDADES WAS MOBILIZED TO DO FARM LABOR. MALE PROFESSORS & STUDENTS WERE SENT TO PINAR DEL RIO TO CUT CANE & FEMALE PROFESSORS & STUDENTS TO FARMS IN HAVANA PROVINCE.
FAREWELL TO FIDEL
THE NEW MAN
THE WOMEN FROM THE SCHOOL OF LETTERS (INCLUDING MONICA & ME) WERE SENT TO THE TOWN OF GÜINES & HOUSED IN THE "RESIDENCIAL MAYABEQUE"— TWO WAREHOUSES OF MINCIN, THE MINISTRY OF INTERNAL COMMERCE.
"...THERE ARE NO BORDERS IN THIS STRUGGLE TO THE DEATH. WE CANNOT BE INDIFFERENT TO WHAT HAPPENS ANYWHERE IN THE WORLD, BECAUSE A VICTORY BY ANY COUNTRY OVER IMPERIALISM IS OUR VICTORY, JUST AS ANY COUNTRY'S DEFEAT IS A DEFEAT FOR ALL OF US..." — ALGERIA, FEB. 1965
"AT THE RISK OF SEEMING RIDICULOUS, LET ME SAY THAT THE TRUE REVOLUTIONARY IS GUIDED BY A GREAT FEELING OF LOVE... OUR VANGUARD REVOLUTIONARIES MUST IDEALIZE THIS LOVE OF THE PEOPLE, THE MOST SACRED CAUSE, & MAKE IT ONE & INDIVISIBLE. THEY CANNOT DESCEND, WITH SMALL DOSES OF DAILY AFFECTION, TO THE LEVEL WHERE ORDINARY MEN PUT THEIR LOVE INTO PRACTICE..." — MAN & SOCIALISM IN CUBA, 1965

GÜINES
¡PINCHEN!!
¡AY, LA MUGRE! I CAN'T STAND THE FILTH!
WHO TOOK MY COMB??
OUR BARRACKS IN GÜINES WERE BARE CEMENT BLOCKS, MEANT FOR STORING SACKS OF FOOD. THE BARRACKS HAD NOW BEEN OUTFITTED WITH ROWS OF BUNK BEDS.
Z-Z-Z..!!
"EL CUARTO DE LA LOCURA," "THE CRAZY ROOM," WAS A SMALL SEPARATE ANNEX WHERE THE PROFESSORS SLEPT. VICENTINA ANTUÑA, THE SCHOOL DIRECTOR, HAD THE LUXURY OF HER OWN COT.

OUR WORK BRIGADES TOOK TURNS WORKING IN THE FIELDS, CLEANING THE BARRACKS & DOING KITCHEN DUTY. EVERY DAY THE FARMER & GOVERNMENT REP. JUANITO & HIS DRIVER WOULD COME FOR US BEFORE DAWN & TAKE US TO THE FIELDS. OUR MISSION WAS TO CLEAN & PREPARE ROWS & THEN TO PLANT MALANGA, AS WELL AS HARVEST TOMATOES, POTATOES & BONIATO. THE WORK WAS BACKBREAKING, THE SUN INTENSE & OUR HANDS BURNED FROM BLISTERS. TO SPUR PRODUCTIVITY, WE WERE URGED TO COMPETE TO BE THE BRIGADE THAT BROUGHT IN THE HIGHEST YIELDS.
THE CHINESE STUDENTS FROM THE FOREIGNERS PROGRAM ALWAYS WON *LA EMULACIÓN SOCIALISTA*. THEY NEVER TOOK BREAKS, NEVER GOOFED OFF, NEVER SHOWED EXHAUSTION, BUT WORKED LIKE ARMY ANTS. SMALL WONDER, THEY WERE COMMUNIST PARTY CADRES SENT BY THE CHINESE GOVERNMENT TO BECOME AN ELITE CORPS OF TRANSLATORS.

MIRTA AGUIRRE— OUR SANITATION ENGINEER

THE CAMP ORGANIZERS HAD NEGLECTED TO THINK OF THE NEED FOR TOILETS. MIRTA AGUIRRE, DISTINGUISHED PROFESSOR OF RHETORIC & SPANISH LITERATURE, AS WELL AS A PROMINENT OLD GUARD PSP COMMUNIST, STEPPED UP TO SAVE THE DAY. SHE SINGLE-HANDEDLY DUG A DEEP PIT & OUR ONE-HOLE LATRINE WAS BORN.

WE EAGERLY LOOKED FORWARD TO MAIL FROM LOVERS BACK HOME OR IN OTHER WORK CAMPS & SOMETIMES CHANGED THEIR GENDERS FOR SAFETY'S SAKE.

¡OIGAN, OIGAN! MY CHICHO WROTE!

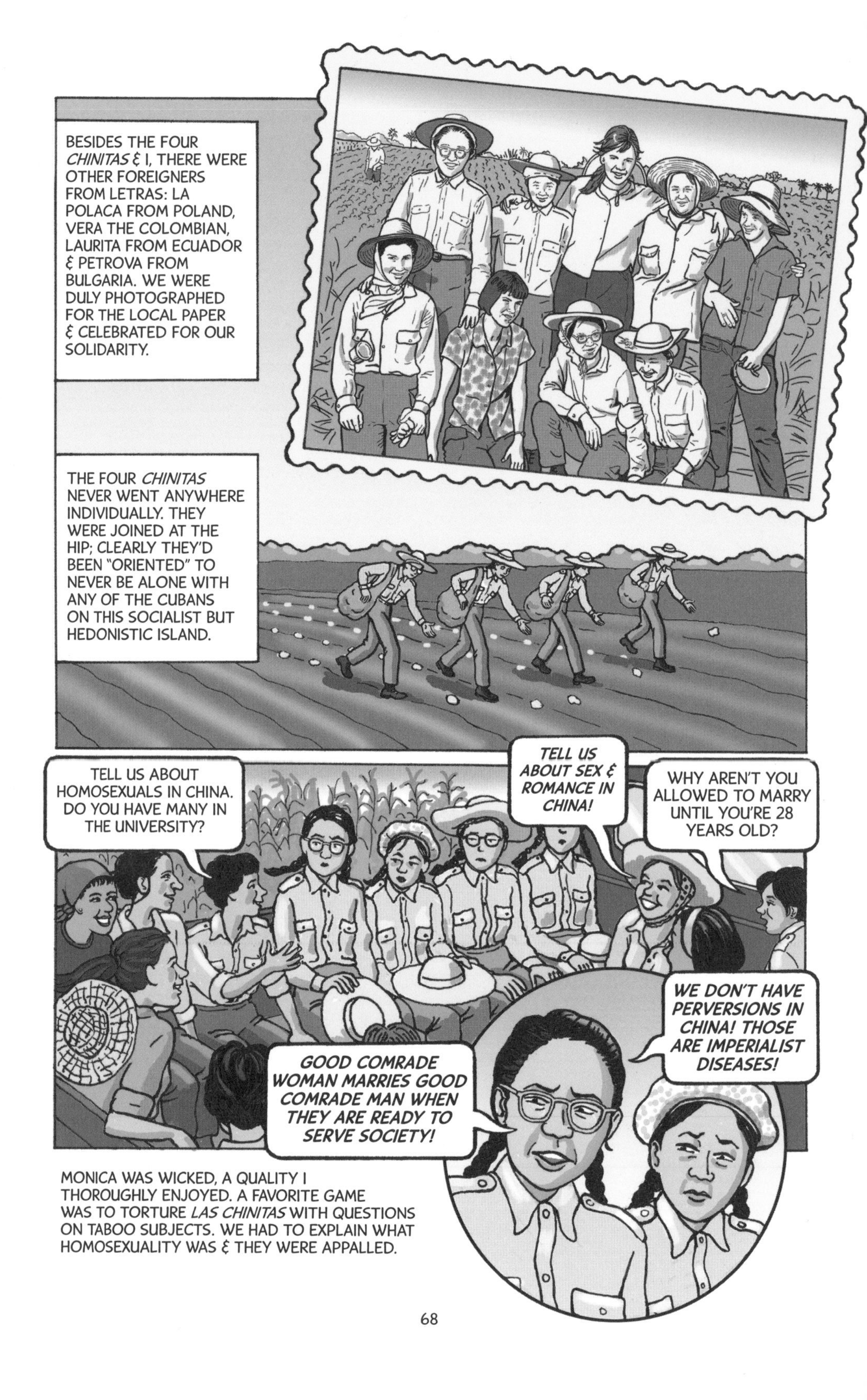

BESIDES THE FOUR *CHINITAS* & I, THERE WERE OTHER FOREIGNERS FROM LETRAS: LA POLACA FROM POLAND, VERA THE COLOMBIAN, LAURITA FROM ECUADOR & PETROVA FROM BULGARIA. WE WERE DULY PHOTOGRAPHED FOR THE LOCAL PAPER & CELEBRATED FOR OUR SOLIDARITY.
THE FOUR *CHINITAS* NEVER WENT ANYWHERE INDIVIDUALLY. THEY WERE JOINED AT THE HIP; CLEARLY THEY'D BEEN "ORIENTED" TO NEVER BE ALONE WITH ANY OF THE CUBANS ON THIS SOCIALIST BUT HEDONISTIC ISLAND.
TELL US ABOUT HOMOSEXUALS IN CHINA. DO YOU HAVE MANY IN THE UNIVERSITY?
TELL US ABOUT SEX & ROMANCE IN CHINA!
WHY AREN'T YOU ALLOWED TO MARRY UNTIL YOU'RE 28 YEARS OLD?
GOOD COMRADE WOMAN MARRIES GOOD COMRADE MAN WHEN THEY ARE READY TO SERVE SOCIETY!
WE DON'T HAVE PERVERSIONS IN CHINA! THOSE ARE IMPERIALIST DISEASES!
MONICA WAS WICKED, A QUALITY I THOROUGHLY ENJOYED. A FAVORITE GAME WAS TO TORTURE *LAS CHINITAS* WITH QUESTIONS ON TABOO SUBJECTS. WE HAD TO EXPLAIN WHAT HOMOSEXUALITY WAS & THEY WERE APPALLED.

AY, JUANITO... I'D REALLY LIKE TO RIDE YOUR HORSE...
ARGGG.
SO YOU THINK I COULD BORROW IT JUST FOR A LITTLE WHILE?
ARGGG.
HMMM?
OH, BLISS! I LOVED TO RIDE HORSES & TOOK EVERY OPPORTUNITY...
¡COÑO! SPLIT PEA MUSH AGAIN! UGH!
THE CAMP FOOD WAS ALWAYS FOUL...
¡VAYA, QUE RICO!
...SO PACKAGES FROM HOME WERE TREASURED.
INEXPLICABLY, THE LOCAL MOVIE THEATER IN THIS COUNTRY VILLAGE, GÜINES, WAS SHOWING A JEAN-LUC GODARD FILM, SO ON SUNDAY AFTERNOON, OUR HALF-DAY OF REST, SOME OF US RELAXED OGLING THE WOMEN IN "VIVRE SA VIE."
"¡EL QUE COME VERDOLAGA SIEMPRE CAGA, CAGA BLANDITO!"
"MALANGA GANGA MALANGÁ"
NANCY MOREJÓN, A POET & ONE OF THE FEW DARK-SKINNED STUDENTS IN OUR SCHOOL, MADE UP HILARIOUS NONSENSE RHYMES WE LUSTILY BELTED OUT WITH IMPROVISED MELODIES.

I WAS HAPPY. I FELT LIKE I BELONGED, THAT WE WERE ALL VERY VIRTUOUS FOR TAKING PART IN THE REVOLUTIONARY PROCESS & THAT THINGS COULD ONLY GET BETTER, WITH OUR HELP, FOR THE *CAMPESINOS*, THE FARMERS & PEASANTS. WE RETURNED TO HAVANA IN THE BEST OF SPIRITS.

LA DEPURACIÓN—THE GREAT PURGES OF 1965

WE CAME BACK TO SCHOOL TO A NEW LANDSCAPE...

OH, MY GOD! HAVE YOU SEEN THIS?!?

IN MAY OF '65, WE STARTED TO READ AGGRESSIVE ARTICLES IN THE STUDENT WEEKLY "ALMA MATER," IN THE COMMUNIST YOUTH MAGAZINE "MELLA" & IN THE DAILY PAPER "JUVENTUD REBELDE"—FIERCE CONDEMNATION OF *"LA LACRA SOCIAL,"* (THE SCUM OF SOCIETY), HOMOSEXUALS & *"ENFERMITOS"* (HIPPIE TYPES), ANY MALE WHO WORE SANDALS OR HAD LONG HAIR, ANYONE WHO SHOWED INSUFFICIENT ENTHUSIASM FOR REVOLUTIONARY ACTIVITIES LIKE MILITIA DUTY OR FARM LABOR, AS WELL AS THOSE KNOWN TO BE RELIGIOUS.

MAYO 31 DE 1965
NUM. 325 15 CTS.
mella

HALF THE SCHOOL OF LETTERS WILL BE PURGED!

WE ARE WAGING A REVOLUTION AGAINST THE EXPLOITERS, AGAINST THE ENEMIES OF THE PEOPLE, & THOSE WHO, IN ONE WAY OR ANOTHER, REPRESENT THE IDEOLOGY OF THOSE ASPIRING TO BRING BACK THE PAST. THEY MUST NO LONGER FIND HARBOR IN OUR UNIVERSITIES, WHERE THE ENGINEERS TO DIRECT OUR FACTORIES, WHERE INTELLECTUALS & THOSE WHO WILL ADMINISTER OUR NATIONAL CULTURAL LIFE, WHERE THE MEN ON THE FRONT LINES IN THE STRUGGLE FOR COMMUNISM, ARE FORMED.

THE GREAT STUDENT BATTLE

...WE, THE STUDENT YOUTH ORGANIZATIONS OF OUR COUNTRY, HAVE DECIDED TO PRESENT TO YOU THE NEED TO EXPEL FROM OUR SCHOOLS ALL THOSE ELEMENTS INCAPABLE OF FINDING INSPIRATION IN THE WORK OF THE REVOLUTION, IN THE SACRIFICE OF OUR MARTYRS, IN THE HEROISM OF OUR YOUTH—THOSE WHO HAVE TURNED THEIR BACKS ON THE REVOLUTIONARY PROCESS & THAT REPRESENT THE IDEOLOGY OF THE ENEMIES OF THE PEOPLE.

...THOSE THAT DEMONSTRATE CERTAIN DEVIATIONS WHICH REVEAL PETIT BOURGEOISIE WEAKNESSES, APATHETIC TO THE REVOLUTIONARY ACTIVITIES OF OUR STUDENT BODY, MUST ALL BE EXPELLED BEFORE THEY REACH THE UNIVERSITY. THEY MUST TAKE ON THE HONORABLE TASK OF JOINING OUR GLORIOUS ARMED FORCES. THIS WAY THEY MAY FILL THE HOLES THEY NOW HAVE IN THEIR DOSSIERS THAT MAKE IT IMPOSSIBLE TO ENTER OUR UNIVERSITIES.

CHICA, WHAT ABOMINABLE PROSE!
UNBELIEVABLE!

YOU THE STUDENTS MUST BE THE ONES TO CARRY OUT THESE ORIENTATIONS THAT CONCERN US ALL.

YOU KNOW VERY WELL WHO THEY ARE. YOU HAVE HAD TO STRUGGLE AGAINST THEM MANY TIMES, & SURELY HAVE ASKED YOURSELVES WHEN THE OPPORTUNITY WOULD COME TO DEMAND AN ACCOUNTING FROM THEM.

THE MOMENT HAS NOW COME TO APPLY, WITH RESPONSIBILITY, THE POWER OF THE WORKER & PEASANT CLASSES AGAINST THEIR ENEMIES.

OUT WITH THE COUNTERREVOLUTIONARIES & HOMOSEXUALS IN OUR SCHOOLS!

WE SHALL WIN THE BATTLE OF SCHOOL PROMOTIONS!

WHEREVER, HOWEVER & FOREVER—COMMANDER-IN-CHIEF, WE AWAIT YOUR ORDERS!

UJC-UES

FATHERLAND OR DEATH, WE SHALL WIN!

DPTO. DE PERSONAL
NO SÉ QUE TIENE DE MALO ESA GENTE
"EL FLAUTISTA DE HAMELIN"
4
El hijo del machetero lo saludó de esta manera: "Pipo, yo hice una zafra de papalotes".
MELLA, Nº. 326, MAY 31, 1965

SOON NEWS SPREAD ABOUT *LA DEPURACIÓN*, THE "PURIFICATION" PURGES BEING CONDUCTED IN OTHER SCHOOLS OF THE UNIVERSITY. WE BRACED OURSELVES FOR THE CALAMITY AT LETRAS. FRIENDS IN THE ARQUITECTURE SCHOOL & SOME OF THE SCIENCE SCHOOLS AT CUJAE (LA CIUDAD UNIVERSITARIA JOSÉ ANTONIO ECHEVERRÍA), TOLD US WHAT HAD HAPPENED THERE.

THIS INDIVIDUAL IS A HOMOSEXUAL!!! SOCIAL SCUM! THERE'S NO ROOM FOR DEVIANTS IN THE UNIVERSITY OF HAVANA! IT'S TIME TO THROW THEM OUT!
¡FUERA!!! ¡FUERA!!! ¡FUERA!!!
¡MARICÓN!!! ¡CONTRARREVOLUCIONARIO!!!
THE PURIFICATION PURGES INCLUDED MASS MEETINGS PRESIDED OVER BY STUDENT GOVERNMENT REPS, THE FEU (FEDERACIÓN ESTUDIANTIL UNIVERSITARIA) & THE UJC (UNIÓN DE JOVENES COMUNISTAS).
AFTER A PUBLIC SHAMING, THE ACCUSED WERE SUMMARILY EXPELLED.
TO PROTEST ON SOMEONE ELSE'S BEHALF WAS OUT OF THE QUESTION—AN AUTOMATIC SOCIAL & POLITICAL SUICIDE.

AS IT TURNED OUT, THE MASS PURGES NEVER CAME TO LETRAS. OUR DIRECTOR, VICENTINA ANTUÑA, HAD IMPECCABLE REVOLUTIONARY CREDENTIALS THAT GAVE HER & HER SCHOOL SOME INMUNITY & EVEN THE APPARENT PROTECTION OF FIDEL CASTRO HIMSELF. SHE HAD PLAYED A ROLE IN THE URBAN INSURRECTION BEFORE THE TRIUMPH OF THE REVOLUTION, HARBORING ARMS FOR THE 26 OF JULY MOVEMENT. BUT MANY INDIVIDUALS WERE EXPELLED ANYWAY, IF NOT PUBLICLY SHAMED.

PORQUE HAY QUE TENER EN CUENTA QUE FLORITO ERA "REVOLUCIONARIO"...
...PORQUE YO TENDRÉ MIS DEBILIDADES, PERO SOY MUY MARXISTA... ¡VAYA!

SIN EMBARGO, CADA DÍA QUE PASABA ENCONTRABA MENOS COMPRENSIÓN... Y EL POBRE FLORITO NO PODÍA MENOS QUE COMPARAR:
CUBA:
EL MUNDO LIBRE:
TODOS A LA RECOGID DE CAFE
THE CHATTANOO
SE EDITA EN NEW YORK UNA REVISTA DEDICADA ESPECIALMENTE A LOS HOMOSEXUALES.
...Y HAY QUE SEGUIR DÈPURANDO... ¡NO QUEREMOS GUSANOS NI CORROMPIDOS EN LA UNIVERSIDAD!
...Y FLORITO AL FIN COMPRENDIÓ...
¡PROTÉGEME, JOHNNY! ¡SOY UN PERSEGUIDO POR LOS COMUNISTAS!
US
CAL 45
—mella 21—

MELLA Nº 325 MAY 24, 1965

ALLEN GINSBERG & THE DEATH OF "THE BRIDGE"

IN JANUARY 1965, THE AMERICAN POET ALLEN GINSBERG CAME TO CUBA AS A JUDGE FOR A POETRY PANEL FOR THE CASA DE LAS AMERICAS LITERARY CONTEST. IT DIDN'T TAKE LONG BEFORE THE SHIT HIT THE FAN & GINSBERG WAS DEPORTED.

THE NORTEAMERICANOS AMIGOS DE CUBA WERE TOLD BY ICAP THAT ALLEN GINSBERG WAS IN TOWN & WERE DIRECTED TO SOCIALIZE WITH HIM. SO ANGELA BOYER, ONE OF A SMALL FLOCK OF FEMALE TRANSLATORS, HOSTED A PARTY FOR HIM AT HER APARTMENT IN VEDADO. THIS EVENT WAS ONE I DIDN'T WANT TO MISS.
¡ALERTA!
26 de JULIO
FIDEL CASTRO
I'VE BROUGHT SOME MUSIC FROM THE STATES THAT YOU JUST HAVE TO HEAR—BOB DYLAN & JOAN BAEZ. THEY'RE FANTASTIC.
THIS MUSIC IS SO GREAT..! WAS IT HARD TO BRING INTO THE COUNTRY?
FIDEL CA
BOB DYLAN
OH, SOME DINGLEBERRY AT CUSTOMS WASN'T HAPPY & OBJECTED, BUT I GOT THEM THROUGH.
A DINGLEBERRY? WHAT'S *THAT?*
AAH! A DINGLEBERRY IS A SMALL PIECE OF SHIT, DRY & FORGOTTEN, THAT'S HANGING FROM THE HAIRS OF YOUR ANUS.
THANKS! THAT'S THE BEST INSULT I'VE EVER HEARD.
YOU'RE WELCOME! AND NOW I MUST LEAVE. I'M MEETING SOME PEOPLE...
GINSBERG EXTRACTED HIMSELF GRACIOUSLY & HIT THE STREET.

GINSBERG ROAMED NIGHT TIME VEDADO & SOON WAS APPROACHED BY SEVERAL YOUNG POETS, FRIENDS OF JOSÉ MARIO, THE FOUNDER & LIFE FORCE OF EL PUENTE PUBLISHING HOUSE. THIS COUNTER-CULTURAL SHOESTRING ENTERPRISE HAD PUBLISHED WORKS OF POETRY & FICTION SINCE 1961. MARIO HAD BEEN A LETRAS STUDENT FOR A WHILE & NOW DEDICATED HIMSELF FULL TIME TO WRITING & PUBLISHING HIS & OTHER YOUNG WRITERS' WORKS, WITH RELUCTANT RECOGNITION FROM HAVANA'S CULTURAL ESTABLISHMENT.
ALLEN GINSBERG! WE WANTED TO MEET YOU. COME HAVE A DRINK WITH US. WE'RE WRITERS & WANT TO TALK WITH YOU ABOUT "HOWL."
23
OH SURE! BUT FIRST, CAN YOU HELP ME GET SOMETHING FOR THESE AWFUL CRAB LICE I PICKED UP IN MEXICO?
HA! HA! OF COURSE! COME ON. HERE'S A PHARMACY THAT'S OPEN. WE'LL GET SOME "SOLDIERS' CREAM."
FARMACIA
THEY MET UP WITH THE REST OF THEIR GROUP—INCLUDING JOSÉ MARIO—& WENT TO THE ATELIER CLUB, A TINY HOLE-IN-THE-WALL ON 17TH & 6TH STREET.
TELL US ABOUT THE BEATNIKS.
NOW TELL ME ABOUT SEXUAL FREEDOM IN CUBA.
TELL ME ABOUT THE REVOLUTION.
WHAT ABOUT MARIJUANA?
WHAT'S *"FILIN"* MUSIC?
WHO ARE THE *"ENFERMITOS"* (THE SICKOS)?
SO WHY DID THEY LET ME INTO THE COUNTRY IF PEOPLE ARE PERSECUTED FOR THE WAY THEY DRESS?
THEY TOLD GINSBERG ABOUT THE PURGES IN THE ART SCHOOLS, THE UNIVERSITY, THE PERSECUTION OF HOMOSEXUALS. THE NEXT DAY, GINSBERG TOOK THEM TO HIS HOTEL ROOM AT THE RIVIERA, AFTER ARGUING WITH THE ELEVATOR OPERATOR, AS CUBANS WERE FORBIDDEN TO ENTER FOREIGNERS' ROOMS.
LOOK ALLEN, WE'VE BROUGHT YOU SOME OF THE BOOKS WE'RE PUBLISHING AT EL PUENTE.

NEXT A REPRESENTATIVE OF THE COMMUNIST PARTY NEWSPAPER, "HOY," WALKED INTO THE HOTEL ROOM TO INTERVIEW GINSBERG.

TELL US, MR. GINSBERG, WHAT WOULD YOU SAY IF YOU MET FIDEL CASTRO?
WHY, I'D TELL HIM TO STOP THE EXECUTIONS. INSTEAD OF EXECUTING PEOPLE, THEY SHOULD BE PUNISHED BY SERVING AS ELEVATOR BOYS IN THIS HOTEL... I'D TELL HIM HE SHOULDN'T PERSECUTE *"ENFERMITOS,"* HE SHOULD ALLOW THE FREE SALE OF MARIJUANA SINCE IT'S A LOT LESS DANGEROUS THAN ALCOHOL.
...& THAT HE SHOULDN'T PERSECUTE HOMOSEXUALS BECAUSE COMMUNISM IS A MATTER OF THE HEART & I BELIEVE HOMOSEXUALITY IS, TOO.

IN THE DAYS THAT FOLLOWED, IT DIDN'T TAKE LONG FOR THESE YOUNG POETS TO BE ARRESTED, ACCUSED OF "CONSORTING WITH FOREIGNERS." WHEN GINSBERG FOUND OUT, HE TRIED TO INTERVENE WITH THE CULTURAL AUTHORITIES. JOSÉ MARIO WAS FREED, ONLY TO BE ARRESTED OVER & OVER AGAIN, AS WERE ALL OF HIS FRIENDS & ALMOST EVERYONE WHO HAD COME IN CONTACT WITH ALLEN GINSBERG WITHOUT APPROVAL.

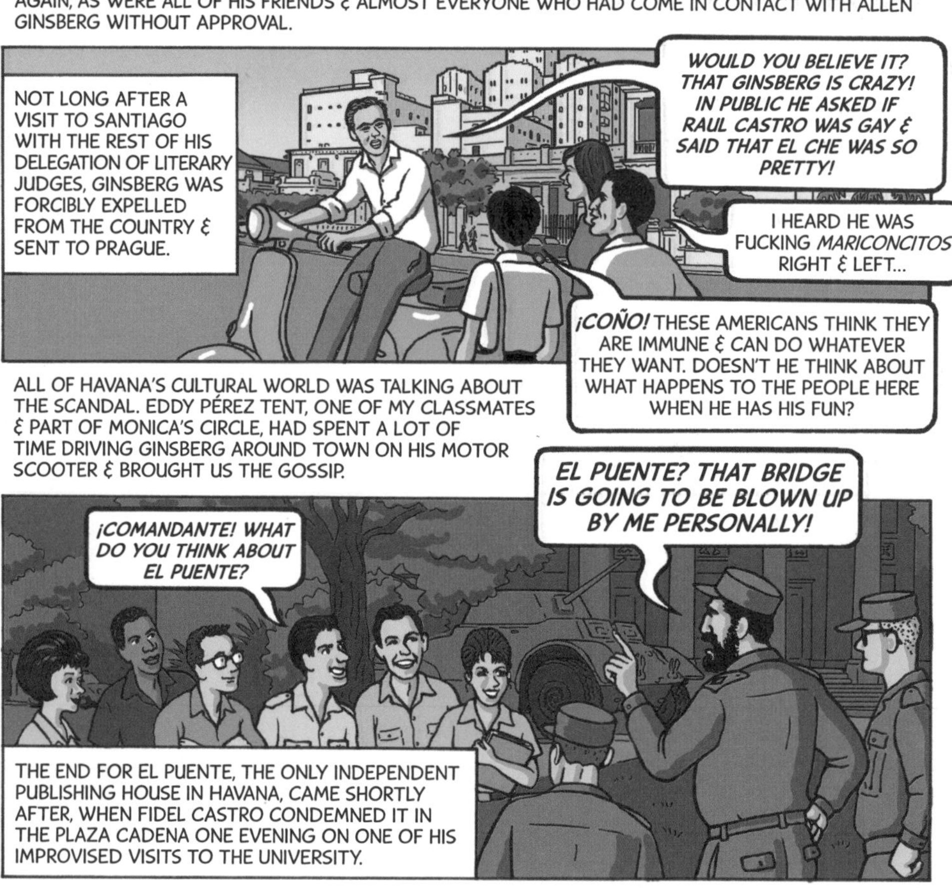
NOT LONG AFTER A VISIT TO SANTIAGO WITH THE REST OF HIS DELEGATION OF LITERARY JUDGES, GINSBERG WAS FORCIBLY EXPELLED FROM THE COUNTRY & SENT TO PRAGUE.
WOULD YOU BELIEVE IT? THAT GINSBERG IS CRAZY! IN PUBLIC HE ASKED IF RAUL CASTRO WAS GAY & SAID THAT EL CHE WAS SO PRETTY!
I HEARD HE WAS FUCKING *MARICONCITOS* RIGHT & LEFT...
¡COÑO! THESE AMERICANS THINK THEY ARE IMMUNE & CAN DO WHATEVER THEY WANT. DOESN'T HE THINK ABOUT WHAT HAPPENS TO THE PEOPLE HERE WHEN HE HAS HIS FUN?
ALL OF HAVANA'S CULTURAL WORLD WAS TALKING ABOUT THE SCANDAL. EDDY PÉREZ TENT, ONE OF MY CLASSMATES & PART OF MONICA'S CIRCLE, HAD SPENT A LOT OF TIME DRIVING GINSBERG AROUND TOWN ON HIS MOTOR SCOOTER & BROUGHT US THE GOSSIP.
¡COMANDANTE! WHAT DO YOU THINK ABOUT EL PUENTE?
EL PUENTE? THAT BRIDGE IS GOING TO BE BLOWN UP BY ME PERSONALLY!
THE END FOR EL PUENTE, THE ONLY INDEPENDENT PUBLISHING HOUSE IN HAVANA, CAME SHORTLY AFTER, WHEN FIDEL CASTRO CONDEMNED IT IN THE PLAZA CADENA ONE EVENING ON ONE OF HIS IMPROVISED VISITS TO THE UNIVERSITY.

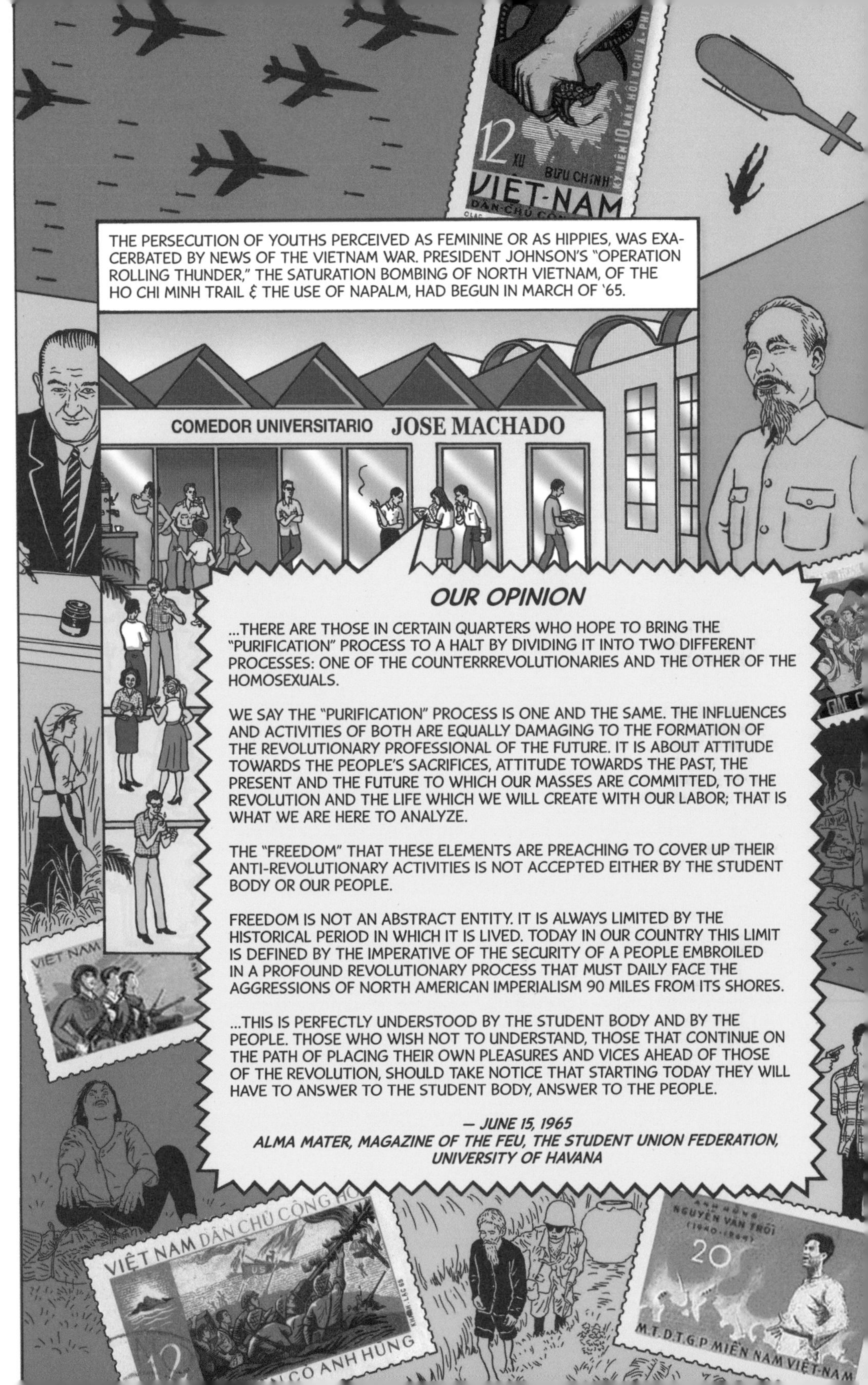
12
XU
BƯU CHÍNH
VIỆT-NAM
THE PERSECUTION OF YOUTHS PERCEIVED AS FEMININE OR AS HIPPIES, WAS EXACERBATED BY NEWS OF THE VIETNAM WAR. PRESIDENT JOHNSON'S "OPERATION ROLLING THUNDER," THE SATURATION BOMBING OF NORTH VIETNAM, OF THE HO CHI MINH TRAIL & THE USE OF NAPALM, HAD BEGUN IN MARCH OF '65.
COMEDOR UNIVERSITARIO JOSE MACHADO
OUR OPINION
...THERE ARE THOSE IN CERTAIN QUARTERS WHO HOPE TO BRING THE "PURIFICATION" PROCESS TO A HALT BY DIVIDING IT INTO TWO DIFFERENT PROCESSES: ONE OF THE COUNTERRREVOLUTIONARIES AND THE OTHER OF THE HOMOSEXUALS.
WE SAY THE "PURIFICATION" PROCESS IS ONE AND THE SAME. THE INFLUENCES AND ACTIVITIES OF BOTH ARE EQUALLY DAMAGING TO THE FORMATION OF THE REVOLUTIONARY PROFESSIONAL OF THE FUTURE. IT IS ABOUT ATTITUDE TOWARDS THE PEOPLE'S SACRIFICES, ATTITUDE TOWARDS THE PAST, THE PRESENT AND THE FUTURE TO WHICH OUR MASSES ARE COMMITTED, TO THE REVOLUTION AND THE LIFE WHICH WE WILL CREATE WITH OUR LABOR; THAT IS WHAT WE ARE HERE TO ANALYZE.
THE "FREEDOM" THAT THESE ELEMENTS ARE PREACHING TO COVER UP THEIR ANTI-REVOLUTIONARY ACTIVITIES IS NOT ACCEPTED EITHER BY THE STUDENT BODY OR OUR PEOPLE.
FREEDOM IS NOT AN ABSTRACT ENTITY. IT IS ALWAYS LIMITED BY THE HISTORICAL PERIOD IN WHICH IT IS LIVED. TODAY IN OUR COUNTRY THIS LIMIT IS DEFINED BY THE IMPERATIVE OF THE SECURITY OF A PEOPLE EMBROILED IN A PROFOUND REVOLUTIONARY PROCESS THAT MUST DAILY FACE THE AGGRESSIONS OF NORTH AMERICAN IMPERIALISM 90 MILES FROM ITS SHORES.
...THIS IS PERFECTLY UNDERSTOOD BY THE STUDENT BODY AND BY THE PEOPLE. THOSE WHO WISH NOT TO UNDERSTAND, THOSE THAT CONTINUE ON THE PATH OF PLACING THEIR OWN PLEASURES AND VICES AHEAD OF THOSE OF THE REVOLUTION, SHOULD TAKE NOTICE THAT STARTING TODAY THEY WILL HAVE TO ANSWER TO THE STUDENT BODY, ANSWER TO THE PEOPLE.
— JUNE 15, 1965
ALMA MATER, MAGAZINE OF THE FEU, THE STUDENT UNION FEDERATION, UNIVERSITY OF HAVANA
VIET NAM
VIỆT NAM DÂN CHỦ CỘNG HÒA
12
CÔ ANH HÙNG
NGUYỄN VĂN TRỖI
20
M.T.D.T.G.P MIỀN NAM VIỆT-NAM

OVNIVERSIDAD DE LA HABANAO
TWO YEARS EARLIER, WHILE I WAS STILL IN HIGH SCHOOL, FIDEL GAVE A SPEECH THAT PREPARED THE GROUND FOR THE PURGES NOW UPON US. HE SPOKE ON THE EVE OF MARCH 13, 1963, AT THE "ESCALINATA," THE GRAND STEPS FRONTING THE QUAD OF HAVANA UNIVERSITY.
...THERE IS A SPECIMEN TO BE FOUND OUT THERE, A BI-PRODUCT WE MUST STRUGGLE AGAINST—THAT YOUNG MAN, 16, 17, 18 YEARS OLD, WHO NEITHER STUDIES NOR WORKS. HE'S A LUMPEN, HANGS OUT ON STREET CORNERS, IN BARS, GOES TO THE THEATER & TAKES CERTAIN LIBERTIES, & FALLS INTO LIBERTINE BEHAVIOR. WHAT DOES A YOUNG PERSON WHO NEITHER STUDIES NOR WORKS THINK ABOUT LIFE? DOES HE EXPECT TO LIVE AS A PARASITE? AS A BUM? OFF OF OTHERS? IF THE IMPERIALISTS DON'T WELCOME THEM OVER THERE, WELL, THEY BETTER BE PREPARED TO WORK!
CLAP! CLAP! CLAP!
THEY ARE SHAMELESS!... ALWAYS REMEMBER..! JUST AS THE REVOLUTION UNITES THE BEST, THE FIRMEST, THE MOST ENTHUSIASTIC & THE MOST VALUABLE, SO THE COUNTERREVOLUTION UNITES THE WORST, FROM THE BOURGEOIS TO THE MARIJUANA DEALER, FROM THE KILLER TO THE THIEF, FROM THE OWNER OF A SUGAR MILL TO THE PROFESSIONAL BUM & THE PERVERT. ALL THESE ELEMENTS COME TOGETHER TO DO BATTLE AGAINST LEGALITY, THE REVOLUTION & SOCIETY... NEVER FORGET!...
CLAP! CLAP! CLAP!
THE LIMP-WRISTED, FIDEL! THE HOMOSEXUALS!
YOU DIDN'T LET ME FINISH THE IDEA!
MANY OF THESE BUM "PEPILLOS," CHILDREN OF THE BOURGEOISIE, GO AROUND WITH PANTS THAT ARE TOO TIGHT (LAUGHTER), SOME WITH A GUITAR & AN ELVIS PRESLEY ATTITUDE & THEY'VE TAKEN THEIR LIBERTINE BEHAVIOR TO SUCH EXTREMES THAT THEY WANT TO GO TO PUBLIC PLACES & ORGANIZE THEIR EFFEMINATE SHOWS RIGHT IN THE OPEN. LET NO ONE CONFUSE THE SERENITY OF THE REVOLUTION WITH WEAKNESSES OF THE REVOLUTION. BECAUSE OUR SOCIETY CANNOT GIVE SPACE TO THESE DEGENERATES!
CLAP! CLAP! CLAP!
A SOCIALIST COUNTRY CANNOT PERMIT THIS TYPE OF DEGENERACY!

LIFE AT LETRAS WENT ON, WHILE THE POLITICAL WITCH-HUNT SWIRLED THROUGH THE UNIVERSITY. STUDENTS FROM "BROTHER" COUNTRIES —POLAND, BULGARIA, ALBANIA & ROMANIA— RAN A BRISK BUSINESS SELLING BLACK MARKET LEATHER & VINYL BRIEFCASES.

TAKE A LOOK AT THE LINING! I HAVE TWO OF THESE, TOP QUALITY!
HMM... HOW MUCH?
GOT ANYTHING TO OFFER?
I'VE GOT A NECKLACE AT HOME. I'LL BRING IT TOMORROW. WE'LL TALK.
MAYO

SOMETIMES THE VIETNAMESE STUDENTS AMAZED US.

¡DIOS MÍO! THEY'RE HOLDING HANDS! THE'D BE LYNCHED IF THEY WERE CUBANS...

AT THE SIERRA MAESTRA HOTEL & CLUB FOR FOREIGN *TÉCNICOS,* RUSSIAN HOUSEWIVES MINED THEIR CONTACTS TO OBTAIN GOLD FROM CUBANS WHO WERE DESPERATE FOR CASH TO BUY BLACK MARKET FOOD. FOR A WHILE, I EXCHANGED PRIVATE LESSONS IN CONVERSATIONAL ENGLISH FOR INTRO CLASSES IN ELEMENTARY RUSSIAN WITH THE WIFE OF ONE OF TED'S RUSSIAN COLLEAGUES. WE MET AT HER APARTMENT ONCE A WEEK FOR CLASSES WITH TEA & SWEETS.

Что это такое?
Это карандаш.
CUBANS DON'T HAVE HARD CURRENCY, BUT THEY DO HAVE GOLD, OLD FAMILY JEWELRY, YOU KNOW?
IF YOU HEAR OF ANYONE WHO WANTS TO SELL, I'M VERY INTERESTED.
MMM... OH SURE, ¡DA! ¡DA!
¡LIKE HELL I WILL... ¡THAT'S EXPLOITATION!

GUANABO BEACH
BECAUSE OF A PERMANENT HOUSING SHORTAGE, MOST OF MY FRIENDS LIVED WITH THEIR PARENTS. THE OPTIMAL WAY TO BE FREE, TO GET AWAY FROM THE FAMILY, TO MAKE LOVE, OR TO RELAX TOGETHER AWAY FROM PRYING EYES WAS TO POOL OUR MONEY & RENT A CABAÑA ON THE THE BEACH, A LUXURY, BUT WE DID IT WHENEVER WE COULD.

GUANABO, A FEW MILES TO THE EAST OF HAVANA, WAS ONE OF OUR FAVORITE PLACES. THE NERVE-WRACKING PART WAS GETTING THERE WITHOUT BEING SEEN BY MEMBERS OF THE UNIVERSITY UJC. IT WAS OFTEN ALREADY KNOWN WHO WAS GAY, OF COURSE. THE GAME WAS NOT TO GET CAUGHT OR TO BE SEEN ALONE TOO OFTEN WITH SOMEONE OF THE SAME SEX. THE WEAPON OF CHOICE FOR RUINING A FELLOW STUDENT WAS AN ACCUSATION OF BEING GAY OR COUNTERREVOLUTIONARY.

THERE WAS NOWHERE TO BUY FOOD, OR LIQUOR, OR CIGARETTES AT THE BEACH, SO WE BROUGHT OUR OWN & COOKED IN OUR CABAÑA, WHICH CAME EQUIPPED WITH THE BASICS.

CITA
L CINE...
ÑOS DE
ISTAS
ECTUA-
BAR-
O CON
...
RÍA
NTIGUA
ISULS
LLENA DE SEXO, DE CON-
FLICTOS Y SENSITIVIDAD:
EL LOBO! Y EL PROFUNDO
COMPLEJO QUE SE OCUL-
TA TRAS SU OBSESIÓN DE
COMERSE A LA MUCHACHA.
O MENOS ASÍ...
LAS
CAPERUCITAS
SE
COSECHAN
EN
PRIMAVERA

BUT THE BEACH COULDN'T PROTECT US FROM THE STORMS AT SCHOOL, AS THE PURIFICATION CAMPAIGN RAGED ON. A TASTE FOR FOREIGN FILMS, EVEN FROM "BROTHER COUNTRIES" LIKE CZECHOSLOVAKIA, WAS NOW SUSPECT. "THE HOP PICKERS," FROM 1964 (*"EL AMOR SE COSECHA EN VERANO"*, OR "LOVE IS HARVESTED IN THE SUMMER"), WAS A ROMANTIC COMEDY ABOUT NON-CONFORMIST YOUTH & WAS IDENTIFIED WITH THE LIMP-WRISTED DILETTANTES OF THE CULTURAL WORLD.

"MELLA" MAGAZINE SNEERED THAT IN THE HANDS OF A FOREIGN FILMMAKER, "LITTLE RED RIDINGHOOD" WOULD BECOME "LITTLE HOODS ARE HARVESTED IN THE SPRING."

¿A DÓNDE VAS, NIÑA?
VOY AL CABARET DE MI ABUELA. ESTOY CANTANDO ALLÍ EN EL SHOW.

CONTINUAN LOS MISTERIOSOS CRIMENES DE EL LOBO

WHAT IS TO BE DONE WITH COUNTERREVOLUTIONARY WORMS?

"WE MUST BOIL THEM!"

—*MELLA*, JUNE 7, 1965

¡HAY QUE HERVIRLOS!

COMO DIJO EL FILÓSOFO MEDIEVAL PRUDENCIO GOLLEJO, AL AGUA DE POZO HAY QUE HERVIRLA... PERO ES QUE HAY "MICROBIOS" MUCHO MÁS PELIGROSOS QUE LAS AMEBAS... Y A ESOS TAMBIÉN HAY QUE HERVIRLOS...
EN ESA TAREA ESTÁN AHORA LOS JÓVENES ESTUDIANTES UNIVERSITARIOS Y TAMBIÉN LOS DE LOS PRE-UNIVERSITARIOS, LOS DE LOS INSTITUTOS DE ADMINISTRACIÓN Y COMERCIO E INSTITUTOS TECNOLÓGICOS.
NUESTRO PUEBLO ESTÁ PLENAMENTE DE ACUERDO CON ESTA MEDIDA DE PROFILAXIS...

WHAT IS TO BE DONE WITH THE SOCIAL MISFITS WHO REFUSE TO INTEGRATE INTO THE REVOLUTION? THE DEADBEATS WHO WON'T WORK OR STUDY? THE RELIGIOUS? THE PERVERTS?
WE PROPOSE AN OBLIGATORY UNARMED FORCE, A PRODUCTION FORCE, SEPARATE FROM THE SMO (OBLIGARORY MILITARY SERVICE).
YES! WE'LL CALL IT THE UMAP, UNIDADES MILITARES DE AYUDA A LA PRODUCCIÓN!
UMAP
ONE DAY IN NOVEMBER 1965, OUR FRIEND GUSTAVO VENTOSO DISAPPEARED.
MANDARIN
FARMACIA
IN THE EARLY AFTERNOON, GUSTAVO (AN EXEMPLARY CLASSICS STUDENT) & DR. NICOLAS FARRAY (OUR LATIN PROFESSOR) WERE TALKING AT THE CORNER OF L & 23RD STREET ON LA RAMPA. WE SOON LEARNED THAT GUSTAVO HAD DISAPPEARED & FEARED THE WORST. RUMORS WERE FLYING ABOUT THE SUDDEN EMERGENCE OF FORCED LABOR CAMPS, THE "MILITARY UNITS TO AID PRODUCTION."
FAGGOTS!
HUNGER!
HUNGER!
WATER!

UMAP: forja de ciudad.
Brillante iniciativa de cuadros militares
Fidel les dio el nombre. Un ejército más con que cuenta el pueblo para defenderse
RECIENTEMENTE tuvimos oportunidad de recordar
toda nitidez unos párrafos del discurso que
ximo dirigente, comandante Fidel Castro,
lectuales. Esos párrafos son:
"Es precisamente el hombre
de sus semejantes,
lucionarios.
EMPRESA CONSOLIDADO
FARMACIA
TURNO MARTES
útiles a la sociedad, es produciendo" refiere
unión de los integrantes de las UMAP. En las U
rteto vanguardia de esta quincena está integ
Rey de Rojas y Arcadio Lópe
EL MUNDO, APRIL 14, 1966
NO ONE HEARD FROM GUSTAVO FOR SIX MONTHS. HIS FAMILY & FRIENDS DIDN'T KNOW IF HE WAS ALIVE OR DEAD.
FARMACIA
edida muy grande, esto SMO de ayuda a la
se debe al comandante Ernesto Casillas.
de la provincia de Camagüey y miembro del
al que vemos departiendo con un recluta
COMANDANTE ERNESTO CASILLAS, WHO CONTROLLED THE MANY UMAP CAMPS IN CAMAGÜEY PROVINCE, CHATS WITH A SUBORDINATE.

"THE TWO CURRENTS OF WORLD REVOLUTION SHALL BE REPRESENTED HERE, THE ONE BORN OF THE OCTOBER REVOLUTION & THE NATIONAL LIBERATION MOVEMENTS."
— BEN BARKA, OCTOBER 3, 1965
OCT. 3 & 4, 1965— THE COMMUNIST PARTY & GRANMA, THE OFFICIAL PARTY PAPER, ARE BORN.
HOY
REVOLUCION
SEGUNDA EDICION
Granma
No hay sacrificio, combate o proeza que no estén representados en el Comité Central
THE TRICONTINENTAL
CONFERENCE OF AFRICAN, ASIAN, & LATIN AMERICAN PEOPLES
JANUARY 1966
FIDEL INVITED THE WORLD'S MOST PROMINENT REVOLUTIONARIES TO THIS SUMMIT FOR THE UNIFICATION OF THE WORLD'S ANTI-COLONIAL MOVEMENTS, WITH CUBA AT THE HELM.
AS THE FOREIGN CORRESPONDENT FOR "DAS ANDERE DEUTSCHLAND," MY MOTHER LENORE HAD THE TIME OF HER LIFE INTERVIEWING & MINGLING WITH FAMOUS REVOLUTIONARIES AT THE RECEPTIONS THAT SHE & TED ATTENDED.
HAVE YOU HEARD? THEY'RE PICKING UP THOUSANDS & SENDING THEM TO THE UMAP! THEY'RE ALL MEN SO FAR. MARIJUANEROS, JEHOVAH'S WITNESSES, CATHOLICS, FLAMING FAGGOTS & OTHERS LIKE GUSTAVO.
I HEARD THE OLD LADIES FROM LETRAS ARE TRYING TO GET GUSTAVO OUT... BUT IT'S NOT HAPPENING. I HEARD THEY PULLED EVERY STRING THEY COULD.
MEANWHILE, AT THE SCHOOL OF LETTERS, WE COUNTED ON THE GRAPEVINE, RADIO BEMBA, FOR NEWS ABOUT THE UMAP.
A STORY CIRCULATED THAT AN INMATE KNOWN AS ELLEGUÁ DIDN'T FEEL WELL ONE DAY & REFUSED TO GO TO WORK...

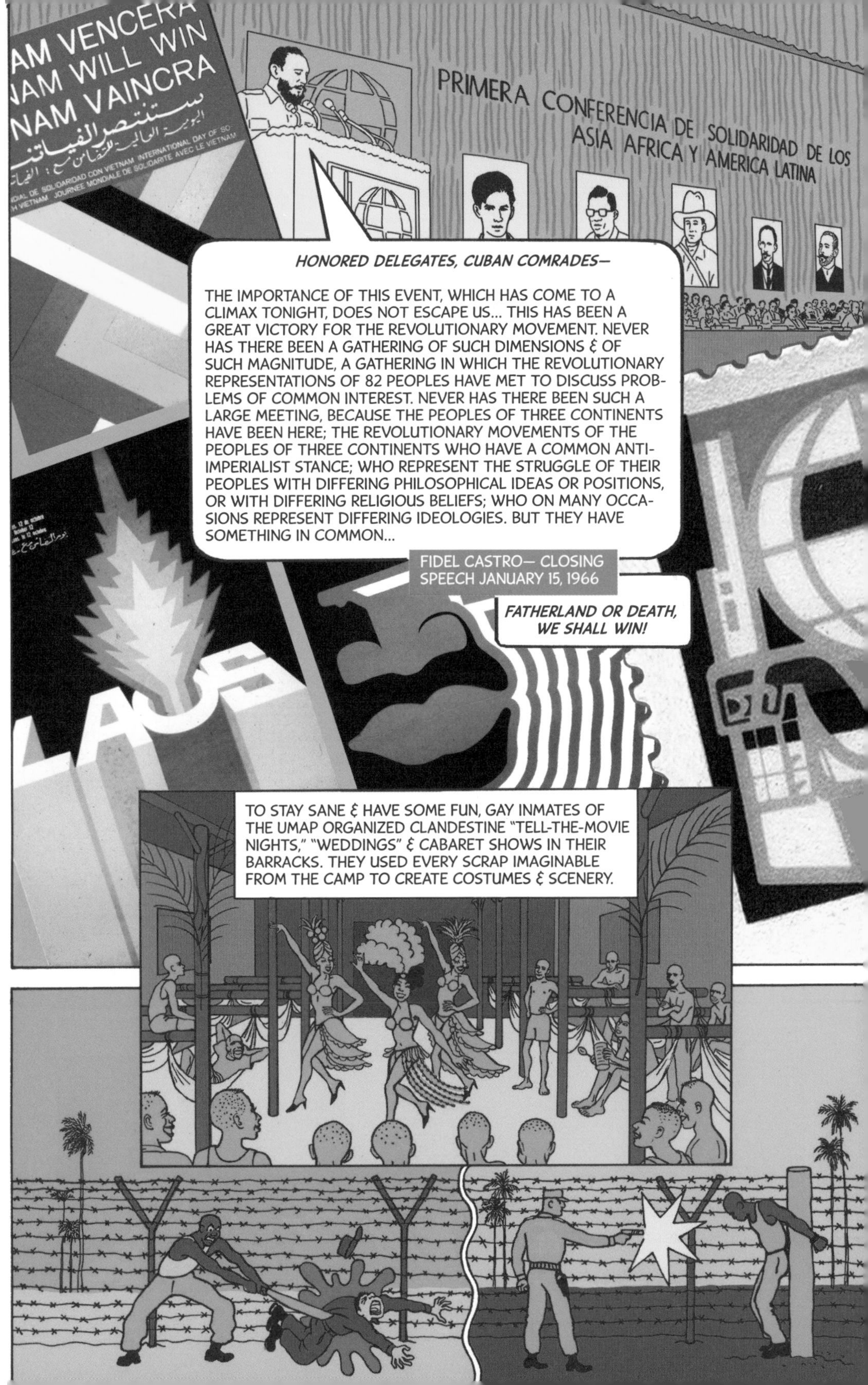

AM VENCERA
NAM WILL WIN
NAM VAINCRA
PRIMERA CONFERENCIA DE SOLIDARIDAD DE LOS
ASIA AFRICA Y AMERICA LATINA
HONORED DELEGATES, CUBAN COMRADES—
THE IMPORTANCE OF THIS EVENT, WHICH HAS COME TO A CLIMAX TONIGHT, DOES NOT ESCAPE US... THIS HAS BEEN A GREAT VICTORY FOR THE REVOLUTIONARY MOVEMENT. NEVER HAS THERE BEEN A GATHERING OF SUCH DIMENSIONS & OF SUCH MAGNITUDE, A GATHERING IN WHICH THE REVOLUTIONARY REPRESENTATIONS OF 82 PEOPLES HAVE MET TO DISCUSS PROBLEMS OF COMMON INTEREST. NEVER HAS THERE BEEN SUCH A LARGE MEETING, BECAUSE THE PEOPLES OF THREE CONTINENTS HAVE BEEN HERE; THE REVOLUTIONARY MOVEMENTS OF THE PEOPLES OF THREE CONTINENTS WHO HAVE A COMMON ANTI-IMPERIALIST STANCE; WHO REPRESENT THE STRUGGLE OF THEIR PEOPLES WITH DIFFERING PHILOSOPHICAL IDEAS OR POSITIONS, OR WITH DIFFERING RELIGIOUS BELIEFS; WHO ON MANY OCCASIONS REPRESENT DIFFERING IDEOLOGIES. BUT THEY HAVE SOMETHING IN COMMON...
FIDEL CASTRO— CLOSING SPEECH JANUARY 15, 1966
FATHERLAND OR DEATH, WE SHALL WIN!
LAOS
TO STAY SANE & HAVE SOME FUN, GAY INMATES OF THE UMAP ORGANIZED CLANDESTINE "TELL-THE-MOVIE NIGHTS," "WEDDINGS" & CABARET SHOWS IN THEIR BARRACKS. THEY USED EVERY SCRAP IMAGINABLE FROM THE CAMP TO CREATE COSTUMES & SCENERY.

IN THE SUMMER OF 1966, TED & HIS DEPENDENTS WERE ENTITLED TO A GOVERNMENT-PAID VACATION TO THEIR COUNTRY AS PART OF HIS FOREIGN *TÉCNICO* CONTRACT. SO THEY WENT TO THE STATES FOR ABOUT SIX WEEKS, VIA CANADA, ON A CUBAN FREIGHTER. THIS CONFLICTED WITH MY UNIVERSITY SCHEDULE, SO I STAYED BEHIND & HAD THE APARTMENT TO MYSELF.

OH FREEDOM! MONICA & *EL GRUPO* MOVED IN. WE DECIDED TO CELEBRATE THIS WONDERFUL RESPITE FROM PARENTS & THROW A PARTY.

HEY, I HAVE AN IDEA! HOW ABOUT I BRING A SMALL PROJECTOR FROM WORK & SHOW THIS OLD PORNO FILM I FOUND IN THE VAULTS?
COMANDANTE EN JEFE ¡ORDENE!
HOW FUNNY! I'VE NEVER SEEN ONE! LET'S DO IT!
HMM... OK, BUT WE HAVE TO BE CAREFUL. NOT A WORD TO ANYONE. WE COULD GET EXPELLED.
UNFORTUNATELY SOMEONE BLABBED & THE NEWS SPREAD LIKE WILDFIRE.
DID YOU HEAR ABOUT THE GRINGA'S PARTY?
¡DIÓS MÍO! WILL THEY DARE?
¡COÑO! HAVE YOU HEARD WHAT THOSE PERVERTS ARE PLANNING TO DO?
HI EVERYBODY! I HEARD WE'RE HAVING A SCHOOL PARTY...
WHO THE HELL INVITED THAT BITCH? THEY'VE SENT HER TO SPY ON US, HA HA!
THE YOUNG COMMUNIST UNION DEPLOYED SOMEONE TO CRASH OUR PARTY.
WE GLEEFULLY WAITED HER OUT. FINALLY EXHAUSTED, SHE LEFT IN DEFEAT AT 3 AM, & THEN WE SET UP THE PROJECTOR...
SNIFF! THIS IS SO DISAPPOINTING!
¡CARAJO! YOU CAN'T SEE A DAMN THING!
ALAS, OUR FORAY INTO SIN WAS NOT TO BE.

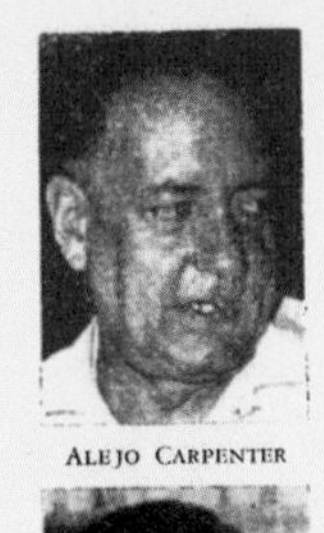

ALEJO CARPENTIER

CARTA DE NERUDA A LOS CUBANOS

QUERIDOS compañeros:

Por infundada me extraña profundamente la preocupación que por mí ha expresado un grupo de escritores cubanos.* Los invito a tener en cuenta no sólo las especulaciones y mutilaciones de mis textos por cierta prensa yanqui, sino con mucha mayor razón la opinión de los comunistas norteamericanos.

Ustedes parecen ignorar que mi entrada a los Estados Unidos, al igual que la de escritores comunistas de otros países, se logró rompiendo las prohibiciones del Departamento de Estado, gracias a la acción de los intelectuales de izquierda. En los Estados Unidos y en los demás países que visité, mantuve mis ideas comunistas, mis principios inquebrantables y mi poesía revolucionaria. Tengo derecho a esperar y reclamar de ustedes, que me conocen, que no abriguen ni difundan inadmisibles dudas a este respecto. En los Estados Unidos y en todas partes, he sido escuchado y respetado sobre la base inamovible de lo que soy y seré siempre: un poeta que ... u vida y su obra al servicio de ... arte tengo una inquietud más ... ie se están tratando diferencias

... ner el acento en la responsabi- ... ollo de la necesaria unidad an- ... y todas las fuerzas revolucio- ... des, como lo he hecho a través ... revolución cubana. Fraternal-

PABLO NERUDA

NICOLÁS GUILLÉN

ONE DAY GUSTAVO SUDDENLY APPEARED & TOLD US WHAT HAD HAPPENED TO HIM IN THE UMAP.

I'M HERE ON A 15-DAY PASS. I HAVE TO GO BACK. THERE'S NO PLACE TO HIDE. I HAVE NO CHOICE. THEY WATCH EVERYBODY.

...DE LOS CUBANOS

... cionario ... vechadas ... lados en ... ktos por ... nos atu- ... icio que ... y en su ... perialista continental"; unidad

WE LIVE IN DISGUSTING BARRACKS, BEHIND BARBED-WIRE FENCES & GUARD TOWERS. THE FOOD IS ATROCIOUS & THE OFFICERS PUNISH PEOPLE BY MAKING THEM STAND NAKED ALL NIGHT IN A DUG-OUT PIT.

WHEN MY SENTENCE IS OVER, I AM LEAVING THE COUNTRY HOWEVER I CAN. I CAN'T LIVE HERE ANYMORE.

FERNÁNDEZ RETAMAR

MIGUEL BARNET

JULY 1966—PABLO NERUDA, REVERED POET & HIGH-RANKING CHILEAN COMMUNIST—VISITED THE INTERNATIONAL PEN CLUB IN NEW YORK CITY. THE CUBAN GOVERNMENT INSTRUCTED ALL PROMINENT CUBAN INTELLECTUALS TO SIGN AN OPEN LETTER DENOUNCING NERUDA & PUT HIS REVOLUTIONARY CREDIBILITY INTO DOUBT. NERUDA RESPONDED & TO HIS DYING DAY NEVER FORGAVE THE CUBANS FOR THIS INSULT & INDIRECT ATTACK ON THE CHILEAN COMMUNIST PARTY, WHICH ADVOCATED "PEACEFUL CO-EXISTANCE" WITH THE WEST.

JOSÉ TRIANA

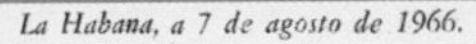

La Habana, a 7 de agosto de 1966.

* Ver POLÍTICA, Nº 151, Págs. 37, 38, 39 y 40.

ALFREDO GUEVARA

POLÍTICA, MEXICAN NEWS MAGAZINE, AUGUST 15, 1966

TED, LENORE & THE KIDS RETURNED TO CUBA. AFTER WORK, TED RESUMED HIS VOLUNTEER BROADCASTS, TRANSMITTED TO THE STATES, ON RADIO HAVANA CUBA.

RADIO HABANA
CUBA

I CAN SAY THAT THE INDIVIDUAL FREEDOM PICTURE HERE IS ABOUT AS CLOSE TO THE AMERICAN LIBERAL INTELLECTUAL'S IDEAL OF UTOPIA AS YOU CAN GET WITHOUT COMPLETELY DISRUPTING THE ECONOMY...

ARTISTS NOT ONLY WRITE & PAINT WHAT THEY PLEASE, BUT SOME MANAGE TO TURN OUT SOME PARTICULARLY HORRIBLE FAR-OUT JUNK, AT GOVERNMENT EXPENSE. AS FAR AS I KNOW, THERE ARE NO PARTICULAR FAVORITES OF EITHER THE GOOD OR THE BAD; ALL RECEIVE THEIR STIPEND AS ARTISTS.

GOVERNMENT POLICY ABOUT WHAT WAS EXPECTED OF ARTISTS & WRITERS, WHAT WOULD BE ALLOWED IN THE ARTS, BOTH IN STYLE & CONTENT, HAD BEEN DICTATED BY FIDEL IN 1961 DURING A FAMOUS MEETING WITH CUBA'S INTELLECTUALS: *"CON LA REVOLUCIÓN TODO, CONTRA LA REVOLUCIÓN NADA"*— "WITH THE REVOLUTION EVERYTHING; AGAINST THE REVOLUTION, NOTHING."

IN 1965, THIS IS HOW THE COMMUNIST YOUTH MAGAZINE "MELLA" INTERPRETED THIS POLICY.

Pucho
DIBUJOS: VIRGILIO
TEXTOS: URRA
¡AH... MUY ACADÉMICO!
¡QUÉ ANTICUADO!
¡QUÉ HORROR! ¡UNA MUJER DESNUDA!
...Y SIN TERMINAR!
¡QUÉ PROSAICO!
¡OH! ¡ESTO SÍ ES ARTE!
¡QUÉ LÍNEAS! ¡QUÉ COLORIDO!
¡ES UN AGUAFUERTE!
NO... ES UN PASTEL...
NO... NO... ES UN ÓLEO...
A MÍ ME PARECE QUE ES UNA ACUARELA...
¡ES UN "PUCHO"!

MELLA, OCT. 4, 1965— MAGAZINE OF THE UJC NEWSPAPER JUVENTUD REBELDE.

A CHRISTMAS TREE AT THE SCHOOL OF LETTERS

CHRISTMAS EVE IN CUBA WAS TRADITIONALLY A BELOVED HOLIDAY, CELEBRATED WITH A FAMILY MEAL OF ROAST PORK, *YUCA CON MOJO* (CASSAVA SAUTEÉD WITH LEMON & GARLIC SAUCE), *CONGRÍ* (RICE & RED BEANS), FRIED PLANTAINS, & SPANISH *TURRÓN* CANDIES & OTHER DELICACIES. AFTER THE REVOLUTION CAME TO POWER, CHRISTMAS BECAME ASSOCIATED WITH *EL IMPERIALISMO YANQUI*, & IN '69 WAS OFFICIALLY ABOLISHED, FOR INTERFERING WITH THE SUGAR HARVEST. CHRISTMAS TREES BECAME FORBIDDEN.

WOULD YOU BELIEVE IT? THE SCHOOL ISN'T GOING TO HAVE ANY DECORATIONS AT ALL. NOT EVEN FOR NEW YEAR'S.
A CHRISTMAS TREE IS WHAT WE SHOULD HAVE... HEH HEH.
WE COULD MAKE OUR OWN...
OH, REALLY? WITH WHAT & WHERE?
A GOOD TREE BRANCH & SOME CONDOMS!
YEEESSSS! I HAVE A BIG BOX OF REALLY AWFUL CHINESE ONES.
COME ON! LET'S FIND A BRANCH. WE'LL HIDE IT NOW IN AN ART CLOSET & SET IT ALL UP TONIGHT IN THE MUSEUM.
UFFF!!!
SHHH!!!
THE NEXT MORNING OUR LOBBY LOOKED VERY FESTIVE.
¡QUE BARBARIDAD!
THIS MUST BE THE WORK OF COUNTER-REVOLUTIONARIES!
¡CARAMBA!
WHO ARE THESE DEGENERATES..?
THEY NEVER CAUGHT US. OUR CHRISTMAS SURPRISE WAS A COMPLETE SUCCESS.

MIRAMAR

WHENEVER I WAS HOME AT OUR FAMILY APARTMENT & FREE OF SCHOOLWORK, NIKKI & I WOULD HOLE UP TOGETHER FOR HOURS ON END. SHE WAS MISERABLE AT SCHOOL & MY ROOM BECAME HER OASIS. BOOKS & SONGS IN ENGLISH BECAME HER PASSION.

LISTEN, I'VE PUT MUSIC TO "THE OWL & THE PUSSYCAT."
"...PUSSY SAID TO THE OWL YOU ELEGANT FOWL, HOW CHARMINGLY SWEET YOU SING. OH, LET US BE MARRIED, TOO LONG WE HAVE TARRIED..."
KAFKA
WAIT! SHOW ME AGAIN!
NOW LET'S SING DADDY'S FAVORITE, "THE KEEPER OF THE EDDYSTONE LIGHT."
"MY FATHER WAS THE KEEPER OF THE EDDYSTONE LIGHT, & HE SLEPT WITH A MERMAID ONE FINE NIGHT. OUT OF THIS UNION THERE CAME THREE, A PORPOISE & A PORGY & THE OTHER WAS ME..."
KEVIN WAS 8 YEARS OLD NOW & AN EXPERIENCED EXPLORER. FREE OF SUPERVISION, HE ROAMED HAVANA AFTER SCHOOL, ALL ON HIS OWN. HE HAD HIS SECRETS (CIGARETTES!) & KNEW HIS WAY AROUND THE RIVERBANK OF THE FETID ALMENDARES RIVER, FOR WHICH HE OFTEN PAID A HEAVY PRICE.
OW!!! I CAN'T STAND IT!!! STOP, STOP!!!!
HOLD STILL, CHILD! THIS MUST BE DRAINED!!!

CHAPTER 3

The Sierra Maestra

HUMANITIES GOES TO THE COUNTRYSIDE—SOCIAL RESEARCH IN THE SIERRA MAESTRA MOUNTAINS
JANUARY 1967— CARLOS AMAT, THE DEAN OF HUMANITIES, INFORMED THE STUDENT BODY THAT THIS MARCH, FOR A LITTLE OVER TWO WEEKS, STUDENTS & FACULTY OF THE SCHOOLS OF LETTERS & ART, LIBRARY SCIENCE, HISTORY, & JOURNALISM WOULD BE DEPLOYED ALL OVER THE COUNTRY TO CONDUCT TWO SOCIAL RESEARCH PROJECTS CALLED *"CARA AL CAMPO,"* "FACING THE COUNTRY."
I WAS ASSIGNED TO THE GROUP GOING TO THE SIERRA MAESTRA MOUNTAINS IN THE PROVINCE OF SANTIAGO, QUITE NEAR THE AREA WHERE FIDEL CASTRO CONDUCTED HIS GUERRILLA WAR AGAINST THE BATISTA DICTATORSHIP.
THE NEW INSTITUTIONS OF THE REVOLUTION ARE ASKING FOR INVESTIGATIONS RELATED TO THE SOCIO-ECONOMIC DEVELOPMENT OF THE COUNTRY. SO, THE OBJECTIVE OF THIS PROJECT IS TO OFFER CONCRETE SOLUTIONS THAT CHANNEL REVOLUTIONARY ACTION FOR OUR COUNTRY COMMITED TO MOVING FROM UNDERDEVELOPMENT TO DEVELOPMENT.
COMPAÑEROS, YOU'VE BEEN DIVIDED INTO GROUPS OF STUDENTS & TEACHERS THAT WILL GO TO 12 DESTINATIONS ALL OVER THE COUNTRY. LISTEN AS WE CALL OUT YOUR NAMES.

THROUGH DOOR-TO-DOOR INTERVIEWS WITH THE PEASANT POPULATION, WE WERE TO CONDUCT A LINGUISTIC STUDY & A SOCIO-POLITICAL SURVEY OF OPINIONS, AS WELL AS WRITE DESCRIPTIONS OF ALL THE FAMILIES & SINGLE HOUSEHOLDS IN OUR ASSIGNED AREAS.

HMM... GOOD. NO ONE FROM MONICA'S GROUP. I COULD USE SOME TIME AWAY & ON MY OWN.
LATELY, I'D BEEN FEELING STIFLED IN THE CLOSE-KNIT GROUP OF MONICA'S FRIENDS, ESPECIALLY AS I WAS HER GIRLFRIEND. I WANTED MORE INDEPENDENCE...

HEY! WHY DON'T WE CREATE A PUPPET TROUPE SO WE CAN OFFER SOMETHING BESIDES INTERVIEWS TO THE *CAMPESINOS* IN THE SIERRA?
GREAT IDEA! WHO'D ORGANIZE IT?
I WILL!

OK, I CAN SHOW YOU HOW TO MAKE SOME SIMPLE FLAT PUPPETS...
... & THESE THREE-DIMENSIONAL PAPER MACHÉ ONES.
I'D LIKE TO BE ABLE TO TEACH THE *CAMPESINO* TEACHERS HOW TO MAKE THEIR OWN PUPPETS, TOO.
HERE, I'LL GIVE YOU SOME OF THESE & YOU CAN PAINT & DRESS THEM.
Las Preciosas Ridículas
TEATRO NACIONAL DE GUIÑOL

FROM OUR SIERRA GROUP I RECRUITED MARTUGENIA, NATALIA, IRENE, RODRIGO & ANDRÉS. OUR SCHOOL DIRECTOR VICENTINA ANTUÑA AGREED & EVEN ASKED FOR HELP FROM THE GUIÑOL NACIONAL DE CUBA. THEY SET US UP WITH MANOLO, ONE OF THEIR PRINCIPAL PUPPETMAKERS.

¡FANTÁSTICO! COULD WE MAKE A BUGS BUNNY-LIKE HEAD OUT OF THIS ONE?
THIS CAT? *SURE!* WHY NOT?
ANOTHER DAY.
I'LL FINISH THE HEAD; YOU CAN MAKE THE CLOTH BODY.
LA CAPERUCITA ROJA

CHONGOLO, OUR MASTER OF CEREMONIES WAS BORN. WHEN WE FELT WE HAD ENOUGH PUPPET HEADS, WE MOVED TO MY APARTMENT & CREATED THEIR BODIES, READ SOURCE MATERIAL & PLANNED OUR PRODUCTIONS.

SO WE'LL DO INTERIAN'S "THE WHITE DAISY" FOR THE SMALL KIDS...
AND MAYBE "STONE SOUP?"
HEY! LET'S IMPROVISE A FEW OF THESE FRENCH FARCES! THEY'RE PERFECT!
YEAH, AFTER CHONGOLO WARMS UP THE CROWD & INTRODUCES THE TROUPE.
NOW WHAT SHALL WE DO FOR A CURTAIN?
FARSAS

I PACKED ALL OUR EQUIPMENT INTO AN OLD SUITCASE THAT TED & LENORE WERE WILLING TO SPARE & HEADED FOR OUR DEPARTURE SPOT. MY GROUP TRAVELED FOR 22 HOURS BY BUS, A GRUELING TRIP, TO SANTIAGO DE CUBA ON THE SOUTHERN COAST, 600 MILES TO THE EAST.

IN THE EARLY 1970S, DURING THE MASSIVE REPRESSION CARRIED OUT BY ARMY LT. LUIS PAVÓN TAMAYO, AS PRESIDENT OF THE *CONSEJO NACIONAL DE CULTURA,* THE LEGENDARY FOUNDERS, THE CAMEJOS & MOST OF THE GUIÑOL, WERE PURGED & CRUELLY OSTRACIZED.

THE SIERRA MAESTRA MOUNTAINS
WE HAD A FINAL ORIENTATION MEETING AT SCHOOL & WERE GIVEN OUR FORMS TO FILL OUT, WITH INSTRUCTIONS FOR TEN AREAS OF STUDY. THEN WE HEADED OUT.
"1. RURAL COMMUNITIES— STUDY OF THE ECONOMY, EDUCATION, POPULAR CULTURE, MASS MEDIA, TRANSFORMATION OF SMALL FARMERS INTO AGRICULTURAL WORKERS, PROBLEMS WITH FOOD, HYGIENE, HEALTH, HOUSING...
"2. URBAN COMMUNITIES— MIGRATION, URBANIZATION, PROBLEMS OF HOUSING, FOOD, AREAS OF IRRITATION...
"3. POLITICAL THEMES— TRANSFORMATION OF THE SUBJECT, INTEGRATION WITH THE REVOLUTION, PARTICIPATION OF THE MASSES IN VOLUNTARY AGRICULTURAL WORK, PRESTIGE OF POLITICAL ORGANIZATIONS, MASS ORGANIZATIONS, ETC.
SIGH...
"9. SOCIAL PATHOLOGIES— STUDIES ON DELINQUENCY (CAUSES, FREQUENCY ZONES, EVOLUTION), REEDUCATION OF COMMON & COUNTERREVOLUTIONARY PRISONERS, STUDIES ABOUT HOMOSEXUALITY..."

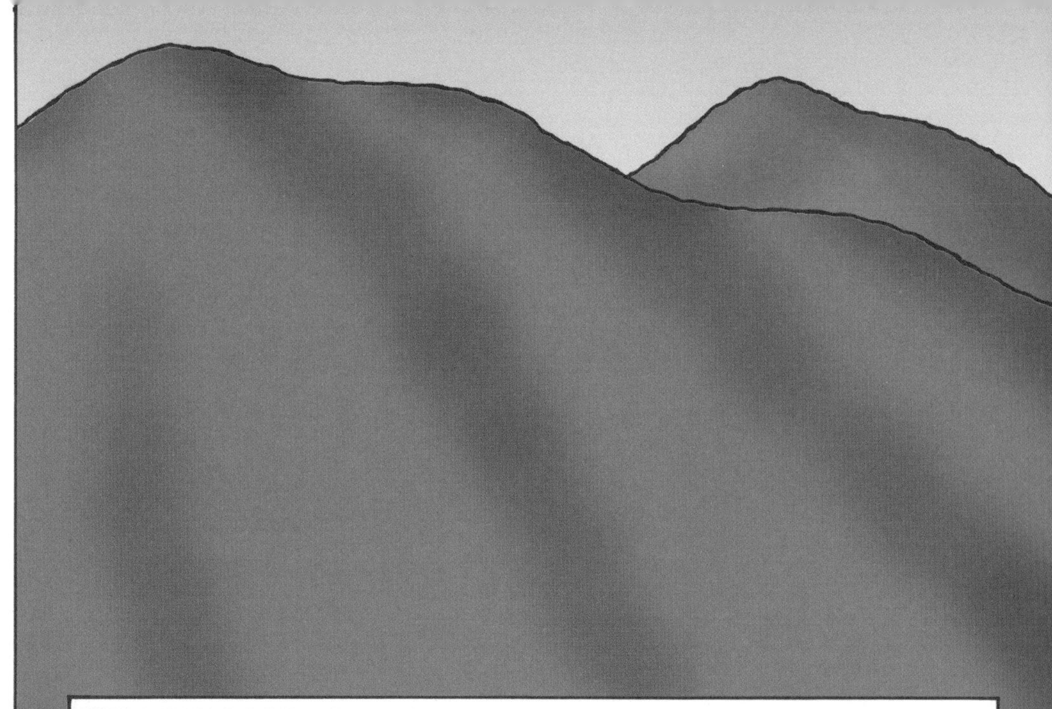

WITH STARS IN OUR EYES, WE FELT SO ROMANTICALLY REVOLUTIONARY: OFF TO HELP THE PEASANTS, DOCUMENT WHAT THEY LACKED & WHAT THE REVOLUTION DID RIGHT. WE WOULD DO GOOD DEEDS WITH OUT PUPPET THEATER...

MMM...LOTS OF MEMBERS OF THE "GUILD"* IN THIS BUNCH. HAVE YOU NOTICED?
OH, YEAH, BUT WATCH YOUR BACK WITH SONIA & JACINTO...

OUR LEADER & FACULTY ADVISOR WAS DR. ISABEL MONAL, OUR PROFESSOR OF HISTORIC MATERIALISM" & MARXISM-LENINISM. A VETEREN OF THE 26 OF JULY MOVEMEMT, SHE HAD WORKED IN FIDEL CASTRO'S ORGANIZATION SINCE BEFORE THE TRIUMPH OF THE REVOLUTION & THEN HELD AN IMPORTANT POST IN THE EMERGING CULTURAL ESTABLISHMENT, AS A FOUNDER OF THE *TEATRO NACIONAL* IN JUNE, 1959.

LISTEN UP, EVERYBODY! WE'RE ALMOST IN SANTIAGO! WE'LL STAY OVERNIGHT IN PARTY BARRACKS & HEAD OUT AT DAWN FOR THE MOUNTAINS, SO BE PREPARED & BE PUNCTUAL!

* "TO BE A MEMBER OF THE GUILD" (ESTAR EN EL GREMIO) MEANT THAT SOMEONE WAS GAY.

OUR CARAVAN OF OLD BUSES FANNED OUT TO THE FAR CORNERS OF THE COUNTRY. AFTER THE OVERNIGHT IN SANTIAGO, OUR GROUP TOOK OFF THE NEXT MORNING FOR CHIVIRICO, A SMALL TOWN ON THE COAST AT THE FOOT OF THE SIERRA MAESTRA MOUNTAINS.

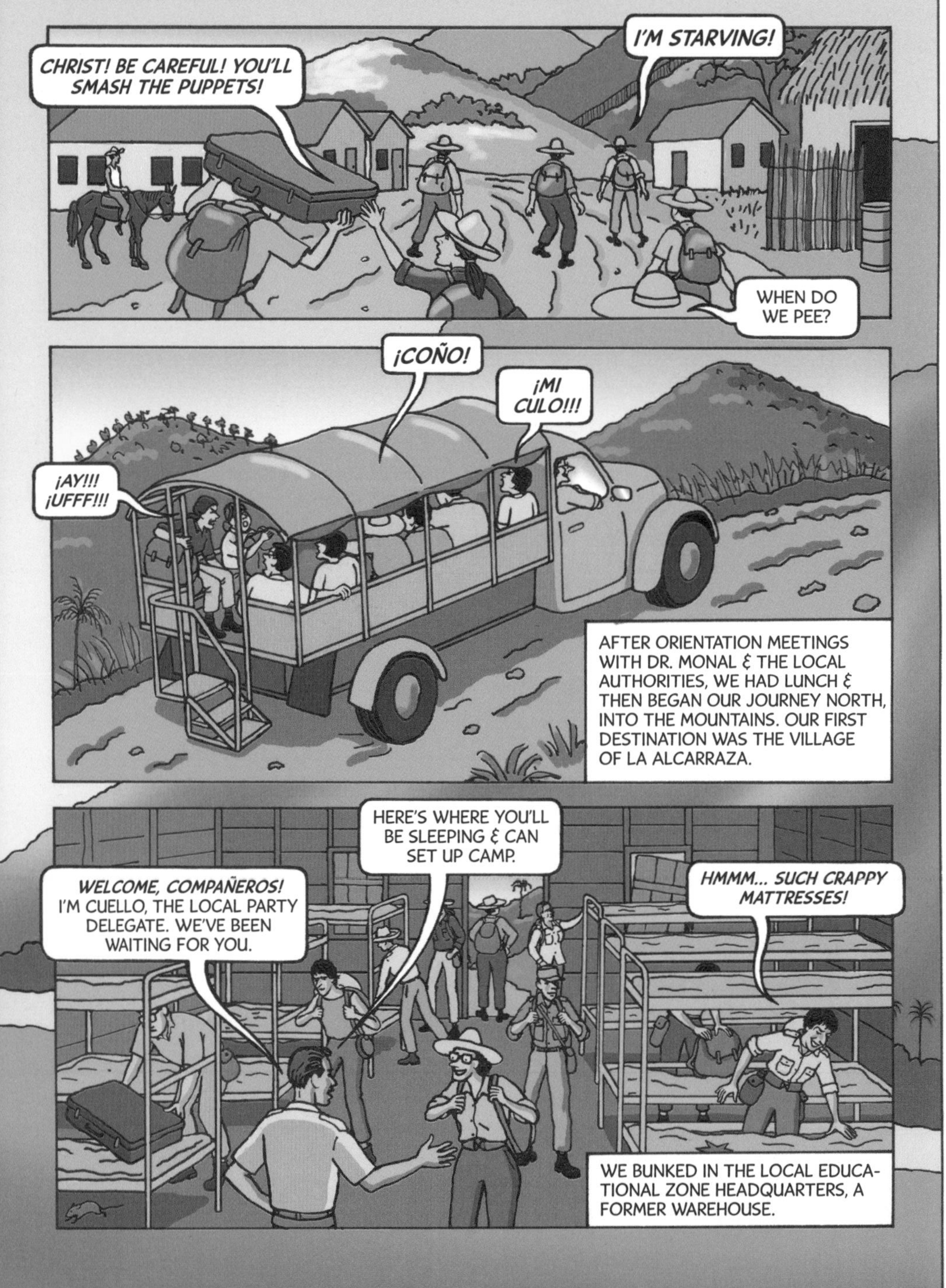

CHRIST! BE CAREFUL! YOU'LL SMASH THE PUPPETS!
I'M STARVING!
WHEN DO WE PEE?
¡COÑO!
¡MI CULO!!!
¡AY!!! ¡UFFF!!!
AFTER ORIENTATION MEETINGS WITH DR. MONAL & THE LOCAL AUTHORITIES, WE HAD LUNCH & THEN BEGAN OUR JOURNEY NORTH, INTO THE MOUNTAINS. OUR FIRST DESTINATION WAS THE VILLAGE OF LA ALCARRAZA.
WELCOME, COMPAÑEROS! I'M CUELLO, THE LOCAL PARTY DELEGATE. WE'VE BEEN WAITING FOR YOU.
HERE'S WHERE YOU'LL BE SLEEPING & CAN SET UP CAMP.
HMMM... SUCH CRAPPY MATTRESSES!
WE BUNKED IN THE LOCAL EDUCATIONAL ZONE HEADQUARTERS, A FORMER WAREHOUSE.

IN HAVANA BANANAS ARE CALLED *PLATANITOS*. WHAT DO YOU CALL THEM HERE?
WHY, THOSE ARE *GUINEITOS DE TAHITI.*
THAT SAME DAY, WE SET OFF RIGHT AWAY TO CONDUCT OUR FIRST TRIAL INTERVIEWS & LINGUISTIC SURVEYS WITH PEASANTS LIVING NEAR TOWN.
THE NEXT MORNING WE WASHED IN LA ALCARRAZA RIVER —FIRST THE WOMEN, THEN THE MEN— OUR FIRST BATH SINCE LEAVING HAVANA.
YOU ALL BEHAVE, NOW!
WE REHEARSED OUR PROGRAM & GOT OUR ORIENTATION FOR THE DAYS AHEAD.
ALRIGHT EVERYBODY! LISTEN UP! TOMORROW WE'LL START ROTATING PARTNERS!
WELL, SO AFTER YOU'VE GATHERED ALL YOUR MATERIALS, OLD POSTERS, STRING, MAGAZINES, FLOUR & WATER, MAYBE COCONUT SHELLS... YOU CAN START CREATING CHARACTERS FOR YOUR STORIES...
EVERY MOUNTAIN TEACHER A PUPPETEER!
THIS WAS MY TRIAL BY FIRE, MY FIRST CLASS FOR THE TEACHERS OF LA ALCARRAZA ZONE ON HOW TO MAKE SIMPLE PUPPETS OUT OF AVAILABLE MATERIALS.

OHHHHH!!!! NO ASPIRIN... I'VE GOT TO GET OUT OF HERE..!
¡COÑO! THESE CRAMPS ARE KILLING ME!
I KNOW SHE'S GOT HER CANTEEN OF RUM HERE SOMEWHERE...
JUST MY LUCK, THAT NIGHT I CAME DOWN WITH MY MONTHLY TORMENT...
OH! HELP!
GULP! GULP! GULP!

THE NEXT MORNING DR. MONAL DISPATCHED A SEARCH PARTY...
WHERE'S THAT GRINGA?!?
DOCTOR! UP HERE! SHE'S PASSED OUT UNDER A TREE!
GRINGUITA! WHAT'S WRONG?
JESUS! SHE'S FINISHED ALL THE RUM!!!
DURALGINA! GET THE EMERGENCY KIT!!!
ALL RIGHT, CRAZY GRINGA! LOWER YOUR PANTS. THIS WILL FIX YOU!
WHAT!?! YOU'RE NOT A MEDICAL DOCTOR! DON'T YOU TOUCH ME!!!
HOLD HER DOWN!!! KEEP STILL, GRINGA!
DIÓS! HER BUTT'S SO TIGHT, SHE'S BROKEN THE NEEDLE!
ALL RIGHT, NOW! ONE MORE TIME!
"DAME LA MANO Y DANZAREMOS, DAME LA MANO Y ME AMARÁS. COMO UNA SOLA FLOR SEREMOS, COMO UNA FLOR Y NADA MÁS..."
THAT MORNING WE PERFORMED IN LA ALCARRAZA'S SCHOOL PATIO. WE BORROWED HEAVILY FROM THE MUSICAL REPERTOIRE OF TERESITA FERNÁNDEZ AT ONE OF OUR FAVORITE BOHEMIAN NIGHT CLUBS IN HAVANA, EL COCTEL. THE HANGOVER WAS EPIC...

LUNCH WAS DELICIOUS & VERY WELCOME.
MMM! HORSEMEAT STEW & SARDINES!

LUCÍA & MARTUGENIA WERE ASSIGNED TO STUDY LA CARIDAD, A TINY HAMLET HIGHER UP IN THE MOUNTAINS. AFTER A LONG HIKE, THEY REACHED THE HOME OF SANTA, THE LOCAL WOMEN'S FEDERATION LEADER & HER FAMILY. AFTER THE OBLIGATORY CUPS OF COFFEE, THEY OPENED THE SUBJECT CAUTIOUSLY, WHAT DIFFICULTIES MIGHT THE PEOPLE HERE BE HAVING? AN UNNECESSARY PRECAUTION. SANTA & HER MEN COULDN'T STOP TALKING.

WE'RE FIDELISTAS HERE! BUT THERE ARE MANY PROBLEMS...
THERE'S NO ELECTRICITY!
EVERY OTHER VILLAGE SCHOOL HAS BEEN ADOPTED, BUT OURS NOT!
WE DON'T GET ANY INFORMATION HERE. ONLY ONE COPY OF THE MAGAZINE "MUJERES" REACHES THE INFORMANTE, OUR TOWN CRIER.
WE WERE ASSIGNED 40 PESOS TO BUILD OUR SCHOOL, & WE DID IT WITH $33. BUT WE'VE GOTTEN NO NAILS TO FINISH THE BUILDING. NO NOTEBOOKS, NO BOOKS AT ALL.
SOME OF OUR RATIONS ARE BEING STOLEN BY CORRUPT BUREAUCRATS WHO WRITE THINGS IN OUR RATION BOOKS THAT WE NEVER BOUGHT.
WE'VE GOT RADIOS WE CAN'T USE BECAUSE THERE ARE NO BATTERIES. THEY ONLY GIVE THEM OUT IN LA ALCARRAZA.
WE'VE GOT NO DOCTORS OR CLINICS HERE. ONLY IN CHIVIRICO. SO MANY WOMEN HAVE GIVEN BIRTH IN THE BUSES TRYING TO GET TO CHIVIRICO. THE BUS DRIVERS HAVE BECOME MIDWIVES.
THERE'S NOT ENOUGH MILK. OUR CHILDREN GET ONLY THREE CANS EACH PER WEEK.
OUR CHILDREN HAVE PARASITES & NO SHOES. THEY ONLY GIVE OUT ONE PAIR A YEAR.
NEWS TRAVELED FAST THAT THERE WERE STRANGERS FROM HAVANA IN THE AREA. WE WERE OVERWHELMED WITH PEOPLE WHO WANTED TO TELL US THEIR PROBLEMS & HOLD TOWN MEETINGS TO TALK ABOUT EVERYTHING.
IS IT TRUE THAT THE VIETNAMESE ARE FIGHTING WITH THE AMERICANS?

IN EVERY HAMLET THAT WE VISITED, PEOPLE APPROACHED US. THEY WANTED "THE FIDEL PEOPLE FROM THE BIG CITY" TO HEAR ABOUT LIFE HERE. TO OUR DISMAY, A FAMILY GOAT WAS SLAUGHTERED IN OUR HONOR & THEN COOKED INTO A DELICIOUS *CHILINDRÓN DE CHIVO* STEW.

THE POPULAR TRIBU-NALES ARE UNFAIR! THEY ABUSE THEIR POWER OVER US!
WE'VE GOT LOTS OF PROBLEMS WITH COMPAÑERO CUELLO, OUR PARTY DELEGATE...
AFTER HURRICANE FLORA IN '63, THINGS BECAME VEY BAD HERE. HOMES WERE DESTROYED & NEVER REBUILT.
WE'VE GOT BAD PROBLEMS WITH THE ANAP (NATIONAL ASSOCIATION OF SMALL FARMERS).
THEY'RE NO HELP. THEY WON'T BUY OUR LAND, THEY DON'T SOLVE ANYTHING!
OUR CROPS WERE RUINED BY A HERD OF CATTLE. WE GOT NO COMPENSA-TION AT ALL! AND THEY SANCTIONED US!
WE'RE NOT ALLOWED TO PLANT WHEN WE WANT. SEEDS GET HERE TOO LATE, ESPECIALLY CORN.
THE ANAP BOSSES ARE ARROGANT!
WE'RE FORCED TO EAT WILD ANIMALS BECAUSE THERE'S NOT ENOUGH FOOD... WILD PIGS, HAWKS... JUTÍAS!
MOST OF THE PEASANTS OF THIS ZONE HAD TAKEN PART IN THE INSURRECTION AGAINST BATISTA. THEY HAD TREMENDOUS FAITH IN FIDEL & IN THE ARMY, BUT NOT THE PARTY.
ONE NIGHT A RAINSTORM SOAKED THROUGH THE DECREPIT ROOF OF OUR CAMP. WE WERE ABOUT TO HEAT UP SOME PRECIOUS CHOCOLATE THAT IRENE HAD BROUGHT FROM HOME, WHEN SUDDENLY –THERE WAS A KNOCK ON THE DOOR...

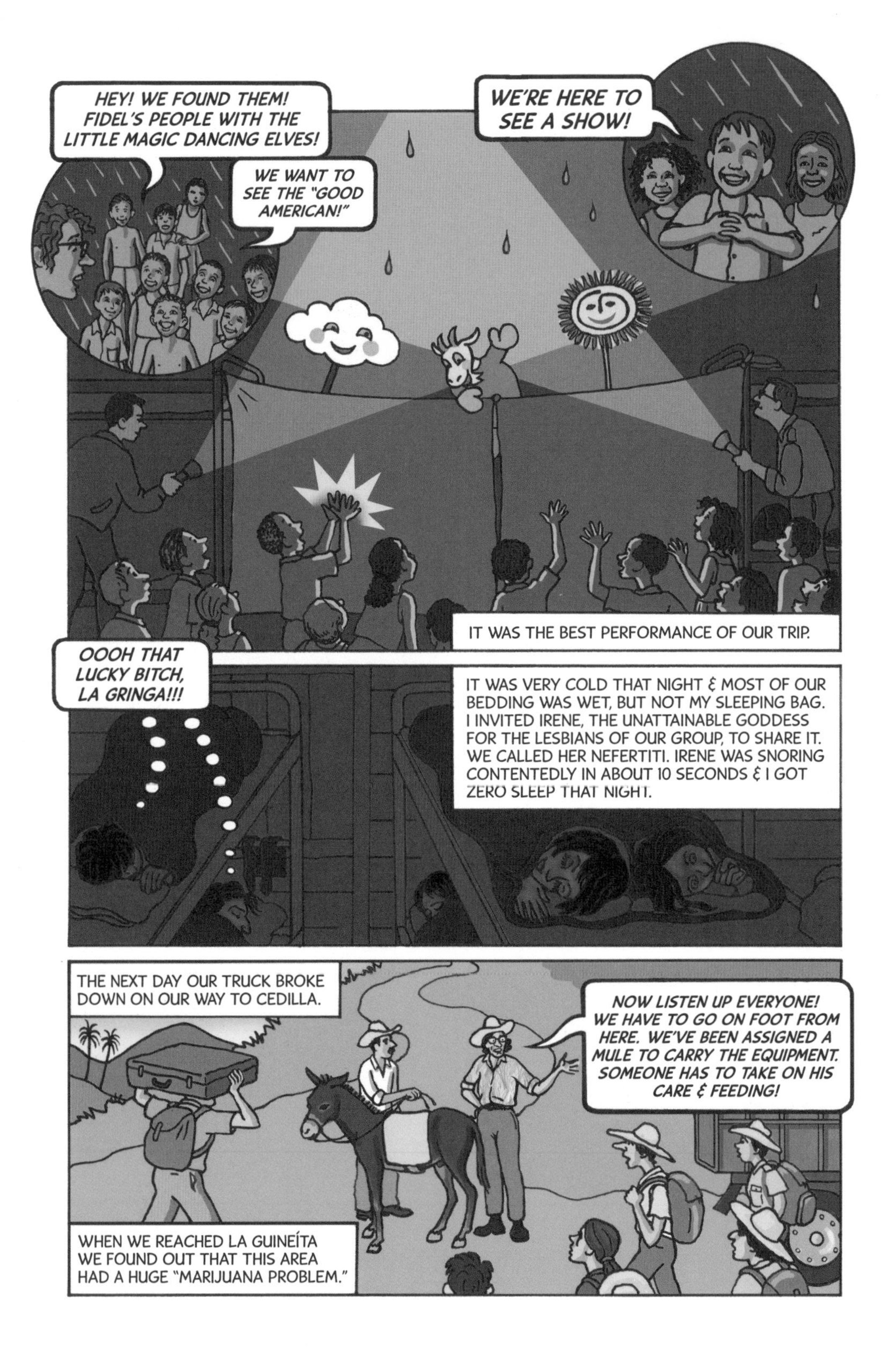
HEY! WE FOUND THEM! FIDEL'S PEOPLE WITH THE LITTLE MAGIC DANCING ELVES!
WE WANT TO SEE THE "GOOD AMERICAN!"
WE'RE HERE TO SEE A SHOW!
IT WAS THE BEST PERFORMANCE OF OUR TRIP.
OOOH THAT LUCKY BITCH, LA GRINGA!!!
IT WAS VERY COLD THAT NIGHT & MOST OF OUR BEDDING WAS WET, BUT NOT MY SLEEPING BAG. I INVITED IRENE, THE UNATTAINABLE GODDESS FOR THE LESBIANS OF OUR GROUP, TO SHARE IT. WE CALLED HER NEFERTITI. IRENE WAS SNORING CONTENTEDLY IN ABOUT 10 SECONDS & I GOT ZERO SLEEP THAT NIGHT.
THE NEXT DAY OUR TRUCK BROKE DOWN ON OUR WAY TO CEDILLA.
NOW LISTEN UP EVERYONE! WE HAVE TO GO ON FOOT FROM HERE. WE'VE BEEN ASSIGNED A MULE TO CARRY THE EQUIPMENT. SOMEONE HAS TO TAKE ON HIS CARE & FEEDING!
WHEN WE REACHED LA GUINEÍTA WE FOUND OUT THAT THIS AREA HAD A HUGE "MARIJUANA PROBLEM."

AFTER A GOOD NIGHT'S SLEEP IN LA GUINEÍTA, WE LEFT FOR LIMONCITO, HIKING FOR SEVERAL BACKBREAKING HOURS. FINALLY WE GOT TO THE VILLAGE STORE WITH OUR MULE & HAD LUNCH.

EL SOL, EL SOL QUISIERAMOS QUE USTED Y SU CALOR, DESPIERTA A MARGARITA CON LUZ Y CON AMOR!
CARACOL, CARACOL! SACA TUS CUERNOS AL SOL!
WE PUT ON A PERFORMANCE OF "LA MARGARITA," IMPROVISED A FRENCH FARCE & SANG SONGS. LUCÍA AS ALWAYS, FORGOT HALF OF HER LINES. BUT THE CHILDREN HERE WERE VERY STRANGE. SOMETHING WAS GOING ON IN THIS VILLAGE.

WHAT THE HELL IS THAT ALL ABOUT!?!
WE HURRIED TO PACK OUR EQUIPMENT ON THE MULE & GOT OUT OF THERE. TO KEEP UP OUR SPIRITS, WE SANG SPANISH ZARZUELAS ALL THE WAY. FINALLY WE MADE IT TO OUR NEW ENCAMPMENT IN A LOCAL SCHOOL & SLEPT LIKE LOGS.

WE WERE NOW FINISHED IN THE ZONA OF LA ALCARRAZA. WE PACKED OUR KNAPSACKS & OUR PUPPET EQUIPMENT, SAID GOODBYE TO OUR MULE & HEADED SOUTH, BACK TO CHIVIRICO ON THE COAST.

HELP!!!
¡COÑO! ¡LA COMIDA! ¡THERE GOES THE FUCKING COFFEE!!!

WE WERE MET BY VICENTINA ANTUÑA, & MIRTA AGUIRRE.
¡MUCHACHOS!!!
HEY! HERE'S A SONG FOR THAT LITTLE GIRL WITH THE GRAY HAIR!

WE BATHED IN THE CARIBBEAN SEA & FOR LUNCH FEASTED ON LOCAL WHITE CHEESE, A BLESSED GIFT FROM THE PROFESSORS. WE WERE SICK OF BOILED EGGS & SARDINES. WE THANKED THEM WITH A PERFORMANCE.

PEOPLE! THAT'S THE SAME KNIFE EMILIO JUST USED TO SHAVE DOWN THE CORN ON HIS FOOT!

ON TO MADRUGÓN TO SLEEP, PERFORM & REPAIR OUR PUPPETS. LATER WE FANNED OUT TO STUDY NEIGHBORING HAMLETS & RECONVENED IN AJÍ ABAJO. WE HEARD THERE WERE "RELIGIOUS CONFLICTS" IN THE AREA... MANY SEVENTH-DAY ADVENTISTS LIVED HERE.
WE'RE FROM HAVANA...
YES, I KNOW. *YOU'RE ASKING EVERYBODY LOTS OF QUESTIONS!*
PEOPLE SAY THE GOVERNMENT WANTS TO TAKE OUR CHURCH AWAY. *IT'S ALL WE HAVE!*
THE LOCAL TEACHER WAS CONDUCTING A CHILDREN'S EVENT AT SCHOOL. WHEN WE ARRIVED, HE TRIED TO CONVINCE THEM TO JOIN THE PIONEROS, THE REVOLUTIONARY CHILDREN'S ORGANIZATION.
ONCE UPON A TIME, THERE WAS A MAN WHO CLIMBED UP ON A TABLE & WOULDN'T GET DOWN. HE SAID HE WAS GOD.
HE MADE EVERYBODY ADORE HIM & BRING HIM FOOD. HE WAS JUST A TRICKSTER, DON'T YOU SEE?
THAT NIGHT THE MILITARY CHIEF OF THE ZONE, LIEUTENANT MORINO & THE TEACHER, ASKED US TO PERFORM A SHOW AT THE SAME TIME AS A CHURCH SERVICE, TO DRAW AWAY THE CHILDREN.
I WANT TO SMASH THE CHURCH! IT KEEPS 'EM FROM BECOMING "INTEGRATED" INTO THE REVOLUTIONARY PROCESS.
¡NO, NO, NO, COMPAÑERO! IT DOESN'T WORK THAT WAY. WE DON'T WANT TO ALIENATE THEM THROUGH CONFRONTATION...

EARLY NEXT MORNING WE SET OUT WEST ALONG THE COAST FOR OCUJAL, WITH SURI, THE NEW DRIVER, WHOM LIEUTENANT MORINO HAD ASSIGNED US. ALONG THE WAY WE MADE A STOP TO COMMISSION A 15-LB. BLACK MARKET CHEESE FOR PICKUP ON THE WAY BACK. OUR BUTTS BECAME SO SORE FROM THE ROUGH TRIP THAT WE STOOD MOST OF THE WAY HOME.

HERE, TRY OUR SMOKED MILK. WE CAN SELL YOU SOME OF THIS, TOO.
¡MMM! ¡RIQUÍSIMA!
AFTER THAT EVENING'S PERFORMANCE, MARTUGENIA & I WENT DOWN TO THE RIVER TO BRUSH OUR TEETH...
MY *PAREJA* TREATS ME LIKE A CHILD...
MAYBE IT'S TIME TO SPREAD YOUR WINGS & LEAVE THE NEST..?
WE COMPARED NOTES ON OUR LOVE LIVES & CONFIDED THAT WE WERE RESTLESS & READY TO MOVE ON FROM OUR RELATIONSHIPS AT HOME. WE BOTH HAD LOVERS OLDER THAN OURSELVES.
IT WAS QUITE DARING TO TALK OPENLY DURING THESE TIMES OF THE PURGES & THE WITCH-HUNTS, DANGEROUS TO BE FRANK WITH SOMEONE NEW, BUT WE FELT A WARM CAMARADERIE HERE & TALKED UNTIL MIDNIGHT.
¡AY DIÓS! LOOK AT THE TIME! WE HAVE TO GET BACK.
YEAH, WE WOULDN'T WANT THEM TO WONDER ABOUT US... WOULD WE?

¡CRISTO! THE DOOR'S LOCKED!
COME ON. WE'LL FIND AN OPEN WINDOW WITH MY CAPITALIST FLASHLIGHT.
LIKE HUCK & TOM!
SHHH!
SEVERAL DAYS & HAMLETS LATER, WE REACHED LA ZARZA, & WERE RECEIVED AT THE REGIONAL CADRE SCHOOL OF THE COMMUNIST PARTY, IN A MODERN TWO-STORY RANCH-STYLE VILLA. THEY WERE WAITING FOR US WITH A GLORIOUS MEAL OF REAL FOOD, HOSTED BY LA TÉCNICA DE EDUCACIÓN DE LA ESCUELA DEL PARTIDO.
COMPAÑERA, WHAT IS GOING ON IN LIMONCITO? THE CHILDREN WERE SO HOSTILE. THEY EVEN THREW ROCKS AT US...
THERE'S A LOT OF BITTERNESS IN LIMONCITO. BOTH THE ADULTS & THE CHILDREN...
YOU SEE... THERE WAS AN UPRISING AGAINST THE REVOLUTION IN THE AREA. IT WAS SUPPRESSED, OF COURSE. MANY OF THE NEIGHBORS IN THE ZONE PARTICIPATED. THEY WERE FOLLOWERS OF CAPITÁN LUGO.
PLUS, THIS ZONE WAS HEAVILY BOMBED BY THE BATISTA GOVERNMENT DURING THE INSURRECTION.
THEN LATER... FOR SOME MYSTERIOUS REASON, A LOT OF ABNORMAL PEOPLE WERE BORN IN THIS TOWN... CHILDREN WITH BIRTH DEFECTS, AWFUL THINGS...
NOW THEY DON'T TRUST ANYONE.

AFTER A COUPLE MORE DAYS, WE RETURNED TO SANTIAGO & CITY LIGHTS. WE PASSED THE TIME SINGING. A BIG FAVORITE WAS DRA. MONAL'S OLD COLLEGE SONG FROM HER DAYS AS A GRADUATE STUDENT.

I WISH I WERE A FASCINATING BITCH, I'D NEVER BE SO POOR, I'D BE SO VERY RICH! I'D LIVE IN A HOUSE WITH A BIG RED LIGHT, SLEEP ALL DAY & WORK ALL NIGHT!
AND ONCE A MONTH I'D TAKE A HOLIDAY JUST TO DRIVE THE CUSTOMERS WILD! I WISH I WERE A FASCINATING BITCH INSTEAD OF AN ILLEGITIMATE CHILD!

MIRTA AGUIRRE

AFTER WE CAME DOWN FROM THE MOUNTAINS AT THE END OF MARCH, I SPENT MORE & MORE TIME WITH MARTUGENIA. WE WERE JUST FRIENDS, THOUGH I'D KNOWN SINCE THE SIERRA I WAS INTERESTED IN MORE THAN THAT.

ONE DAY MIRTA AGUIRRE'S SISTER YOLANDA INVITED US TO ATTEND HER YOUNG DAUGHTER'S BIRTHDAY PARTY. COULD WE PUT ON A PUPPET SHOW FOR THE GUESTS?
¡GRINGA! LET'S DO IT!! WE HAVE TO SEE IF ANY OF THE OTHERS WILL, TOO.
MMM! MAYBE THE AGUIRRE WILL BE THERE. LET'S PLAN A PROGRAM!

MIRTA AGUIRRE WAS A LEGENDARY FIGURE AT THE SCHOOL OF LETTERS. SHE PLAYED FAVORITES & I WAS HAPPY TO BECOME ONE OF THEM. WOE TO THOSE WHO FELL IN HER DISFAVOR. THIS WAS A CHANCE TO SEE HER IN HER HOME LIFE. I COULD HARDLY WAIT.

"HAY GOLPES EN LA VIDA TAN FUERTES... YO NO SÉ"
"PUEDO ESCRIBIR LOS VERSOS MÁS TRISTES ESTA NOCHE."
OUR SHOW WAS A GREAT SUCCESS.
QUICK! LOOK! THERE'S THE AGUIRRE'S LOVER, THE RUSSIAN DANCER!
WE RACED UP THE STAIRS TO THE SECOND FLOOR. THERE SHE WAS, ANNA LEONTIEVA, THE WHITE RUSSIAN, WHO RAN A BALLET FEEDER SCHOOL FOR THE NATIONAL BALLET.
HELLO! I HOPE YOU ENJOYED OUR SHOW.
LA AGUIRRE HURRIED AFTER US TO DO DAMAGE CONTROL. HER PRIVATE LIFE WAS STRICTLY OFF-LIMITS.
ALL RIGHT, GIRLS. COME DOWNSTAIRS FOR SOME REFRESHMENTS. WE'RE SERVING THE CAKE.

DID YOU KNOW? LEONTIEVA'S MOTHER BELONGED TO A RUSSIAN IMPERIAL BALLET SCHOOL & ANNA DANCED WITH THE ORIGINAL BALLET RUSSE. THEY CAME TO CUBA IN THE FORTIES & NEVER LEFT.
HA! AT LAST WE'VE SEEN HER. WOW, WHITE RUSSIANS WHO RAN FROM ONE REVOLUTION ONLY TO BE CAUGHT UP IN ANOTHER... ***TOO BAD WE CAN'T ASK THE AGUIRRE ABOUT THAT!***

MIRTA HAD SUBLIME POLITICAL CREDENTIALS, HAVING EARNED HER PLACE IN COMMUNIST HEAVEN DURING THE BLOODY DICTATORSHIP OF CUBA'S 5TH PRESIDENT, GERARDO MACHADO. SHE HAD SMUGGLED THE ASHES OF JULIO ANTONIO MELLA FROM MEXICO CITY INTO HAVANA IN 1933. MELLA, THE CHARISMATIC FOUNDER OF THE CUBAN COMMUNIST PARTY, WAS MURDERED IN MEXICO & HIS FOLLOWERS WERE DETERMINED TO BRING HIS REMAINS BACK TO CUBA.

SHE INVITED US TO HER HOME FROM TIME TO TIME TO DISCUSS LIFE & POLITICS UNTIL TWO OR THREE IN THE MORNING. FOR US SHE WAS LIVING PROOF THAT YOU COULD BE A REVOLUTIONARY, AN INTELLECTUAL & A LESBIAN AT THE SAME TIME.
¡DOCTORA! TELL US THE STORY ABOUT MELLA'S BONES...
JULIO ANTONIO MELLA
WELL... WE TOOK HIS ASHES, SMASHED THE BONE FRAGMENTS, & HID THEM IN THE HEM OF MY DRESS. I WALKED RIGHT THROUGH IMMIGRATION.
WE GOT PAST THE POLICE. IT WAS A COMPLETE SUCCESS.
ADUANA
SHE HAD THE REPUTATION OF AN IMPLACABLE STALINIST, BUT SHE NEVER CLOSED HER DOOR TO US.

BANAO

AFTER SIX WEEKS OF CLASSES (I WAS NOW IN MY SECOND YEAR AFTER AN INITIAL "PRE-CURSO" IN 1964/65), THE STUDENTS OF HUMANIDADES WERE AGAIN SENT TO THE COUNTRY, FOR A MONTH, TO DO AGRICULTURAL WORK AT THE EXPERIMENTAL-FARM-COMPLEX BANAO, A VAST AGRICULTURAL ZONE ABOUT HALFWAY BETWEEN TRINIDAD & SANCTI SPIRITUS.

THIS WAS ONE OF FIDEL CASTRO'S PET PROJECTS. BANAO HAD A "MICRO-CLIMATE" WITH SUPPOSEDLY UNIQUE CONDITIONS THAT PERMITTED THE FARMING OF CROPS NORMALLY GROWN IN NORTHERN CLIMES, SUCH AS APPLES, PEACHES, STRAWBERRIES & ASPARAGUS.

¡COÑO! CHICKPEAS EVERY DAY! WHEN WILL THEY PUT ANY SEASONING INTO THIS CRAP?
UGH! I'M NOT EATING THIS SHIT. I'LL STICK TO STRAWBERRIES... I DON'T CARE IF IT'S FORBIDDEN.
THE LETRAS PROFESSORS ASSIGNED TO WATCH OVER US WERE NERVOUS WE MIGHT RAISE THE IRE OF THE OTHERS IN THIS GIANT WORK CAMP; SO MANY LETRAS WOMEN WERE VISIBLY BUTCH. THEY GAVE US VEILED WARNINGS TO BEHAVE OURSELVES, TERRIFIED OF ANY SCANDAL THAT COULD TARNISH LETRAS' ALREADY SUSPECT REPUTATION.

MY GROUP LIVED IN STUDENT CAMP NO. 6, ONE OF MANY CAVERNOUS BARRACKS, ALONG WITH THOUSANDS OF YOUNG FACTORY WORKERS & OTHER UNIVERSITY & VOCATIONAL STUDENTS. LETRAS PEOPLE WORKED LONG HOURS EVERY DAY HARVESTING MOSTLY STRAWBERRIES THAT WERE DESTINED FOR EXPORT & FOR FLAVORING ICE-CREAM. WE ALSO HARVESTED ASPARAGUS, WHICH I ATE RAW, IN THE FIELD, ALONG WITH INDUSTRIAL QUANTITIES OF FRESH STRAWBERRIES, LACED WITH FERTILIZER & EARTH.

SLURP! SLURP! MMM!!!
¡ASÍ, MAMI, ASÍ!
I CAN'T BELIEVE IT!
THE PROFESSORS NEEDN'T HAVE WORRIED. THE WORKING-CLASS WOMEN IN OUR BARRACK WERE MUCH TOO BUSY TO PAY ATTENTION TO US.
OH! OH! OH!
HIJA DE PUTA, SHUT THAT OFF! YOU WANNA GET STABBED?
THERE WAS HOT & HEAVY ACTION GOING ON UNDER THE BLANKETS IN SEVERAL BUNKS & NOBODY DARED SAY BOO; THESE WERE TOUGH BROADS. WE FOUND THIS HYSTERICALLY FUNNY. SO MUCH FOR THE SOCIALIST MORALITY OF THE WORKING CLASS.
¡ANDA PA'L CARÁ!

NIKKI & CALLE 8

MY SISTER NIKKI FELT LIKE A FREAK AT HER CUBAN SCHOOL. SHE HAD NO SCHOOL FRIENDS AT ALL FROM 1ST THROUGH 5TH GRADE. SHY & RESERVED, SHE COULDN'T COPE WITH CUBAN EXUBERANCE & CHAOS, WHILE OUR SUNNY & OUTGOING BROTHER KEVIN THRIVED.
SHE FINALLY FOUND A FRIEND, AN ICELANDIC GIRL JUST HER AGE, AT THE POOL AT THE SIERRA MAESTRA HOTEL SOMETIME IN '66 OR '67.
WHAT SCHOOL DO YOU GO TO?
MISS POWER'S HILLSIDE SCHOOL.
ELIN WAS THE DAUGHTER OF A UNITED NATIONS PHYSICAL OCEANOGRAPHER STATIONED IN CUBA WITH HIS FAMILY. THEY LIVED NEARBY, IN AN APARTMENT BUILDING ON THE BANKS OF THE ALMENDARES RIVER IN MIRAMAR.
DO THEY SPEAK ENGLISH AT HILLSIDE?
OH, YES!
I HATE MY SCHOOL. CLASSES ARE BORING... PEOPLE ARE ROUGH & RUDE.
WHY DON'T YOU GET YOUR PARENTS TO MOVE YOU TO HILLSIDE?

ONE DAY, FORMER NEIGHBORS IN OUR BUILDING, THE BARUCHS, LEFT CUBA & ABANDONED THEIR CAT IN THE GARDEN. DESPERATE & STARVING, HE SHOWED UP AT OUR KITCHEN DOOR, DAY AFTER DAY.

SHIT, THERE'S THAT AWFUL CAT AGAIN!
THE POOR THING'S SO HUNGRY. PLEASE LET ME FEED HIM!
ABSOLUTELY NOT! I'M NOT FEEDING TWO CATS! ONE IS ENOUGH.
GET AWAY! RAUS!

I'D LIKE THAT MORE THAN ANYTHING.
BUT MY PARENTS... THEY'RE NOT GOING TO LET ME...
THE STUDENTS AT HILLSIDE, THE ONLY PRIVATE SCHOOL IN HAVANA NOW, WERE MOSTLY CHILDREN OF DIPLOMATS & TECHNICIANS EMPLOYED BY INTERNATIONAL ORGANIZATIONS. IT WAS FOUNDED IN 1965 & RUN BY MISS POWERS WHO HAD BEEN LIVING IN CUBA SINCE THE '50S.

NIKKI HAD EARNED EXCELLENT GRADES IN HER CUBAN SCHOOL. SHE WORKED ON LENORE FOR MONTHS.

YOU HAVE TO LET ME GO TO HILLSIDE. OH, PLEASE, PLEASE!
YOUR FATHER ISN'T GOING TO SPEND HIS MONEY ON PRIVATE SCHOOL WHEN THERE ARE PERFECTLY WONDERFUL CUBAN SCHOOLS.
ARE YOU CRAZY? THE DIPLOMATS' SCHOOL? WHERE THOSE FASCISTS SEND THEIR SPAWN?
TEDDY, THE CHILD IS SO UNHAPPY! I'M WORRIED ABOUT HER.

AT LAST, NIKKI PREVAILED, HER FIRST STEP OUT OF CUBA AND HER PARENTS' WORLD.

JOSÉ, HERE'S TEN PESOS FOR YOU. GET RID OF THAT CAT. YOU KNOW WHAT TO DO.
WHAM!!!

SANTA MARÍA DEL MAR
WHILE I WAS WORKING AT BANAO, OUR SCHOOL HAD SENT MARTUGENIA TO THE CITY OF GUANTANAMO ON A *"TRABAJO SOCIAL"* RESEARCH TEAM.

AFTER WE RETURNED TO HAVANA, I PERSUADED MARTUGENIA TO GO WITH ME TO SANTA MARÍA DEL MAR BEACH. WE COULDN'T AFFORD A *CABAÑA,* SO WE SET OUT ON A DAY TRIP.

WE PICKED A SPOT NEAR A HOTEL THAT PERMITTED NON-GUESTS IN IT'S RESTAU-RANT FOR LUNCH, WHICH MOST DID NOT.

WE HAD SUCH A GOOD TIME, WE FORGOT THE HOUR & DIDN'T NOTICE UNTIL AFTER DARK.

GRINGA! IT'S ALMOST MIDNIGHT & THE LAST BUS ALREADY LEFT FOR HAVANA!
WELL, WE CAN'T STAY HERE. LET'S HEAD FOR THE HIGHWAY.
I HATE TO TELL YOU THIS, BUT WE'RE NEVER GOING TO MAKE IT ALL THE WAY ON FOOT.

MAYBE WE CAN STAY IN ALAMAR. IT SHOULD BE COMING UP SOON...
WHO DO I KNOW THERE?
I'VE GOT IT! NORMA & HER FAMILY LIVE IN ALAMAR!
WE BOTH HAD RECENTLY DRIFTED APART FROM OUR *COMPROMISOS,* SO WE FELT WILD & FREE OUT HERE ON THE ROAD.
LOOK! SEE THE GLOW ON THE HORIZON? THAT'S HAVANA.
ALAMAR IS RIGHT OVER THERE...
THERE'S A COLONY OF FOREIGN *TÉCNICOS,* & NORMA'S FROM ARGENTINA.
NO ONE FROM SCHOOL WILL SEE US.
MRS. SMIRCIC! IT'S ME, MARTUGENIA! I AM SO SORRY TO DISTURB YOU. WE WERE LOOKING FOR NORMA. WE MISSED THE LAST BUS FROM SANTA MARÍA... & WE WONDERED...
OH, YOU POOR DEARS! NORMA'S NOT HERE, BUT YOU CAN TAKE HER ROOM. I'M SORRY, THERE'S JUST ONE BED. COME RIGHT THIS WAY.

WE EMERGED FROM NORMA'S HOUSE THE NEXT DAY AS A COUPLE, BLISSFULLY UNAWARE OF THE STORM THAT WAS BREWING. IT WAS A HAPPY SUMMER.
SANTA MARIA

CALLE ÁNIMAS

MARTUGENIA WAS A FREE SPIRIT, BLESSED WITH A QUICK WIT & A WONDERFULLY TWISTED SENSE OF HUMOR. AS A REVOLUTIONARY & AS A POPULAR YOUNG INSTRUCTOR IN THE ENGLISH DEPARTMENT, THIS SOMETIMES GOT HER INTO TROUBLE.

GRINGUITA! I HAVE TO GO REPORT FOR DUTY, BUT I'LL BE FREE AT FIVE. MEET ME IN THE CAFETERIA & WE'LL GO TO MY HOUSE FOR DINNER. ROMELIA'S MAKING *ARROZ CON POLLO* TODAY.
I JUST GOT PAID! ELENA BURKE IS PLAYING LATER TONIGHT AT THE GATO TUERTO. WE COULD GET A DRINK AT THE BAR. WANNA GO?
SURE! SOUNDS GREAT.
ROMELIA! YOUR DAUGHTER INVITED ME TO DINNER...
AH... LA GRINGA! OF COURSE! WE'VE GOT TO PUT SOME MEAT ON YOUR BONES, TOO SKINNY!
ROMELIA WAS AN ARDENT FIDELISTA & HEADED THE LOCAL CDR, THE *COMITÉ DE DEFENSA DE LA REVOLUCIÓN* ON HER BLOCK. SHE HAD JUST A FEW YEARS OF FORMAL EDUCATION, & BEFORE THE REVOLUTION, SHE RAN AN UPSCALE HAUTE-COUTURE SHOP, WHERE WITH HER EMPLOYEES, SHE DESIGNED & PRODUCED CLOTHING FOR WEALTHY CLIENTS.

¡AY! I'M SO TIRED. THEY DROVE ME CRAZY AT THE FACTORY TODAY, & I STILL HAVE TO GET THIS DRESS FINISHED FOR MENGANA'S QUINCE PARTY.
ROMELIA & PEDRO ALBERTO, MARTUGENIA'S PARENTS, HAD AN APARTMENT ON CALLE ÁNIMAS AS BOTH THEIR HOME & FOR ROMELIA'S SHOP. AFTER THE TRIUMPH OF THE REVOLUTION, SHE SOLD ALL HER EQUIPMENT, EXCEPT FOR ONE MACHINE, CLOSED THE BUSINESS & OFFERED HER SERVICES TO THE NEW GOVERNMENT.
PEDRO ALBERTO WORKED AS A PHYSICAL EDUCATION TEACHER AT THE BENEFICENCIA, THE CITY ORPHANAGE, RETIRED AS SOON AS HE COULD ARRANGE IT.
HA! YOUR FAULT FOR WORKING FOR THOSE BASTARDS. BUNCH OF CROOKS!
ROMELIA BECAME A PATTERN-MAKER FOR A STATE CLOTHING FACTORY & WORKED AFTER HOURS SEWING FOR HER FAMILY & FRIENDS.
THOSE PEOPLE ACROSS THE STREET... THERE'S BLACK MARKET BUSINESS GOING ON...
AS HEAD OF THE COMITÉ, SHE MADE ALL OF THE NEIGHBOR'S LIVES HER BUSINESS & CAME TO BE THE BOSS OF THE BLOCK. AS A MILICIANA, SHE PUT IN MANY HOURS OF GUARD DUTY AT THE FACTORY.
¡COÑO, ROMELIA! LEAVE THE FRIGGING NEGRITOS ALONE. AT LEAST THEY'RE MAKING A LIVING.
AY! PEDRO ALBERTO! I DON'T WANT TO HEAR ANY OF YOUR GUSANERÍA!
THERE WERE ALWAYS PEOPLE IN THE HOUSE: NEIGHBORS, RELATIVES, OR COMPAÑEROS FROM THE SECCIONAL DE LOS CDR.

HEY! WHAT'S UP, GRINGA?
HEY, SUPERMAN!
PEDRO ALBERTO THOUGHT THE REVOLUTION WAS CRAP & SAID SO. SEMI-RETIRED, HE DIDN'T GIVE A DAMN WHAT ANYBODY THOUGHT.
¡VIEJA! ANY COFFEE LEFT?
PEDRO ALBERTO HAD A STRICT ROUTINE: BREAKFAST & BATH AT HOME...
IT'S ME!
LUNCH AT HIS MISTRESS JENNY'S HOUSE— SHE LIVED NEARBY IN THE NEIGHBORHOOD.
THESE FUCKING COMMUNISTS–THEY STEAL EVERYTHING. WOULD YOU BELIEVE IT?! MY WIFE TURNED OVER ALL THE FAMILY SILVER IN THAT COLLECTION CAMPAIGN LAST WEEK!
AFTERNOONS WITH HIS BUDDIES IN THE PARK TO DISCUSS THE EVENTS OF THE DAY...
QUIET, EVERYBODY! MY MOVIE'S ABOUT TO START. IT'S A GOOD ONE TONIGHT.
THEN HOME FOR DINNER, COOKED & SERVED BY ROMELIA, WITH TV BEFORE & AFTER UNTIL BEDTIME.

IT WAS THE SAME FOR ALL OF MY FRIENDS. ALL HAD A FATHER, A MOTHER, MAYBE SIBLINGS & THEIR FATHER HAD A MISTRESS (OR A MALE LOVER) ON THE SIDE.

ROMELIA SPENT LOTS OF TIME WAITING IN LINES AT THEIR ASSIGNED GROCERY STORE & BUTCHER SHOP. FOR ALL BUT THE PRIVILEGED FEW, ESSENTIALS WERE RATIONED. ROMELIA HAD A NETWORK OF NEIGHBORS & FAMILY FOR ALERTS OF WHEN SUPPLIES CAME IN. THERE WERE NEVER ENOUGH, SO DISCREET BLACK MARKET PURCHASES FILLED THE GAP.

Gracias Fidel
MURAL
ONE DAY, AT HER MINIMAX GROCERY, ROMELIA SAW "THAT JENNY!"
¡PROSTITUTA! GET OUT OF MY STORE!
¡SIN VERGÜENZA!!! SHAMELESS BITCH!
ROMELIA HAD POWER IN THE NEIGHBORHOOD.
ÁNIMAS BECAME MY SECOND HOME & I STAYED OVER COUNTLESS NIGHTS. WE ALL KEPT UP THE FICTION THAT MARTUGENIA & I WERE "JUST FRIENDS."
HERE, GRINGUITA! HURRY UP! THEY'RE TURNING OFF THE WATER SOON, & I HAVE TO FILL THE TUB, OR WE'RE SCREWED 'TIL TOMORROW.
ROMELIA! DID YOU GET ANY MALANGA TODAY?
Guardia
TODOS A LA PLAZA
EMULACION SOCIALISTA
I WAS HAPPY, THEY CALLED ME "THE BANANAFIED AMERICAN," *LA GRINGA APLATANADA*. IT MEANT I BELONGED.

AFTER SCHOOL, TO GO TO ÁNIMAS, WE'D WALK UP THE HILL & AROUND THE UNIVERSITY STADIUM, THEN DOWN CALLE RONDA TO NEPTUNO OR SAN RAFAEL, & FROM THERE ALL THE WAY TO SOLEDAD & ÁNIMAS.
ALONG THE WAY, THERE WERE STILL PLENTY OF OLD *BODEGAS* WITH THEIR FINE EBONY, OPEN-AIR BARS. YOU COULD STOP THERE FOR A BEER & LISTEN TO ÑICO MEMBIELA OR VICENTICO VALDÉS ON THE JUKEBOX WHILE DISCUSSING LITERATURE, OR EXISTENTIALISM, OR—IN WHISPERS—THE UMAP...
MEANWHILE, MUCH WAS HAPPENING IN THE ARTS & CULTURE SCENE. THE SALON DE MAYO AT PABELLÓN CUBA ATTRACTED THE CREAM OF AMERICAN & EUROPEAN AVANT-GARDE ARTISTS. CARLOS FRANQUI, FOUNDING EDITOR OF "REVOLUCIÓN," THE OFFICIAL NEWSPAPER SINCE THE SIERRA MAESTRA, ORGANIZED THIS THUMB-IN-THE-EYE OF SOVIET SOCIALIST REALISM IN CUBA. SOON AFTER, FRANQUI WAS DEMOTED & EXPELLED FROM THE REVOLUTIONARY PANTHEON.
SALON DE MAYO
PABELLON CUBA, LA HABANA, 30 DE JULIO DE 1967
Notas sobre el Arte en la Revolución
JEAN SCHUSTER
ORQUESTA CUBANA DE MUSICA MODERNA

FIDEL STOPS IN AT THE SCHOOL OF LETTERS

ONE FRIDAY IN AUGUST '67, THE SCHOOL OF LETTERS AS WELL AS OTHER HUMANITIES SCHOOLS WERE MOBILIZED TO DO AGRICULTURAL LABOR IN ARIGUANABO, SOUTH OF HAVANA. THE TRUCKS WERE LATE & WE SAT AROUND WAITING FOR THEM TO PICK US UP AT SCHOOL, WHEN SUDDENLY...

HEY LOOK! IT'S FIDEL!
FIDEL! COME TALK TO US!
FIDEL! FIDEL! WE'RE WAITING TO GO TO WORK IN THE FIELDS!
WELL, WHERE ARE YOU STUDENTS HEADED?
ARIGUANABO, FIDEL! COME IN & TALK WITH US!
AH! THAT'S IN SAN ANTONIO DE LOS BAÑOS! I'LL COME IN & TELL YOU ABOUT OUR PLANS FOR THAT AREA.
¡FIDEL! ¡FIDEL! COME TO THE AUDITORIUM!
HEY, WATCH IT, COMPAÑERA!
¡AY DIÓS MÍO! I'VE JUST ELBOWED RAMIRO VALDÉS! SHUDDER!!!

THE DOORS ARE LOCKED!
BREAK THEM OPEN!
WHAT'S YOUR NAME? WHERE ARE YOU FROM?
CONNIE, AN AMERICAN. I'M STUDYING HERE IN LETRAS.
AH, HMMM. WELL, LET ME TELL YOU ABOUT WHAT YOU WILL BE DOING. WE'VE DEVELOPED A REVOLUTIONARY WAY TO PLANT PINEAPPLES! FIRST YOU...
I GOT MY OWN FIVE-MINUTE TUTORIAL.

THEN FIDEL MOUNTED THE STEPS TO THE STAGE, JOINED BY RAMIRO VALDÉS, THE INTERIOR MINISTER; CARLOS AMAT, DEAN OF HUMANITIES; CHOMY, RECTOR OF THE UNIVERSITY; & OUR DIRECTOR, VICENTINA ANTUÑA. FIDEL GAVE A ROUSING SPEECH ON THE VIRTUES OF ARGRICULTURAL WORK & HOW WE WERE ALL GOING TO BE BETTER REVOLUTIONARIES THROUGH OUR EFFORTS FOR THE FATHERLAND. SOON FIDEL & HIS ENTOURAGE SPED OFF & WE LEFT FOR ARIGUANABO.

Precio: cinco centavos

La Habana, sábado 5 de

Despidió Fidel a los estudiantes universitarios que van al agro

Con motivo de iniciarse el plan de trabajo productivo de fin de semana por los estudiantes de las distintas escuelas de la Universidad de La Habana, el Primer Secretario del Comité Central de nuestro Partido y Primer Ministro del Gobierno Revolucionario, comandante Fidel Castro, se reunió con los alumnos de la Facultad de Humanidades momentos antes de partir éstos hacia la región de Ariguanabo. El compañero Fidel les explicó a los jóvenes los importantes planes de desarrollo agrícola de nuestro país y les exhortó a desempeñar un destacado rol en los mismos. En la foto de Arnaldo Santos se observan junto al Jefe de la Revolución al comandante Ramiro Valdés, miembro del Buró Político del Partido; el rector de la Universidad doctor José R. Miyar y a la directora de la Escuela de Letras, doctora Vicentina Antuña.

CHAPTER 4

"Morgan!" & the Malecón

"MORGAN!" & THE MALECÓN

ONE EARLY SEPTEMBER EVENING IN '67, MARTUGENIA & I DECIDED TO GO TO THE MOVIES.

RIVIERA
HOY MORGAN
"MORGAN!"—A BRITISH FILM BY KAREL REISZ—WAS SUSPECTED OF NOT BEING MORALLY SOUND, SO WE WERE EAGER TO SEE IT BEFORE IT DISAPPEARED.
LOOK! LET'S GO SEE "MORGAN!"
HEY, YEAH! I READ IT'S ONE OF THOSE "ANGRY YOUNG MEN" FILMS.
THE PLOT WAS ABOUT TWO LOVERS FROM INCOMPATIBLE SOCIAL CLASSES: WORKING-CLASS MORGAN & HIS UPPER-CLASS WIFE, LEONIE, WHO LEAVES HIM FOR ANOTHER, MORE SUITABLE MAN. MORGAN GOES BERSERK & DOES CRAZY THINGS TO WIN HER BACK, LIKE WEARING A GORILLA SUIT TO HER WEDDING & TERRORIZING THE GUESTS.
IN THE END, REBELLION & ANARCHY HAVE BEEN OVERCOME. MORGAN IS IN AN INSANE ASYLUM, WHERE HE SUCCUMBS TO HIS STALINIST MOTHER'S ORDERLY BELIEFS.
WHEW! I NEED SOME AIR AFTER THAT. LET'S WALK ALL THE WAY HOME ON THE MALECÓN.
WHEN WE LEFT AT MIDNIGHT, WE FELT A BIT LIKE MAD GORILLAS OURSELVES & FORGOT THE NEED FOR CAUTION.

MMM... BEAUTIFUL MOON...
¡OYE! ¡MAMI RICA!
HEY! GET IN THE CAR WITH US & HAVE SOME FUN!
¡UFF!!! GET LOST!
SIGH, WE'D BETTER START WALKING...
¡CHICO! TAKE A LOOK AT THAT. THEY'RE DIRTY DYKES!
LET'S GO KICK SOME BUTT!
¡TORTILLERAS DE MIERDA!

WATCH OUT, BABY!

¡BABY!? DID YOU HEAR THAT? THE DYKE SAID "BABY"! I'M GONNA BREAK HER SKULL!

NO! NO!

¡PUERCAS!
LEAVE HER ALONE!!!

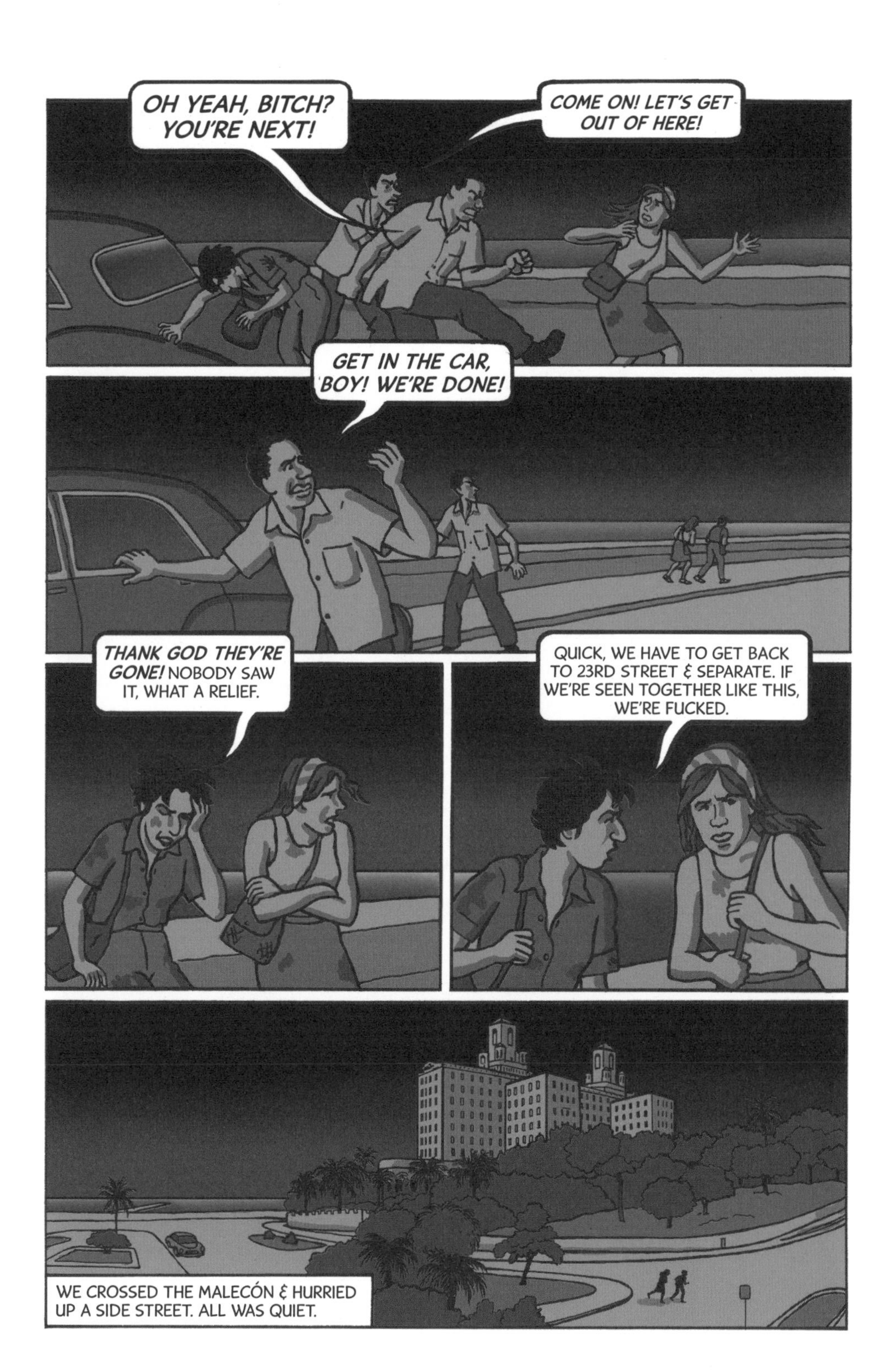
OH YEAH, BITCH? YOU'RE NEXT!
COME ON! LET'S GET OUT OF HERE!
GET IN THE CAR, BOY! WE'RE DONE!
THANK GOD THEY'RE GONE! NOBODY SAW IT, WHAT A RELIEF.
QUICK, WE HAVE TO GET BACK TO 23RD STREET & SEPARATE. IF WE'RE SEEN TOGETHER LIKE THIS, WE'RE FUCKED.
WE CROSSED THE MALECÓN & HURRIED UP A SIDE STREET. ALL WAS QUIET.

STOP! WE'RE POLICE! WE SAW THE ATTACK; PLEASE GET IN OUR CAR. WE'RE TAKING YOU IN TO IDENTIFY THE PERPETRATORS...
HOW THE HELL DID THEY KNOW!!???
WE PICKED UP THOSE TWO MEN.
OH BY THE WAY... THEY ACCUSE YOU OF COMMITTING SEX ACTS ON THE MALECÓN & SAID THEY WERE SO DISGUSTED THAT THEY GOT OUT OF THEIR CAR TO STOP YOU... WHAT DO YOU HAVE TO SAY TO THAT?
ARE YOU CRAZY? WHO WOULD DO THAT? WHY US???
JESUS! IT'S A SET-UP!
THEY'RE FILTHY LIARS, TRYING TO JUSTIFY WHAT THEY JUST DID TO US!!!

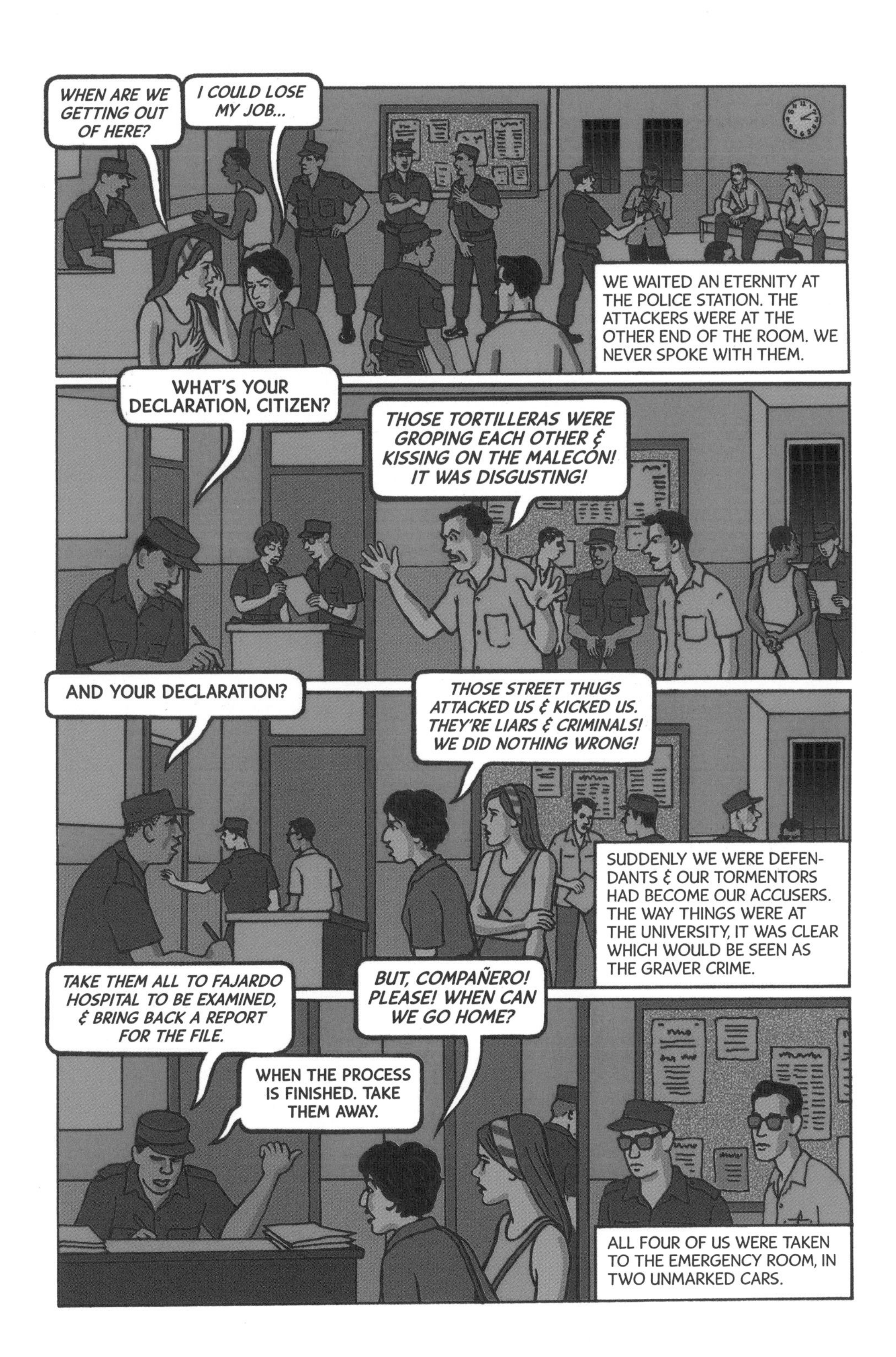
WHEN ARE WE GETTING OUT OF HERE?
I COULD LOSE MY JOB...
WE WAITED AN ETERNITY AT THE POLICE STATION. THE ATTACKERS WERE AT THE OTHER END OF THE ROOM. WE NEVER SPOKE WITH THEM.
WHAT'S YOUR DECLARATION, CITIZEN?
THOSE TORTILLERAS WERE GROPING EACH OTHER & KISSING ON THE MALECÓN! IT WAS DISGUSTING!
AND YOUR DECLARATION?
THOSE STREET THUGS ATTACKED US & KICKED US. THEY'RE LIARS & CRIMINALS! WE DID NOTHING WRONG!
SUDDENLY WE WERE DEFENDANTS & OUR TORMENTORS HAD BECOME OUR ACCUSERS. THE WAY THINGS WERE AT THE UNIVERSITY, IT WAS CLEAR WHICH WOULD BE SEEN AS THE GRAVER CRIME.
TAKE THEM ALL TO FAJARDO HOSPITAL TO BE EXAMINED, & BRING BACK A REPORT FOR THE FILE.
BUT, COMPAÑERO! PLEASE! WHEN CAN WE GO HOME?
WHEN THE PROCESS IS FINISHED. TAKE THEM AWAY.
ALL FOUR OF US WERE TAKEN TO THE EMERGENCY ROOM, IN TWO UNMARKED CARS.

LAST NAME?
PATTERSON.
BRUISES? INJURIES?
I'VE GOT A BROKEN FINGER! LOOK!
MADRE MÍA! DON'T LOOK NOW— THAT'S FRANCISCO DORTICÓS, THE STUDENT BODY PRESIDENT OF THE UNIVERSITY!
WHAT INFERNAL LUCK... DÓRTICOS WAS THE INTERN ON DUTY.
HE DOESN'T KNOW US! MAYBE HE WON'T KNOW TO REPORT US.
NO, BUT HIS WIFE WAS IN YOUR CLASS FOR THE LAST TWO YEARS. IF HE MENTIONS IT TO HER, WE'RE DONE FOR.
SAY AS LITTLE AS POSSIBLE! GOD... HE'S GOING TO FIND OUT YOU'RE AN AMERICAN...
BRUISES? ANY INJURY TO DECLARE?
NO, NOTHING.

FINALLY, THEY LET US GO & TOLD US WE'D BE SUMMONED FOR FUTURE APPEARANCES. WE LEFT IN A PANIC. THIS WAS HAPPENING RIGHT DURING THE PURGES. FEARING EXPULSION & THE LOSS OF MARTUGENIA'S JOB AS AN INSTRUCTOR, WE DECIDED NOT TO SAY A WORD AT SCHOOL. MAYBE IT WOULD ALL JUST GO AWAY.

CONNIE! DINNER'S READY! SET THE TABLE, PLEASE!
YOU GOT THE STRANGEST CALL TODAY, SOMETHING ABOUT A MEETING WITH THE DEAN. YOU'RE SUPPOSED TO CALL BACK.
A WEEK LATER, MARTUGENIA & I WERE SUMMONED BY THE UNIVERSITY AUTHORITIES TO APPEAR & FACE ACCUSATIONS AGAINST US.

MY, THINGS SEEM BUSY FOR YOU AT THE UNIVERSITY. ARE YOUR STUDIES GOING WELL?
WHAT..? OH... YEAH... EVERYTHING'S FINE... UMM... MAY I BE EXCUSED? I HAVE A TEST COMING UP.

FORTUNATELY FOR ME, MY FAMILY HAD LITTLE INTEREST IN MY UNIVERSITY LIFE, OR MY PERSONAL LIFE FOR THAT MATTER, SO THEY REMAINED BLISSFULLY OBLIVIOUS DURING MOST OF THE SCANDAL.

MARTUGENIA WASN'T NEARLY AS LUCKY. THE YOUNGER OF THE ATTACKERS (& NOW OUR ACCUSERS) WAS BY GROTESQUE COINCIDENCE, ENROLLED IN A SPORTS PROGRAM WHERE HER FATHER STILL TAUGHT A CLASS. A FEW DAYS AFTER THE ATTACK, HE BOASTED ABOUT BEATING UP SOME *TORTILLERAS* ON THE MALECÓN...
WOULD YOU BELIEVE IT? ONE OF THE TWO DYKES WAS AN AMERICAN! AT THE UNIVERSITY!
AND THE OTHER ONE?
OH, THE BUTCH! THAT ONE'S CUBAN. BOTH ARE FROM THE SCHOOL OF LETTERS!
TORTILLERA DE MIERDA!!! THAT WAS YOU, WASN'T IT?
GET OUT OF MY HOUSE! I DON'T WANT A QUEER DAUGHTER!
PAPÁ, NO!!! IT'S A LIE!!! WE WERE ATTACKED BY STREET CRIMINALS!
PEDRO ALBERTO WAITED FOR MARTUGENIA TO COME HOME THAT NIGHT...
WHAT YOU NEED IS A BIG DICK!!

WE BOTH BEGAN TO RECEIVE SUMMONSES TO APPEAR AT TRIAL—ONE FOR THE CITY & ONE FOR THE THE UNIVERSITY. THIS NIGHTMARE ENVELOPED US NOW THROUGH MOST OF THE FOLLOWING YEAR... MARTUGENIA, IN CENTRO HABANA, FOUND REFUGE AT AN AUNT'S APARTMENT A FEW BLOCKS AWAY FROM ÁNIMAS. HER MOTHER FINALLY RESCUED HER & BROUGHT HER HOME. I LAY LOW AT MY FAMILY'S APARTMENT IN MIRAMAR.

507
2¢
CORREOS DE CUBA
VOSTOK II
TIEMPO: 25 HORAS
TITOV
Juzgado Correccional Secc. 8va.
Vedado
Anna Veltfort
8 No.507m apto.2 ent.5ta.y
5ta.B. Miramar-Marianao.
PARA USO DEL CARTERO EN
No hay este númer
No se encuentra en hora
Desconocido.
Falleció.
Fecha
LOOK! ¡LA AMERICANA! DID YOU HEAR..?
WHY DOES SHE BOTHER COMING TO SCHOOL & TAKING EXAMS?
EVERYBODY KNOWS SHE'S GETTING EXPELLED!
¡COÑOOO! SHE HAS SOME NERVE SHOWING HER FACE!

WORD QUICKLY SPREAD AT THE UNIVERSITY & BECAME HOT GOSSIP IN OUR BUILDING THAT HOUSED THE SCHOOL OF LETTERS, THE SCHOOLS OF JOURNALISM, HISTORY & LIBRARY SCIENCE.

ON THE DAY OF OUR UNIVERSITY TRIAL, WE CONFERRED & AGREED SHE WAS THE MORE VULNERABLE OF THE TWO. HER JOB WAS IN JEOPARDY. I WAS A STUDENT BUT ALSO THE DAUGHTER OF A FOREIGN PROFESSOR, SO THAT MIGHT AFFORD ME SOME PROTECTION.
WHATEVER HAPPENS, DON'T LET HIM TRICK YOU INTO ADMITTING ANY OF THAT SHIT. DON'T BELIEVE HIM IF HE SAYS I MADE SOME KIND OF CONFESSION. ***NEVER!***
DON'T WORRY. I NEVER WILL. WHO WOULD BE SO STUPID, ANYWAY?

I ENTERED THE INTERROGATION ROOM IN THE LAW SCHOOL BUILDING. MY FACE BURNED WITH FEAR & EMBARRASSMENT.
OUR DEAN, CARLOS AMAT, WAS THE PROSECUTOR & JUDGE OF THE UNIVERSITY TRIAL. THE ADVISORY PANEL INCLUDED OUR DIRECTOR, VICENTINA ANTUÑA, THE STUDENT BODY REPRESENTATIVE MARTINA & A REPTILIAN YOUNG MAN, WHOSE NAME NOW ESCAPES ME. HE REPRESENTED THE YOUNG COMMUNIST UNION, THE "VANGUARD OF CUBAN YOUTH."
PLEASE HAVE A SEAT, CONNIE.

BEFORE HIS ROLE AS A DEAN, AMAT HAD BEEN ONE OF CUBA'S MOST POWERFUL PROSECUTORS OF THE EARLY '60S. HE WAS CHIEF PROSECUTOR AT THE SUMMARY WAR TRIALS OF ALLEGED COUNTERREVOLUTIONARIES & SENT MANY TO THEIR DEATHS IN FRONT OF FIRING SQUADS. HE PROSECUTED OTHER HIGH-PROFILE POLITICAL TRIALS IN FOLLOWING YEARS.

TWO MEN CLAIM TO HAVE SEEN YOU & MARTUGENIA RODRÍGUEZ COMMITTING DEPRAVED HOMOSEXUAL ACTS ON THE WALL OF THE MALECÓN.
WAS THAT TRUE?
ABSOLUTELY NOT. THAT'S AN OUTRAGEOUS LIE. THEY ASSAULTED US WHEN WE REFUSED TO SUBMIT TO THEIR DEMANDS.
ALL RIGHT... BUT NOW I HAVE TO ASK YOU SOMETHING THAT GOES TO THE HEART OF THE MATTER. ARE YOU A HOMOSEXUAL?
THE QUESTION FELT LIKE A FATAL CHECKMATE. IF I FLATLY DENIED IT, I WOULD LOSE ALL CREDIBILITY. I ALREADY HAD A REPUTATION AT SCHOOL AS A SUSPECTED LESBIAN. I HAD TO CONVINCE HIM THAT MARTUGENIA HAD DONE NOTHING WRONG & WASN'T A HOMOSEXUAL HERSELF. IF I ADMITTED I WAS INDEED A HOMOSEXUAL, I'D EARN POINTS FOR HONESTY BUT LEAVE HIM NO CHOICE BUT TO EXPEL ME. I PONDERED THIS CONUNDRUM FOR WHAT SEEMED AN ETERNITY. THE PANEL STARED GLUMLY AT ME. THE SOLUTION CAME TO ME IN A SUDDEN EPIPHANY...
DR. AMAT, I WANT TO BE COMPLETELY HONEST WITH YOU...
...AND THE MOST EXACT & TRUE ANSWER I CAN GIVE YOU IS THAT I REALLY DON'T KNOW IF I AM HOMOSEXUAL...
HMM... I MUST ASK YOU ANOTHER QUESTION, THEN. HAVE YOU EVER ENGAGED IN A HOMOSEXUAL ACT?

DR. AMAT, I ANSWERED YOUR FIRST QUESTION AS BEST I COULD... THE SECOND ONE IS IMPOSSIBLE TO ANSWER BECAUSE BY DEFINITION IT IMPLICATES MORE THAN ONE PERSON.
AS A MATTER OF CONSCIENCE, I CAN'T DO THAT.
I'M BEING AS TRUTHFUL & SINCERE AS I CAN. I'M SORRY, DR. AMAT.
ALL RIGHT, CONNIE. YOU CAN GO NOW. YOU'LL BE CALLED AFTER A COMPLETE INVESTIGATION HAS BEEN MADE.
CALL IN MARTUGENIA, PLEASE.
NO, DR. AMAT, I DIDN'T.
NO, DR. AMAT, THAT'S NOT TRUE.
NO, DR. AMAT, I AM NOT.

NEWS OF THE TRIAL SPREAD SWIFTLY THROUGH THE UNIVERSITY. WORD ALSO GOT OUT THAT MONICA & HER GROUP WERE TALKING ABOUT WRITING TO SARTRE & OTHER PROMINENT EUROPEAN INTELLECTUALS TO DENOUNCE THE HOMOPHOBIC WITCH-HUNTS & TO RALLY INTERNATIONAL SUPPORT FOR CUBANS ACCUSED OF BEING "SOCIAL SCUM," LACRA SOCIAL.

THE WORLD HAS TO KNOW WHAT'S GOING ON IN CUBA!
DON'T BE CRAZY! THEY'LL CRUCIFY US ALL!
MONICA & I HAD A SUMMIT MEETING OF SORTS, BUT WE DIDN'T AGREE ON WHAT COULD BE DONE.

WEEKS LATER, I WAS SUMMONED TO ANOTHER MEETING WITH THE DEAN...

WE'VE DECIDED NOT TO CHARGE YOU WITH ANYTHING, BUT WE WANT YOU TO TAKE A YEAR OFF FROM SCHOOL. THEN YOU CAN RETURN, WHEN THINGS HAVE CALMED DOWN.
I DON'T ACCEPT THAT! WHY SHOULD I BE PUNISHED FOR SOMETHING I NEVER DID?
YOU DON'T ACCEPT? HMMM... I THINK THAT'S UP TO ME.
ALL RIGHT, HERE IS YOUR ALTERNATIVE. YOU CAN CONTINUE IN THE UNIVERSITY UNDER ONE CONDITION. YOU MUST SUBMIT TO TREATMENT BY A PSYCHIATRIST WHOM WE WILL ASSIGN. YOU'LL GO TO WEEKLY SESSIONS.
SIGH... OK, IF THAT'S WHAT I HAVE TO DO. I WANT TO FINISH & GRADUATE.
YOU START ON MONDAY WITH DR. ARMANDO CÓRDOBA, AT 3 PM. HERE'S THE ADDRESS.

MARTUGENIA SURVIVED HER ORDEAL WITH AMAT & WAS ALLOWED TO KEEP HER JOB. WE MET FURTIVELY, AWAY FROM SCHOOL, AWAY FROM OUR HOMES, ALWAYS AFRAID TO RUN INTO ANYONE FROM THE UNIVERSITY.
YOU KNOW, THIS IS ALL ABOUT THE ENEMIES OF LETRAS TRYING TO TAKE OVER THE SCHOOL. WE'RE JUST PAWNS. BUT VICENTINA HAS TOO MUCH PRESTIGE...

I SHOWED UP FOR THE FIRST OF MANY APPOINTMENTS AT THE HOSPITAL COMANDANTE MANUEL FAJARDO & KNOCKED ON DR. CÓRDOBA'S DOOR.

PLEASE HAVE A SEAT.
HOURS OF WAITING WENT BY...
NOW TELL ME WHAT THIS IS ALL ABOUT...
DO YOU FEEL PREDOMINANTLY ATTRACTED TO WOMEN?
NO, I DON'T THINK SO. BUT I WAS CURIOUS.
TELL ME ABOUT YOUR FAMILY...

I ASSUMED THE POINT WAS TO DETERMINE IF I WAS AN INCORRIGIBLE DEVIANT OR SOMEHOW SALVAGEABLE. TO APPEASE THE ENEMIES OF LETRAS, THIS WAS A COMPROMISE MADE FOR THE LIBERALS & CONSERVATIVES IN THE VARIOUS POLITICAL FIEFDOMS INVOLVED—THE PARTY, THE UJC, THE LETRAS DIRECTOR'S CIRCLE & OF COURSE, STATE SECURITY...

AFTER EACH SESSION, I CAREFULLY WROTE DOWN EVERYTHING I HAD SAID, FOR CONSISTENCY THE NEXT TIME.
THERE'S AN INTERESTING YOUTH MOVEMENT IN HOLLAND, THE PROVOS. I WONDER IF YOU'VE HEARD OF IT?
WHAT? WHERE IS THAT GOING?

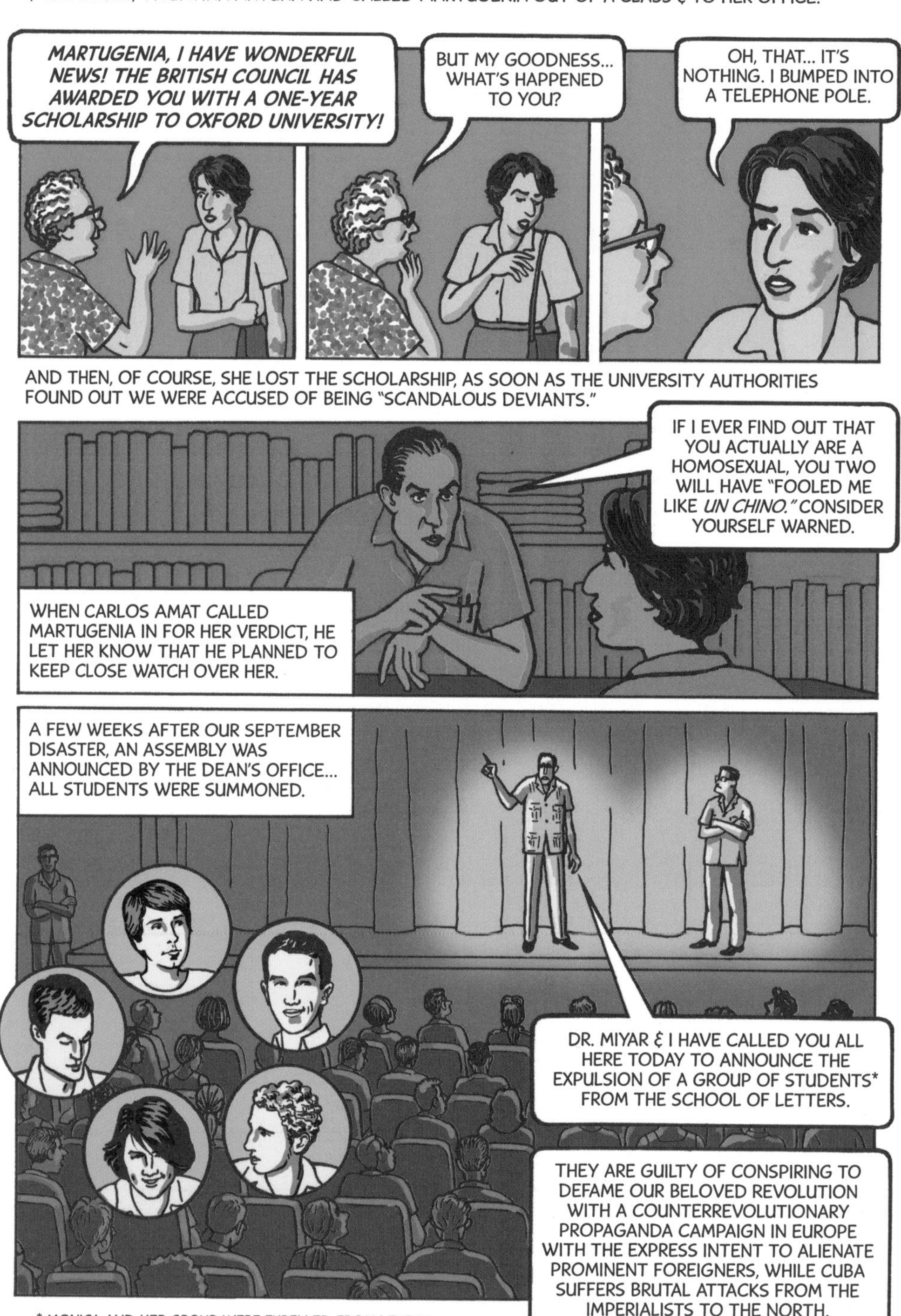
TWO DAYS AFTER THE DISASTER ON THE MALECÓN, BEFORE THE SHIT HIT THE FAN WITH THE DEAN & THE COURT, VICENTINA ANTUÑA HAD CALLED MARTUGENIA OUT OF A CLASS & TO HER OFFICE.
MARTUGENIA, I HAVE WONDERFUL NEWS! THE BRITISH COUNCIL HAS AWARDED YOU WITH A ONE-YEAR SCHOLARSHIP TO OXFORD UNIVERSITY!
BUT MY GOODNESS... WHAT'S HAPPENED TO YOU?
OH, THAT... IT'S NOTHING. I BUMPED INTO A TELEPHONE POLE.
AND THEN, OF COURSE, SHE LOST THE SCHOLARSHIP, AS SOON AS THE UNIVERSITY AUTHORITIES FOUND OUT WE WERE ACCUSED OF BEING "SCANDALOUS DEVIANTS."
WHEN CARLOS AMAT CALLED MARTUGENIA IN FOR HER VERDICT, HE LET HER KNOW THAT HE PLANNED TO KEEP CLOSE WATCH OVER HER.
IF I EVER FIND OUT THAT YOU ACTUALLY ARE A HOMOSEXUAL, YOU TWO WILL HAVE "FOOLED ME LIKE *UN CHINO.*" CONSIDER YOURSELF WARNED.
A FEW WEEKS AFTER OUR SEPTEMBER DISASTER, AN ASSEMBLY WAS ANNOUNCED BY THE DEAN'S OFFICE... ALL STUDENTS WERE SUMMONED.
DR. MIYAR & I HAVE CALLED YOU ALL HERE TODAY TO ANNOUNCE THE EXPULSION OF A GROUP OF STUDENTS* FROM THE SCHOOL OF LETTERS.
THEY ARE GUILTY OF CONSPIRING TO DEFAME OUR BELOVED REVOLUTION WITH A COUNTERREVOLUTIONARY PROPAGANDA CAMPAIGN IN EUROPE WITH THE EXPRESS INTENT TO ALIENATE PROMINENT FOREIGNERS, WHILE CUBA SUFFERS BRUTAL ATTACKS FROM THE IMPERIALISTS TO THE NORTH.

* MONICA AND HER GROUP WERE EXPELLED FROM LETRAS.

JUZGADO CORRECCIONAL DE LA OCTAVA SECCIÓN,, CORNER OF LINEA & M STREET, VEDADO
JUZGADO CORRECCIONAL SECCIONAL 8a
THE TIME CAME FOR THE FIRST OF MANY SESSIONS OF THE PUBLIC TRIAL CONDUCTED BY THE CITY LEGAL SYSTEM. EVERY DAY, FOR CLOSE TO A YEAR, WE ANXIOUSLY WAITED WITH DREAD FOR THE MAIL. IT BECAME A KAFKAESQUE DAISY-CHAIN OF BUREAUCRATIC NIGHTMARES. A SUMMONS WOULD ARRIVE AT EACH OF OUR HOMES, THEN MARTUGENIA & I WOULD APPEAR, THE ACCUSERS WOULD NOT, OR PERHAPS ONLY ONE, SO THE TRIAL WOULD BE POSTPONED. SOMETIMES WE WERE TOLD TO BRING OR SOLICIT ANOTHER PIECE OF PAPER, REQUIRED FOR FILING UNDER GOD KNOWS WHAT STATUTE & WITHOUT IT, THAT DAY'S SESSION WAS POSTPONED AGAIN, FOLLOWED BY YET ANOTHER SUMMONS...
HA! HA! HA!
¡MIRA!! ¡VIENEN LAS TORTILLERAS!! LOOK, LOOK!! HERE COME THE DYKES!!
¡QUE FUERTES LAS COCHINAS ESAS!!! DIRTY STONE DYKES!!!
NOW THEN... YOU TWO ARE CHARGED WITH LEWD, IMMORAL BEHAVIOR ON THE MALECÓN. HOW DO YOU PLEAD?

I DID MY BEST TO SNATCH THE SUMMONSES FOR THE PUBLIC TRIAL OUT OF THE MAILBOX BEFORE MY PARENTS FOUND THEM. ONE DAY I WASN'T SUCCESSFUL...
CONNIE! WHAT ON EARTH IS THIS ABOUT???
OH SHIT! I'M JUST GOING TO DIE RIGHT NOW ON THIS VERY SPOT!
UM... WELL... IT'S A LONG STORY. I WENT TO THE MOVIES ONE NIGHT...
QUATSCH! WHAT NONSENSE! I'M SURE IT WILL ALL GET STRAIGHTENED OUT.
HMM... AH, WELL... IN THE STATES, HOMOSEXUALITY IS FROWNED ON, TOO. I REMEMBER AT SWARTHMORE THERE WAS A TEACHER WHO WAS DISMISSED, MOST UNFORTUNATE...
TO MY SURPRISE & INTENSE RELIEF, TED & LENORE WERE NOT PARTICULARLY PERTURBED. AFTER THIS ONE CONVERSATION, THEY IGNORED THE WHOLE THING.
GOODNESS. HOW UNPLEASANT. WELL, YOU HAVE ALL OUR SUPPORT, DOESN'T SHE, TEDDY?
BUT OF COURSE! YOU'RE OUR DAUGHTER!
AT SCHOOL IT WAS A DIFFERENT STORY. I HAD TO SHOW UP FOR CLASSES & EXAMS. I FELT AS IF THE SKIN ON MY FACE BOILED & BLISTERED EVERY TIME I APPEARED.

WE LEARNED ABOUT WHO OUR FRIENDS WERE & WHO WOULD ABANDON US IN TIMES OF TROUBLE. SOME OF THE PROFESSORS DIDN'T SHUN US; THEY CONTINUED TO GREET US AFFECTIONATELY. OTHERS, UP & COMING ONES, WENT OUT OF THEIR WAY TO AVOID US.

DOCTORA! I NEED TO ASK YOU...
I'M SORRY. I HAVE A MEETING. CAN'T TALK NOW...

MIRTA AGUIRRE & I CROSSED PATHS ON THE STAIRS TO THE LOBBY.
THEY ARE ANGRY WITH YOU.
BUT WHY??? WHAT HAVE WE DONE NOW?
OSTENTACIÓN, CONNIE. *¡OSTENTACIÓN!* BE CAREFUL, YOU TWO...

GOYO, A MATHEMATICS STUDENT & MARTUGENIA'S CLOSE FRIEND, HAND-DELIVERED NOTES & LETTERS BETWEEN US, TRAVELING ACROSS THE CITY TO DO SO.

LA AGUIRRE HAS WARNED US. THE PHONE IS NO GOOD; THEY MUST BE LISTENING. WE'LL HAVE TO STICK TO WRITING NOTES FOR NOW.
AH, YOU'RE A TRUE FRIEND!
CHICO, YOU HAVE TO WAIT & TAKE BACK MY ANSWER.

CHAPTER 5

The Revolutionary Offensive

1968 THE "YEAR OF THE HEROIC GUERRILLERO" BEGAN WITH THE CULTURAL CONGRESS OF HAVANA, JANUARY 4-12. THE DEATH OF CHE GUEVARA IN BOLIVIA JUST MONTHS BEFORE, ON OCTOBER 9, OVERSHADOWED EVERYTHING & SET THE TONE FOR THIS KEY EVENT WHERE THE REVOLUTION'S CULTURAL PARTY LINE WAS PRESENTED FOR THE PERIOD AHEAD.
CLOSE TO 500 PARTICIPANTS FROM ALL OVER THE WORLD— ARTISTS & WRITERS, TROTSKYITES & COMMUNISTS, GUERRILLA FIGHTERS & CULTURAL BUREAUCRATS— CONVERGED IN HAVANA TO PARTICIPATE WITH THEIR CUBAN COUNTERPARTS.
LUMINARIES OF THE WORLDWIDE RADICAL LEFT CAME TO DISCUSS & DEFINE THE BASIC CONFLICT OF THE TIMES AS BETWEEN IMPERIALISM & THE THIRD WORLD & TO DICTATE THE ROLE THAT ALL INTELLECTUALS WERE MORALLY OBLIGED TO TAKE IN SOCIETY, PARTICULARLY IN THIS REVOLUTIONARY SOCIETY.
PRESIDENT DORTICÓS CLOSED THE PREPARATORY SEMINAR OF THE CONGRESS WITH THESE WORDS:
CONGRESO CULTURAL DE LA HABANA
... WE ARE CREATING A NEW SOCIETY, A COMMUNIST SOCIETY; THE LABOR OF CREATION MUST PERMEATE THE MEANING OF YOUR INDIVIDUAL CREATIONS. BY BEING CONSCIOUS OF THIS TRUTH, BY HONORING... THE MEMORY... OF THAT GREAT, REVOLUTIONARY INTELLECTUAL ERNESTO CHE GUEVARA, WE CAN SAY WITH REVOLUTIONARY SATISFACTION... "FATHERLAND OR DEATH!"

THE MICROFRACTION

NO SOONER HAD THE CULTURAL CONGRESS ENDED & ITS INTERNATIONAL PARTICIPANTS GONE HOME THAN THE GOVERNMENT ANNOUNCED THE ARREST & TRIAL OF "LA MICROFRACCIÓN"—34 ALLEGED TRAITORS OF THE REVOLUTION.

DURING A THREE-DAY MEETING OF THE CENTRAL COMMITTEE, RAUL CASTRO READ THE ACCUSATIONS, BEGINNING WITH ANIBAL ESCALANTE, A LEADER OF THE PARTIDO SOCIALISTA POPULAR —THE PRE-1959 COMMUNIST PARTY OF CUBA. HE HAD ALREADY BEEN EXILED TO PRAGUE IN 1962, IN ONE OF THE FIRST PURGES, THE "STRUGGLE AGAINST SECTARIANISM." HE RETURNED IN '64 TO A MINOR PROVINCIAL JOB BUT QUICKLY RECONNECTED WITH HIS NETWORK OF FORMER COLLEAGUES & ORGANIZED A SERIES OF MEETINGS WITH SOME INFLUENTIAL COMMUNISTS IN KEY POSITIONS OF POWER, LIKE THE CDR ORGANIZATION & ESPECIALLY IN THE TRADE UNION MOVEMENT. MANY HAD CLOSE PERSONAL TIES WITH THE SOVIETS & THEIR ALLEGIANCE TO FIDEL, RATHER THAN TO MOSCOW, WAS PUT INTO QUESTION.

MANY OLD PSP PEOPLE WERE UNHAPPY WITH THE DIRECTION THE REVOLUTION WAS TAKING. THEY VIEWED WITH ALARM THE POSITION PRAISING MORAL OVER MATERIAL INCENTIVES, THE ROLE OF VOLUNTARY WORK AS OPPOSED TO SKILLED LABOR, THE ROLE OF GUERRILLA WARFARE NOW DURING THE TIME OF KHRUSHCHEV'S DÉTENTE POLICY.

ESCALANTE WAS ACCUSED OF MEETING WITH A SOVIET NKVD AGENT. THIS SUPPOSEDLY SET OFF AN INVESTIGATION & THEN THE PURGE. HE WAS SENTENCED TO MANY YEARS IN PRISON, AS WERE DOZENS OF THE OLD GUARD COMRADES.

ONE EFFECT OF THIS POLITICAL UPHEAVAL WAS THAT MANY FOREIGNERS WORKING IN CUBA BEGAN TO BE VIEWED SUSPICIOUSLY. THEY WERE INCREASINGLY SUSPECT & CLOSELY WATCHED FOR SIGNS OF FACTIONAL AFFILIATION & THOSE WHO UNCONDITIONALLY ADMIRED MOSCOW WENT OUT OF FAVOR, AS MY FAMILY SOON FOUND OUT.

I CAN'T BELIEVE IT. THEY'RE NOT GOING TO RENEW MY CONTRACT THIS YEAR! I'VE LOST MY JOB...
THEY'VE GIVEN US UNTIL THE END OF THE YEAR TO LEAVE. THE SOONER THE BETTER...
OH, TEDDY! WHAT ARE WE GOING TO DO??? THE APARTMENT, YOUR PAY! EVERYTHING IS PART OF YOUR CONTRACT!
IT'S THOSE SMART-ALECK JERKS IN THE PHYSICS DEPARTMENT!

TED WAS CRUSHED. HE NEVER ACCEPTED THAT HIS CLOSE ASSOCIATION WITH HIS BELOVED SOVIETS WAS TO BLAME. HE LEFT CUBA CONVINCED THAT HE'D SIMPLY LOST HIS JOB BECAUSE HE BELONGED TO A FACTION THAT ADVOCATED AN EXPERIMENTAL HANDS-ON APPROACH AS OPPOSED TO A MORE TRADITIONAL LECTURE FORMAT.

I WANTED TO UNDERSTAND & DECIDED TO SEEK ANSWERS AT MIRTA AGUIRRE'S HOUSE.

DOCTORA, WHY IS IT COUNTERREVOLUTIONARY TO SPEAK WITH SOVIET OFFICIALS NOW? MY PARENTS ARE PRO-SOVIET & MY FATHER'S CONTRACT HASN'T BEEN RENEWED. MY FAMILY HAS TO LEAVE...
AH, I'M GOING TO TELL YOU A STORY, CONNIE...
JOSEPH STALIN DID MANY TERRIBLE THINGS; HE MADE MANY MISTAKES; BUT ABOVE ALL HE SAVED THE WORLD FROM NAZI GERMANY. THE AMERICANS PLAYED A BIG ROLE, BUT WITHOUT STALIN & THE SOVIETS, THE NAZIS WOULD HAVE WON.
AT A PARTICULARLY LOW POINT DURING THE WAR, WHEN THINGS WERE GOING VERY BADLY FOR THE RUSSIANS, STALIN SENT FOR A GENERAL HE'D IMPRISONED SOME TIME BEFORE. HE ORDERED HIM TO GO BACK INTO THE BATTLEFIELD & COMMAND AN IMPORTANT CAMPAIGN FOR THE SAKE OF MOTHER RUSSIA & THE SALVATION OF THE SOVIET UNION.
THE GENERAL OBEYED WITHOUT QUESTION. HE UNDERSTOOD THAT WHAT HAD HAPPENED TO HIM WAS OF NO CONSEQUENCE NEXT TO THE NEED TO DEFEAT HITLER.
THAT GENERAL WAS A TRUE COMMUNIST... YOU HAVE TO KEEP YOUR EYE ON WHAT MATTERS IN THE LONG RUN.
SOCIALISM IS THE FUTURE. IT MUST BE PROTECTED BY ANY MEANS NECESSARY.
WE MUST MAKE SURE THAT WHAT HAPPENED IN HUNGARY IN 1956 NEVER HAPPENS HERE. THERE MUST BE UNITY. THERE CAN BE NO FRACTURES IN THE REVOLUTIONARY LEADERSHIP.
LET'S HAVE SOME COFFEE.
WAIT, I'LL BRING SOME FROM INSIDE. I HAVE TO GET MORE CIGARETTES ANYWAY.

AFTER TOYING WITH THE IDEA OF MOVING TO TANZANIA, TED & LENORE DECIDED THAT TED HAD TO LEAVE RIGHT AWAY & LOOK FOR A JOB IN THE UNITED STATES. THE REST OF THE FAMILY WOULD WAIT HERE IN HAVANA & JOIN HIM WHEN HE HAD FOUND A PLACE TO LIVE & A WAY TO SUPPORT THEM ALL. THEY BARELY HAD ANY SAVINGS.

TED WILL TRY TO GET A JOB IN CALIFORNIA. I DON'T KNOW WHAT WE CAN DO ABOUT YOUR STUDIES. MAYBE SEND YOU LATER ON TO GERMANY? OR ENGLAND?

I'M NOT GOING WITH YOU. HERE I HAVE FRIENDS, I'M IN SCHOOL. I WANT TO GRADUATE. I'M 23 YEARS OLD. I'LL GET ALONG.

LENORE WAS HORRIFIED AT FIRST, BUT REALIZED, WHEN I POINTED IT OUT, THAT I WAS NOW AN ADULT. I SHOULD BE ABLE TO MAKE MY OWN CHOICES. SHE TOOK CHARGE THEN FOR FINDING ME A PLACE TO LIVE & SETTING ME UP WITH A SMALL ACCOUNT IN DOLLARS AT A BANK FOR FOREIGNERS.

MARTUGENIA & I FOUND A WAY TO SEE EACH OTHER DISCREETLY & HAVE A LIFE OUT IN THE WORLD. WE TEAMED UP WITH GOYO & HIS BOYFRIEND & IN PUBLIC PLAYED STRAIGHT COUPLES. THIS EVEN WORKED WITH HER FAMILY.

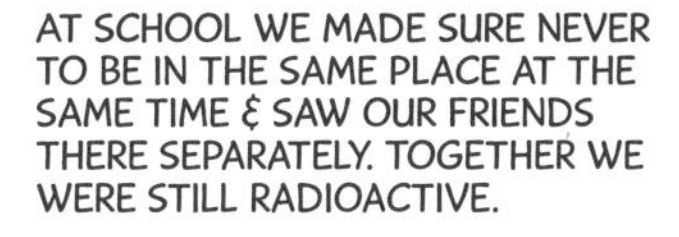

AT SCHOOL WE MADE SURE NEVER TO BE IN THE SAME PLACE AT THE SAME TIME & SAW OUR FRIENDS THERE SEPARATELY. TOGETHER WE WERE STILL RADIOACTIVE.

MAS REVOLUCION — MAS REVOLUCION —MAS REVOLUCION — MAS REVOLUCION

En paz descansen cabarets, cabaretuchos y similares

La noticia corrió como reguerro de pólvora. Los más disímiles comentarios se suscitaron. Algunos se resistían a creerlo. Otros se aferraban a concepciones caducas.

No comprendían qu volución es eso. Una ción renovadora. Qu con todos los vestigio sado. Que rompe de violenta las ataduras cales capitalistas para con fe y esperanza el so futuro. O es que puede formar el hor munista del mañana ciar de sus neurona: men negativo, fruto penetración orientada ner la tesis de que el es malo por naturale por herencia y ego principios.

—oOOo—

Pues sí señores, ¡Q rece! Se acabaron rets y cabaretuchos. res y los barsuchos lo iba a decir a Chic mismo. Que no hab nera, ni cueva, ni e ni matadero, ni gruta ni clubcito, ni barra, ta, ni trampa, ni ant no conociera hasta el último rincón. Que no tenía dificultad en conseguir mesa —inclusive los fines de semana— porque era amigo de todo el mundo. Que sabía en qué lugares a determinadas horas la asistencia era escasa y daba gordas propinas para que el cantinero le cargara el trago, se fuera y no regresara en largo rato. Que dominaba como el minero más experimentado los lugares más oscuros. Donde se pudiera hacer de todo. Que se aprendía de memoria las letras y los números de las victrolas automáticas de música "propia de ocasión".

costeable la existencia de los mismos. La calidad artística y el mensaje cultural dejaba mucho que desear. El público se había acostumbrado a asistir a esos lugares no para presenciar un espectáculo de calidad, educativo y recreativo sino con un propósito radicalmente distinto. El artista se esforzaba en brindar lo mejor de su trabajo, el fruto de su esfuerzo y en la mayoría de los casos se le despreciaba no atendiéndolo, usándolo simplemente como un medio para obtener un fin previsto y calculado.

—oOOo—

En honor a la estricta verdad es correcto señalar que en muchos casos se celebraban natalicios y cumpleaños de casados, con un carácter bien definido en algunos de estos lugares. Esto es cierto. Nadie está en contra de esas manifestaciones sociales propias de seres humanos. Pero lo que nadie puede poner en tela de juicio es que el uso y abuso de un club o cabaret para conquistar una mujer es un método impropio para una juventud enfrascada en la búsqueda de nuevas concepciones en el hombre. Y lo que nadie dejar de reconocer es sa fórmula proviene de euro, obsoleto y decadengen. El amor y las rela entre un hombre y una no pueden, ni deben esndenadas a leyes capis.

—oOOo—

cho estaba desesperado. en sus manos el suple especial del "Alma Ma Este mismo que usted eyendo y se encontró lo nte:

que encontrar nuevas s de diversión. Desarro actividades culturales. populares en lugares ados; círculos, locales s. A través del deporte medio sano de entretento. Paseos en bicicle otos, campings, viajes a ayas. Excursiones, visi museos, teatros, parques, s, jardines botánico y ico, cines, etc. etc. etc.

vas concepciones surgi Premisas y prejuicios tendrán que desaparecer. El largo y metódico proceso de la conquista cabaretera pasará a la historia. Todo tendrá que ser directo. Sin complejos, ni deseos explotados. Hay que orientarse por verdaderos caminos. Hay que sanear el ambiente. Pero sin celibato ni puritanismo. Entiéndase bien. Esto último para los extremistas.

THE REVOLUTIONARY OFFENSIVE

ON MARCH 13, 1968, FIDEL CASTRO UNLEASHED ONE OF HIS MOST RADICAL CAMPAIGNS TO CHANGE CUBAN SOCIETY & ITS ECONOMY—LA OFENSIVA REVOLUCIONARIA— THE REVOLUTIONARY OFFENSIVE. IT OBLITERATED HAVANA NIGHTLIFE &, FROM ONE DAY TO THE NEXT, NATIONALIZED CLOSE TO 60,000 SMALL & MEDIUM-SIZED BUSINESSES. SINCE THE STATE WAS INCAPABLE OF REPLACING OR MAINTAINING SERVICES THAT HAD SUDDENLY BEEN SEIZED, GONE WERE THE NEIGHBORHOOD SHOEMAKERS, CAR MECHANICS, BEAUTY PARLORS, SHOESHINE STANDS, WATCHMAKERS, DRY CLEANERS, *PUESTAS DE FRITAS*— SMALL FAST FOOD STANDS THAT COOKED FRIED SNACKS— & ALL THE REST OF THE EVERYDAY FABRIC OF NEIGHBORHOOD COMMERCE. NEWSPAPERS & MAGAZINES PROCLAIMED A SET OF NEW LAWS—IN FORCE IMMEDIATELY—THAT ORDERED THE CLOSING OF ALL BARS, CABARETS & CLUBS. TO EAT IN A STATE-RUN RESTAURANT MEANT STANDING IN LINE FOR HOURS AT A TIME.

En paz descansen cabarets, cabaretuchos y similares

MAS REVOLUCION — MAS REVOLUCION —MAS REVOLUCION — MAS REVOLUCION

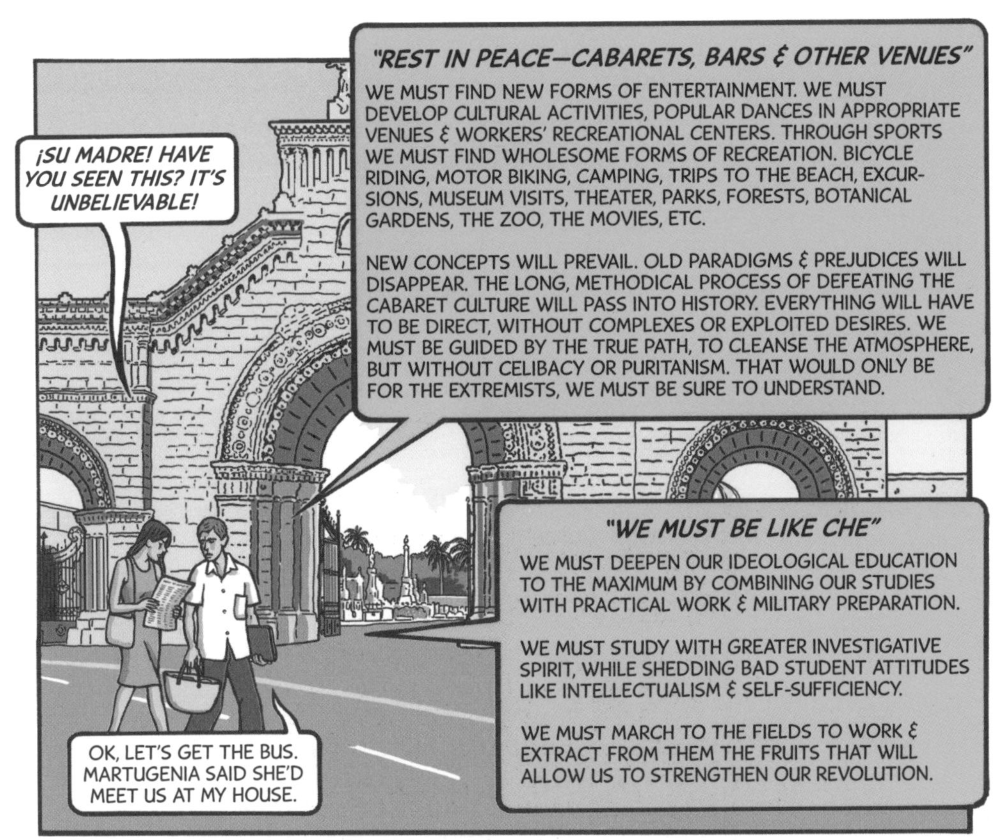
¡SU MADRE! HAVE YOU SEEN THIS? IT'S UNBELIEVABLE!
"REST IN PEACE—CABARETS, BARS & OTHER VENUES"
WE MUST FIND NEW FORMS OF ENTERTAINMENT. WE MUST DEVELOP CULTURAL ACTIVITIES, POPULAR DANCES IN APPROPRIATE VENUES & WORKERS' RECREATIONAL CENTERS. THROUGH SPORTS WE MUST FIND WHOLESOME FORMS OF RECREATION. BICYCLE RIDING, MOTOR BIKING, CAMPING, TRIPS TO THE BEACH, EXCURSIONS, MUSEUM VISITS, THEATER, PARKS, FORESTS, BOTANICAL GARDENS, THE ZOO, THE MOVIES, ETC.
NEW CONCEPTS WILL PREVAIL. OLD PARADIGMS & PREJUDICES WILL DISAPPEAR. THE LONG, METHODICAL PROCESS OF DEFEATING THE CABARET CULTURE WILL PASS INTO HISTORY. EVERYTHING WILL HAVE TO BE DIRECT, WITHOUT COMPLEXES OR EXPLOITED DESIRES. WE MUST BE GUIDED BY THE TRUE PATH, TO CLEANSE THE ATMOSPHERE, BUT WITHOUT CELIBACY OR PURITANISM. THAT WOULD ONLY BE FOR THE EXTREMISTS, WE MUST BE SURE TO UNDERSTAND.
"WE MUST BE LIKE CHE"
WE MUST DEEPEN OUR IDEOLOGICAL EDUCATION TO THE MAXIMUM BY COMBINING OUR STUDIES WITH PRACTICAL WORK & MILITARY PREPARATION.
WE MUST STUDY WITH GREATER INVESTIGATIVE SPIRIT, WHILE SHEDDING BAD STUDENT ATTITUDES LIKE INTELLECTUALISM & SELF-SUFFICIENCY.
WE MUST MARCH TO THE FIELDS TO WORK & EXTRACT FROM THEM THE FRUITS THAT WILL ALLOW US TO STRENGTHEN OUR REVOLUTION.
OK, LET'S GET THE BUS. MARTUGENIA SAID SHE'D MEET US AT MY HOUSE.

SUDDENLY IT WAS SINFUL & FORBIDDEN TO GO TO THE CORNER *BODEGA* & DRINK A BEER AT THE BAR BY THE CURB, WHERE ALL THE NEIGHBORHOOD GUYS USED TO SHOOT THE BREEZE & THE WOMEN WOULD BUY THE FAMILY'S DAILY GROCERIES & LOAF OF BREAD (WHEN THERE WAS BREAD).

I HEARD THERE WAS A LOT OF OPPOSITION TO THE OFENSIVA, & CARLOS RAFAEL WAS THE FIRST ONE TO SAY SO. AND AFTER A BIG ARGUMENT,
FIDEL GOT FURIOUS, SLAMMED HIS FIST ON THE TABLE & BELLOWED *"BY MY COJONES WE WILL INTERVENE AS I SAY!"*

OUR NEW REFUGE WAS GOYO'S HOUSE. HE LIVED IN SANTA FE, A SMALL TOWN TO THE WEST OF HAVANA, WITH HIS MOTHER, ARACELIS. THEY HAD A BIG, TALL AVOCADO TREE & TWO BANANA TREES. HERE WE WERE SAFE FROM THE PRYING EYES OF THE UNIVERSITY.

MANY PEOPLE LOST THEIR JOBS. SOME WERE PAID TO DO NOTHING; SOME WERE ORDERED TO PERFORM AGRICULTURAL WORK INSTEAD; OTHERS WERE LEFT EMPTY-HANDED. THE CLUBS & CABARETS WERE SEALED.

WHAT ABOUT YOUR JOB, ARACELIS?
WELL, IMAGINE... FIRST THEY TOOK AWAY OUR BOARDING HOUSE IN 1960, THEN I GOT THIS JOB AT THE DRY-CLEANERS...
WE DON'T KNOW WHAT'S GOING TO HAPPEN NEXT. THEY SAY IT'S GOING TO BE TAKEN OVER BY THE STATE, BUT WE DON'T KNOW WHO'LL HAVE A JOB.
LOOK AT THIS GREAT FISH I GOT! CUCO CAUGHT IT THIS MORNING. I TRADED SOME AVOCADOS FOR IT. WE'LL HAVE A TASTY DINNER.
AND I BROUGHT COFFEE & TOILET PAPER.
MAS REVOLUCION
GUERRA:
A LA BLANDENGUERIA
AL EGOISMO
AL INDIVIDUALISMO
AL PARASITISMO
AL VICIO
A LA EXPLOTACION
MAS REVOLUCION
TRISTRAM SHANDY
WONDERFUL! WE'LL HAVE HAPPY BELLIES & CULITOS TONIGHT.
¡CARAJO! THIS STUFF IS EVERYWHERE... WHEN IS IT ALL GOING TO END?
MORE REVOLUTION
WAR ON:
WEAKNESS
SELFISHNESS
INDIVIDUALISM
PARASITISM
VICE
EXPLOITATION
MORE REVOLUTION

MORE SUMMONSES TO APPEAR IN COURT ARRIVED EVERY COUPLE OF MONTHS. BUT THERE WAS ALWAYS SOMETHING MISSING, SO NOTHING WAS RESOLVED.

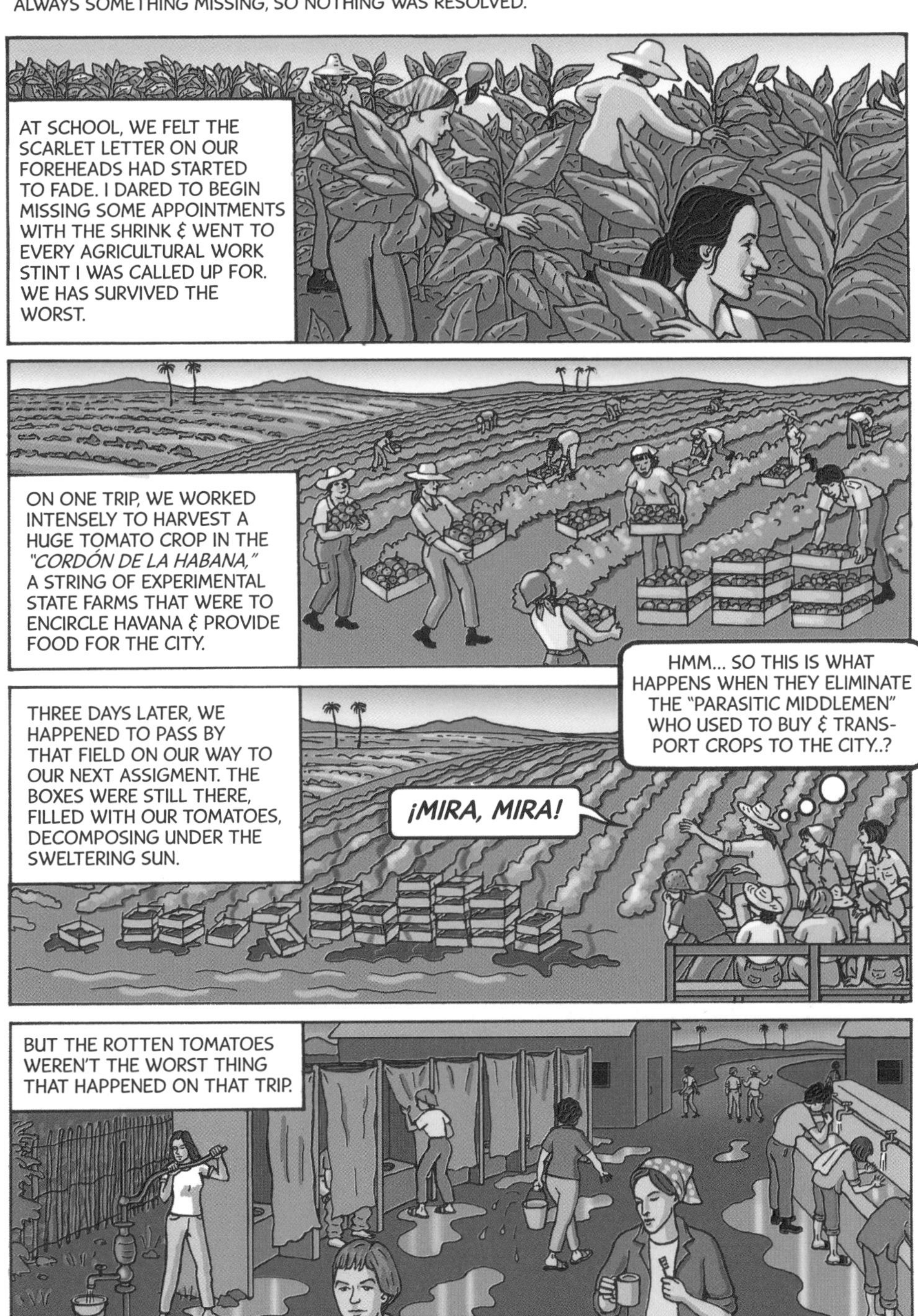

AT SCHOOL, WE FELT THE SCARLET LETTER ON OUR FOREHEADS HAD STARTED TO FADE. I DARED TO BEGIN MISSING SOME APPOINTMENTS WITH THE SHRINK & WENT TO EVERY AGRICULTURAL WORK STINT I WAS CALLED UP FOR. WE HAS SURVIVED THE WORST.
ON ONE TRIP, WE WORKED INTENSELY TO HARVEST A HUGE TOMATO CROP IN THE *"CORDÓN DE LA HABANA,"* A STRING OF EXPERIMENTAL STATE FARMS THAT WERE TO ENCIRCLE HAVANA & PROVIDE FOOD FOR THE CITY.
THREE DAYS LATER, WE HAPPENED TO PASS BY THAT FIELD ON OUR WAY TO OUR NEXT ASSIGMENT. THE BOXES WERE STILL THERE, FILLED WITH OUR TOMATOES, DECOMPOSING UNDER THE SWELTERING SUN.
¡MIRA, MIRA!
HMM... SO THIS IS WHAT HAPPENS WHEN THEY ELIMINATE THE "PARASITIC MIDDLEMEN" WHO USED TO BUY & TRANSPORT CROPS TO THE CITY..?
BUT THE ROTTEN TOMATOES WEREN'T THE WORST THING THAT HAPPENED ON THAT TRIP.

TED HAD LEFT THE COUNTRY BY NOW, TO LOOK FOR WORK IN THE STATES. LENORE & THE KIDS BEGAN PACKING THEIR BELONGINGS INTO HOMEMADE BOXES & LENORE SEARCHED NERVOUSLY FOR AN AVAILABLE FREIGHTER TO SHIP THEM TO CANADA. THE FAMILY RESOURCES DWINDLED OMINOUSLY.

LENORE... I CAN'T GET UP...
BACK FROM THE COUNTRY AT THE END OF JULY, I BECAME MYSTERIOUSLY ILL.
WHAT'S THE MATTER WITH YOU? HOW AM I GOING TO DEAL WITH THE PACKING & ALL THIS DAMN FURNITURE?
I CAN'T LIFT MY HEAD...
A NEIGHBOR CARRIED ME DOWNSTAIRS, SO LENORE COULD CONTINUE PACKING & SELLING WHAT THEY WOULD LEAVE BEHIND.
HELP ME, KEVIN!!!
SMACK, SMACK!!
ONE NIGHT NIKKI HAD ANOTHER OF HER DELIRIOUS NIGHTMARES & LENORE WENT BERSERK. I WANTED TO SAVE HER, BUT I COULDN'T MAKE IT UP THE STAIRS.
OH, TEDDY, I WISH YOU WERE HERE! WAKE UP, NIKKI! SMACK!!!
YOU CAN HAVE THAT COUCH FOR 25...
HEY! SHE'S GOT JAUNDICE! YOU'D BETTER GET HER TO A HOSPITAL!
SASHA! PLEASE! CAN YOU COME AGAIN & CARRY MY DAUGHTER TO THE CAR?

Gramma

La Habana, sábado 24 de agosto de 1968
Año del Guerrillero Heroico

EDICION UNICA

Año 4 / Número 204 / Precio: 5 centavos
Cierre: 5 a. m.

ORGANO OFICIAL DEL COMITE CENTRAL DEL PARTIDO COMUNISTA DE CUBA

EN CHECOSLOVAQUIA SE MARCHABA HACIA UNA SITUACION

CONTRARREVOLUCIONARIA, HACIA EL CAPITALISMO Y

HACIA

RESULTABA

IMP

OSTA, DE

O OCURRIERA

Nosotros

én las divisiones

del Pacto

rialistas yanquis

acrecien

pueblo de Viet

Nam s

divisiones del

NO LIQUOR & LOTS OF REST FOR A YEAR!

IT'S HEPATITIS A... THE DOCTOR SAYS I MUST HAVE GOTTEN IT IN A FILTHY WORK CAMP.

I WAS HOSPITALIZED FOR THREE WEEKS IN THE CLÍNICA ANTONETTI, JUST IN TIME TO MISS THE INVASION OF CZECHOSLOVAKIA ON AUGUST 20. IT WAS VERY BIG NEWS IN HAVANA.

LENORE APPEALED TO THE UNIVERSITY AUTHORITIES TO DELAY THEIR' DEPARTURE BY A MONTH. SHE & MY FRIENDS TOOK TURNS WATCHING OVER ME.

HAVE YOU HEARD, GRINGA? THE SOVIETS JUST INVADED CZECHOSLOVAKIA!

WELL, THERE SURE WON'T BE A "CUBAN SPRING" HERE. THE OFENSIVA TOOK CARE OF THAT...

ON THE 23RD, FIDEL PRONOUNCED HIS POSITION ON THE INVASION. EVERYONE IN CUBA HELD THEIR BREATH.

WE CONSIDERED CZECHOSLOVAKIA TO BE HEADING TOWARD A COUNTERREVOLUTIONARY SITUATION, TOWARD CAPITALISM & INTO THE ARMS OF IMPERIALISM. THIS IS THE OPERATIVE CONCEPT IN OUR FIRST POSITION TOWARD THIS SPECIFIC ACTION TAKEN BY A GROUP OF SOCIALIST COUNTRIES. THAT IS, WE CONSIDER IT WAS UNAVOIDABLE FROM HAPPENING—WHATEVER THE COST—IN ONE WAY OR ANOTHER.

OPERATION HIPPIE, SEPTEMBER 25, 1968

SHORTLY AFTER I GOT OUT OF THE HOSPITAL, THERE WAS A MASSIVE POLICE SWEEP IN EL VEDADO AT COPPELIA, THE ICE CREAM PALACE, AROUND CERTAIN HOTELS & ON LA RAMPA, THE HEART OF WHAT USED TO BE HAVANA'S NIGHTLIFE, BEFORE LA OFENSIVA REVOLUCIONARIA TURNED OUT THE LIGHTS. THIS TIME THE TARGETS WEREN'T ONLY HOMOSEXUALS BUT ALL LONG-HAIRED *"ENFERMITOS"*—YOUNG MEN WHO WORE JEANS, TIGHT *TUBITO* PANTS, OR SANDALS & GIRLS WHO WORE MINISKIRTS. THEY WERE KNOWN TO LISTEN TO FORBIDDEN CAPITALIST MUSIC ON THE "W" STATIONS, LIKE WQAM, TRANSMITTING FROM MIAMI.
...A STRANGE LITTLE PHENOMENON HAS PRESENTED ITSELF IN OUR CAPITAL IN THE LAST FEW MONTHS. GROUPS OF YOUNG PEOPLE, IN THE HUNDREDS SOMETIMES... INFLUENCED BY IMPERIALIST PROPAGANDA, ARE DISPLAYING SHAMELESS BEHAVIOR IN PUBLIC.
THEY'VE TAKEN TO LIVING EXTRAVAGANTLY, IN CROWDS ON CERTAIN STREETS, ON LA RAMPA, IN FRONT OF THE CAPRI...
AND WHAT DO YOU THINK THEY ARE DOING? CORRUPTING 14-, 15-YEAR-OLD GIRLS! PROMOTING PROSTITUTION! SELLING GIRLS TO FOREIGNERS!... LOOKING FOR AMERICAN CIGARETTES & TRANSISTOR RADIOS TO LISTEN TO IMPERIALIST PROPAGANDA!...
OCT. 29— ON THE 8TH ANNIVERSARY OF THE CDRS, THE COMMITTEES FOR THE DEFENSE OF THE REVOLUTION, FIDEL GAVE HIS EXPLANATION...
WHAT DO THEY THINK? THAT WE LIVE IN A LIBERAL BOURGEOIS REGIME? NO! WE HAVE NOT ONE HAIR THAT IS LIBERAL! WE ARE REVOLUTIONARIES! WE ARE SOCIALISTS! WE ARE COLLECTIVISTS! WE ARE COMMUNISTS! AND WHAT DO THEY WANT? TO INTRODUCE A REVIVED VERSION OF PRAGUE?... DID THEY THINK THEY COULD INTRODUCE SUCH SWINISHNESS INTO THE COUNTRY & WE WOULD PERMIT IT?

NUEVO VEDADO, LIFE BY THE ZOO

IN MID-OCTOBER, MY FAMILY LEFT THE COUNTRY. I DROVE THEM TO THE AIRPORT IN THE SKODA I WOULD SOON HAVE TO GIVE UP. THEY HEADED FOR PRAGUE, & THEN ON TO GERMANY TO STAY WITH LENORE'S BROTHER UNTIL THEY COULD RETURN TO THE STATES & JOIN TED. AS IT WAS FORBIDDEN TO TRAVEL TO CUBA—MUCH LESS TO LIVE—IT WAS NECESSARY TO RETURN VIA THIRD COUNTRIES.

WITH THE HELP OF FAMILY FRIENDS, BOB PURDY & AN AUSTRALIAN ARTIST NAMED HARRY READE, I MOVED INTO MY NEW HOME, A SEPARATE MAID'S ROOM IN THE GOVERNMENT-ASSIGNED HOUSE OF AN AMERICAN FAMILY, THE BAILEYS. LIKE TED, HARRY WAS AN ARDENT ADMIRER OF SOVIET SOCIALISM, & WITHIN A YEAR HE ALSO LEFT THE COUNTRY.
OK, THE BED CAN GO HERE, UNDER THE WINDOW.

LENORE WROTE THAT RE-ENTRY INTO THE OUTSIDE WORLD WAS DIFFICULT & PAINFUL FOR HER & THE KIDS. SHE HAD ALWAYS BEEN THE BLACK SHEEP IN HER FAMILY, AS TED HAD BEEN IN HIS. SHE DIDN'T FEEL WELCOME NOW BY OUR GERMAN RELATIVES.

SO, LENORE... I MUST ASK YOU NOT TO TELL THE NEIGHBORS YOU'VE JUST COME FROM CUBA. THEY DON'T LIKE COMMUNISTS HERE. THEY'D BE QUITE SHOCKED.
OH, JOHANNES! SURELY YOU EXAGGERATE!

DURING MY MOVE, MY FRIENDS HAD BEEN AWAY DOING AGRICULTURAL WORK. WHEN AT LAST THEY RETURNED, MY LITTLE ONE-ROOM HOME BECAME A REFUGE FOR THE FOUR OF US.

A PITY YOU HAVE TO TURN THE CAR OVER TO THE BAILEYS. *WE'D BUY THE GAS. WE'D HAVE SUCH FREEDOM!*
I KNOW. I BEGGED MY MOTHER FOR THE SKODA. BUT SHE WOULDN'T LISTEN. SHE SOLD IT TO THEM & THEY'RE SUPPOSED TO PAY ME 30 PESOS A MONTH SO I HAVE MONEY TO LIVE ON.
¡BUENAS! I'VE BROUGHT SOME *CROQUETAS* I MADE THIS MORNING.
LOOK! I GOT MY RATION CARD YESTERDAY. I'LL HAVE MONEY FROM THE SKODA TO BUY FOOD AT THE MINIMAX.
MMM... GREAT HOT PLATE! BRAND NEW!
YEAH! MY FIRST PURCHASE AT THE DIPLO. AND THIS COFFEE! WE CAN MAKE SOME NOW.
THEY LET YOU SHOP AT THE DOLLAR DIPLO???
YEAH! AMAZING. LENORE SET IT UP. I HAVE A DOLLAR ACCOUNT & CAN PAY WITH IT AT THE DIPLO. SHE'LL TRY TO SEND ME 20 DOLLARS A MONTH UNTIL I CAN GET A JOB.
SO BETWEEN ONE THING & ANOTHER, HALF AS A CUBAN & HALF AS A FOREIGNER, I'LL GET BY FOR NOW, WHILE I'M STILL IN SCHOOL.
LOOK! SHE EVEN BROUGHT A CHEESE! I HAVEN'T SEEN THAT IN YEARS!
YES! LET'S HAVE A FEAST!
THE BAILEYS SAID I COULD KEEP A FEW THINGS IN THEIR FRIDGE. WE'LL SEE HOW THAT WORKS OUT.

verde olivo
ORGANO DE LAS FUERZAS ARMADAS REVOLUCIONARIAS

Las provocaciones de Padilla

Por LEOPOLDO AVILA

uel Navarro
l justo tiem-
primera línea
a —en estas
DE OLIVO—
nte generoso,
nálisis, por el
aba un escri-
naba las ore-
s páginas de
despojado de
e iniciar un
uel libro de
conmovían al

blicar, porque en aquellos tiempos,
mente difíciles, el poeta no tenía
posibilidades editoriales que la nuev
ciedad le permite.

Han llovido seis años sobre el
Padilla, hasta ahora, no ha escri
obra, aunque ha anunciado varias
ingenia, eso sí, para permanece
candelero publicando, de tarde
un poema en alguna revista o
do el periscopio con algún vie
en antologías seleccionadas
amigo o por él mismo.

El señor Padilla, antes y
soltar su primer librito sob
tivas de la Revolución ha s

THE BAILEYS BECAME GLACIAL AS THEY SLOWLY REALIZED THEY WERE HARBORING A BUNCH OF QUEERS, BUT MY SEPARATE ENTRANCE ALLOWED US TO STAY OUT OF EACH OTHER'S WAY & THEY LEFT ME ALONE.

WE'VE DECIDED THAT SINCE YOU'RE LIVING FOR FREE IN OUR HOUSE, IT MAKES NO SENSE FOR US TO BE GIVING YOU MONEY EVERY MONTH. HERE'S THE LAST CAR PAYMENT YOU'LL BE GETTING.

!!!??!!!??

OH... SURE, I UNDERSTAND...

FUERA DEL JUEGO HEBERTO PADILLA Premio de poesía "Julián del Casal" UNEAC 1968

NOW HOW AM I GOING TO EAT? I GUESS I'LL STARVE...

CHICA, DON'T WORRY. WE'LL SHARE MY SALARY. YOU PUT IN THE COFFEE & CHEESE. JUAN & GOYO WILL BRING RUM FROM SANTA FE. SCREW THOSE GRINGOS.

SO, DID YOU HEAR ABOUT PADILLA?

LOS SIETE CONTRA TEBAS Antón Arrufat

OUTSIDE THE COCOON OF LA CUEVA DE CONNIE, THE NEXT STORM WAS BREWING IN THE CULTURAL WORLD OF HAVANA. WE GOT THE NEWS THAT HEBERTO PADILLA HAD WON THE ANNUAL JULIAN DEL CASAL POETRY PRIZE AWARDED BY UNEAC, THE ARTISTS' & WRITER'S UNION, FOR HIS BOOK "FUERA DEL JUEGO" & ANTÓN ARRUFAT HAD WON IN THEATER FOR HIS PLAY "LOS SIETE CONTRA TEBAS." EVERYBODY WAS TALKING ABOUT IT.

PADILLA WAS A POET & FORMER DIPLOMAT WHO HAD BEEN AT THE CENTER OF SEVERAL CULTURAL-POLITICAL POLEMICS ALREADY. NOW THIS JURY HAD UNANIMOUSLY VOTED FOR HIS ENTRY, WHICH PROVOKED THE IRE OF THE LEADERSHIP OF THE CULTURAL ESTABLISHMENT, WHO CALLED IT COUNTERREVOLUTIONARY. THE ENSUING SCANDAL & ITS CONSEQUENCES MARKED THE END OF THE ROMANTIC IDYLL BETWEEN MANY INTELLECTUALS & THE REVOLUTIONARY LEADERSHIP.

UNO de los rasgos más interesante sorprendentes de la crítica literaria en general de la literatura en Cuba, su aparente despolitización. Salvo otro ensayo, más o me en muchos

Los enemigos de nuestra cultura son, mente, ésos que han destruido en más de u sión esfuerzos de la Revolución que habría do ser útiles. "Lunes" fue un ejemplo, ya pero demostrativo. Las corrientes —y las liberales y contrarrevolucionarios allí incr lo echaron a pique. También una obra tan la Revolución como la "Escuela de Arte" e

"WITH THE REVOLUTION—EVERYTHING, AGAINST THE REVOLUTION— NOTHING." — FIDEL CASTRO, 1961
THE PADILLA CASE WASN'T THE FIRST FLASH POINT AMONG ARTISTS, INTELLECTUALS, & THE STATE. THESE CONFLICTS STARTED WITH THE SUPPRESSION OF THE 1961 FILM "P.M.," A LIRICAL DOCUMENTARY ABOUT POPULAR NIGHT LIFE IN HAVANA BY SABÁ CABRERA INFANTE & ORLANDO JIMÉNEZ LEAL. IT WAS DEEMED OUT OF STEP WITH THE TIMES (ABOUT 6 WEEKS AFTER THE BAY OF PIGS INVASION). THE FILM DEPICTED STREET FOLKS DRINKING & DANCING LANGUIDLY AS THEY RELAXED ONE PEACEFUL, SENSUOUS EVENING—BUT NO HEROIC MILICIANOS IN THEIR UNIFORMS DEFENDING THE FATHERLAND,
THE CRISIS THIS PROVOKED CULMINATED IN THREE MEETINGS BETWEEN FIDEL CASTRO & LEADING INTELLECTUALS AT THE NATIONAL LIBRARY. THE RULES OF THE GAME WERE SPELLED OUT.
HAVE YOU SEEN THIS WEEK'S 'VERDE OLIVO"? LAST MONTH, THIS *HIJO DE PUTA* "LEOPOLDO AVILA" ATTACKED VIRGILIO PIÑERA & RENÉ ARIZA. NEXT, CABRERA INFANTE & NOW THEY'RE AIMING AT PADILLA.
"LEOPOLDO ÁVILA" — WHO'S THAT?
"VERDE OLIVO'S" THE ARMY, SO WE KNOW WHERE THAT'S COMING FROM... A PSEUDONYM FOR SURE.
verde olivo
THE STALINISTS ARE TAKING OVER.
THESE ATTACKS BY "LEOPOLDO ÁVILA" APPEARED BETWEEN OCTOBER '68 & JANUARY '69. THREE YEARS LATER, PADILLA WAS ARRESTED & LATER STARRED IN A MAJOR SHOW TRIAL.
WELL, I HAVE SOME OTHER NEWS: THE VIEJAS, VICENTINA & MY DEPARTMENT HEAD SAY I SHOULD LEAVE TOWN FOR A YEAR, GO TO THE ISLE OF PINES & SANITIZE MY NAME. THINGS ARE STILL TOO HOT AT SCHOOL.
OH, NO!!! DON'T GO!!!
AND DO WHAT THERE???

IT'LL BE A KIND OF POSTGRAD *TRABAJO SOCIAL*. I'LL BE ORGANIZING WRITERS' WORKSHOPS AROUND THE ISLAND FOR THE CNC, THE NATIONAL CULTURE COUNCIL.
I'LL BE ABLE TO COME HOME ON FURLOUGH EVERY FEW MONTHS.
BESIDES, I CAN'T TAKE THE TENSION AT SCHOOL ANYMORE.

I WAS DEVASTATED. MY FAMILY HAD LEFT; I WAS RECOVERING, BUT STILL WEAK FROM HEPATITIS & HAD JUST STARTED LIFE IN NUEVO VEDADO.
WHEN DO YOU LEAVE?
IN A WEEK...
CAN WE WRITE? NOT THROUGH THE MAIL, I SUPPOSE...
COURSE NOT. WE'LL USE TRAVELERS WE TRUST.
LET'S HAVE A FAREWELL DINNER—THE SUNDAY BEFORE YOU LEAVE.
YES! GRANDMA FLORA IS RAISING BLACK MARKET RABBITS AT UNCLE NENO'S IN EL COTORRO. I CAN BUY ONE ON SATURDAY.
¡BARBARO! FOR HOW MUCH? I'LL ROAST IT AT HOME & BRING IT COOKED.
NOT SURE... MAYBE 20.

ON OUR LAST NIGHT TOGETHER, WE FEASTED ON RABBIT STEW, THE RUM FLOWED, & WE SANG OUR FAVORITE SONGS. "LIBRES HURÍES" WAS A SONG FROM THE 390TH NIGHT OF THE THOUSAND NIGHTS & ONE NIGHT. JUAN HAD PUT IT TO MUSIC, & IT HAD BECOME OUR SECRET ANTHEM.

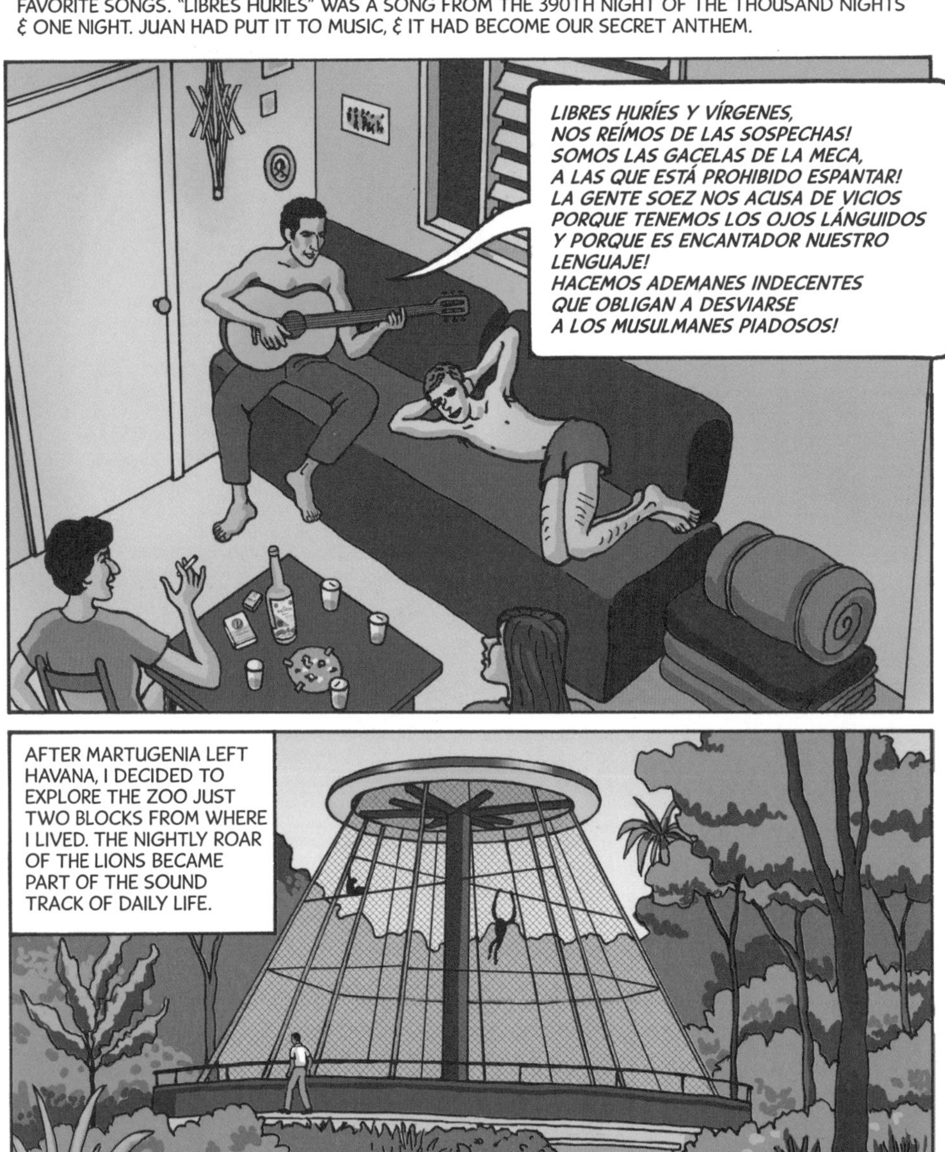
LIBRES HURÍES Y VÍRGENES, NOS REÍMOS DE LAS SOSPECHAS! SOMOS LAS GACELAS DE LA MECA, A LAS QUE ESTÁ PROHIBIDO ESPANTAR! LA GENTE SOEZ NOS ACUSA DE VICIOS PORQUE TENEMOS LOS OJOS LÁNGUIDOS Y PORQUE ES ENCANTADOR NUESTRO LENGUAJE! HACEMOS ADEMANES INDECENTES QUE OBLIGAN A DESVIARSE A LOS MUSULMANES PIADOSOS!
AFTER MARTUGENIA LEFT HAVANA, I DECIDED TO EXPLORE THE ZOO JUST TWO BLOCKS FROM WHERE I LIVED. THE NIGHTLY ROAR OF THE LIONS BECAME PART OF THE SOUND TRACK OF DAILY LIFE.

DON'T GO NEAR THAT ONE! HE'S VICIOUS!
WHOOP! WHOOP!
SURE... I WONDER WHY?
WHOOP! WHOOP!

I MET ONE OF THE VETERINARIANS WHO WORKED AT THE ZOO & ASKED ABOUT MY FRIEND.

DO YOU KNOW THE HISTORY OF THIS GIBBON? HE SEEMS TO WAIT FOR ME & BE HAPPY WHEN I SHOW UP.
OH, YES! HE WAS THE PET OF A RICH AMERICAN; SHE HAD HIM ON HER ESTATE. WHEN THE REVOLUTION TRIUMPHED, SHE LEFT THE COUNTRY & THE APE WOUND UP HERE.
YOU LOOK SORT OF LIKE HER. THE LONG HAIR... YOU MUST REMIND HIM.
I VISITED AS OFTEN AS I COULD.

1969 —THE YEAR OF THE DECISIVE PUSH

AFTER I MOVED TO NUEVO VEDADO, THE CITATIONS TO APPEAR IN COURT STOPPED ARRIVING IN THE MAIL. FOR MONTHS I HELD MY BREATH. THEN THE NEWS TRICKLED OUT THAT THE INFAMOUS UMAP LABOR CAMPS HAD FINALLY BEEN DISMANTLED. TOO MUCH BAD FOREIGN PRESS, IT SEEMED...

ONE OF MY CLASSES WAS A COURSE ON CUBAN ART WITH ADELAIDA DE JUAN. ON FIELD TRIPS TO OLD HAVANA & OTHER *BARRIOS*, WE VISITED DECAYING COLONIAL-ERA BUILDINGS, MANY THAT WERE NOW SLUMS, SUBDIVIDED MULTIPLE TIMES BY THEIR INHABITANTS.
ADELAIDA WAS THE WIFE OF ROBERTO FERNANDEZ RETAMAR, A WRITER & VOICE OF THE OFFICIAL INTELLIGENTSIA. SHE TOOK AN INTENSE DISLIKE TO ME, SO SUFFERING THROUGH HER CLASSES WAS A CHORE. BUT THE FIELD TRIPS WERE WONDERFUL & TOOK US INTO MAGICAL PLACES.

HERNÁN, A FELLOW ART HISTORY MAJOR, BECAME MY STUDY PARTNER & FRIEND. WE EXPLORED THE CITY WITH ART & LITERATURE STUDENTS IN OUR YEAR, INCLUDING NATALIA, SOON TO BE EXPELLED FROM THE COMMUNIST YOUTH, THE UJC, FOR HANGING AROUND WITH QUEERS.

OH, NO! THE URCHINS HAVE SMASHED THE STAINED GLASS!
OH! WHAT A GORGEOUS KITTEN!
YOU LIKE IT? TAKE IT. I CAN'T FEED 'EM ALL.
THANKS! I WILL!

WHEN I GOT HOME, REALITY SET IN. NOW I HAD ANOTHER MOUTH TO FEED. BUT WITH WHAT? MY CUBAN RATIONS & DIPLO DOLLARS WERE NOT GOING TO TAKE CARE OF THIS.

I HOPE THEY HAVE FISH TODAY. I'D BETTER PLAY THIS RIGHT.
MERCADO

I SOON MADE REGULAR TRIPS TO VISIT THE BUTCHER ASSIGNED TO ME IN MY RATION BOOK.

ARMANDO... WHAT HAVE YOU GOT FOR ME TODAY?
FOR YOU, I'VE GOT PLENTY...
MMM... HOW MUCH WOULD YOU LIKE TO GIVE ME... ARMANDO?
HOW MUCH CAN YOU TAKE, AMERICANA?
ALL YOU CAN GIVE ME, ARMANDO...

EVERY TIME THERE WAS FISH, I WALKED OUT WITH A BAG OF FIVE OR SIX MERLUZAS OR MAYBE MACKERELS, MANY TIMES OVER MY QUOTA. ROBIN THE CAT & I WERE HAPPY THEN. OF COURSE, THERE WERE PLENTY OF TIMES WHEN NO FISH ARRIVED AT ALL AT MY BUTCHER SHOP. OFTEN OUR DINNER WAS PLAIN SPAGHETTI WITHOUT ANY SAUCE, FOR EITHER OF US.

SCHOOL WAS A CHALLENGE BECAUSE I WAS WEAK FROM MY ILLNESS & HAD LITTLE TO EAT. I SPENT HOURS WRITING LETTERS & THEN SEARCHING FOR PEOPLE I COULD TRUST TRAVELING TO THE ISLE OF PINES.

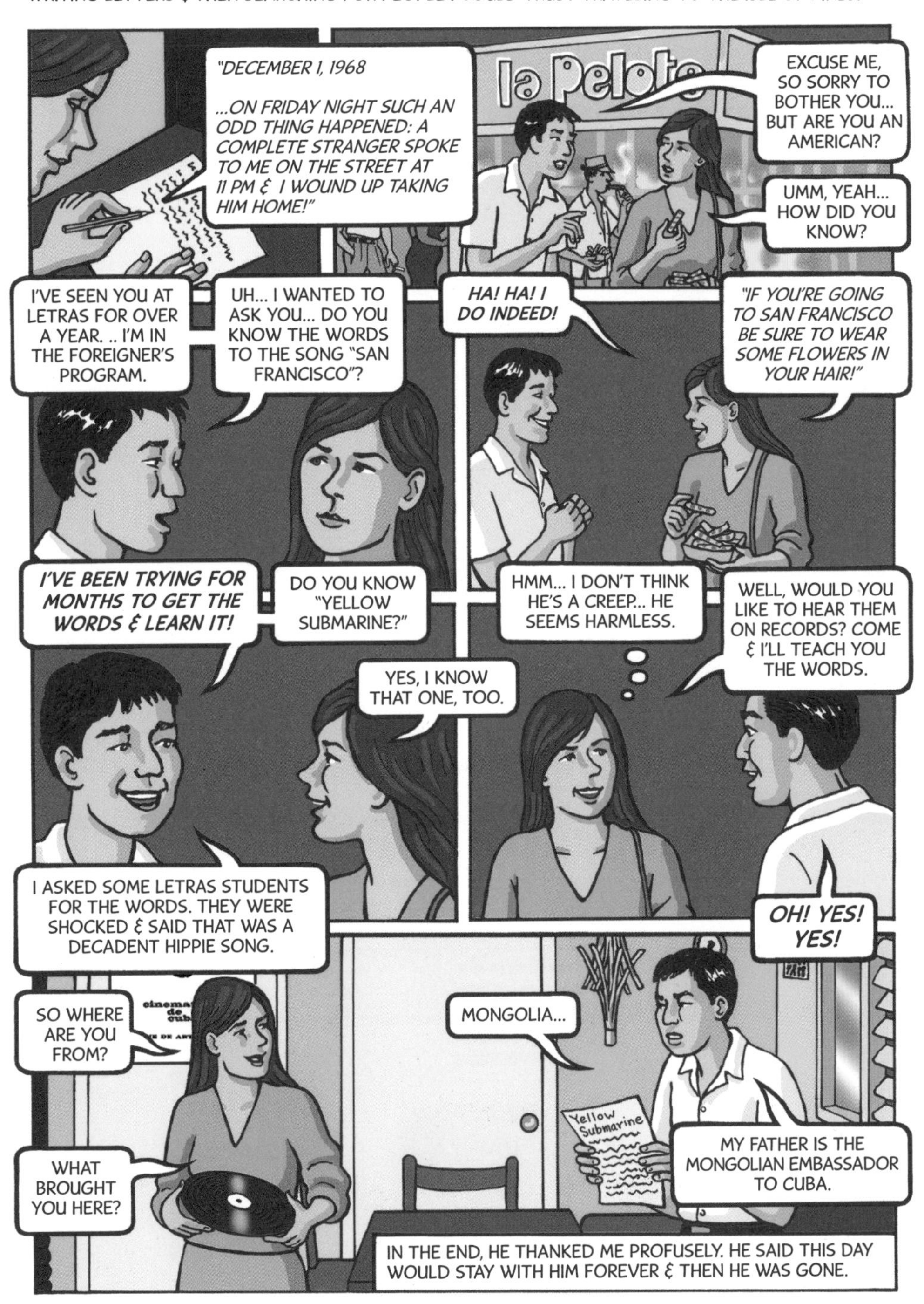
"DECEMBER 1, 1968
...ON FRIDAY NIGHT SUCH AN ODD THING HAPPENED: A COMPLETE STRANGER SPOKE TO ME ON THE STREET AT 11 PM & I WOUND UP TAKING HIM HOME!"
la Pelota
EXCUSE ME, SO SORRY TO BOTHER YOU... BUT ARE YOU AN AMERICAN?
UMM, YEAH... HOW DID YOU KNOW?
I'VE SEEN YOU AT LETRAS FOR OVER A YEAR. .. I'M IN THE FOREIGNER'S PROGRAM.
UH... I WANTED TO ASK YOU... DO YOU KNOW THE WORDS TO THE SONG "SAN FRANCISCO"?
HA! HA! I DO INDEED!
"IF YOU'RE GOING TO SAN FRANCISCO BE SURE TO WEAR SOME FLOWERS IN YOUR HAIR!"
I'VE BEEN TRYING FOR MONTHS TO GET THE WORDS & LEARN IT!
DO YOU KNOW "YELLOW SUBMARINE?"
YES, I KNOW THAT ONE, TOO.
I ASKED SOME LETRAS STUDENTS FOR THE WORDS. THEY WERE SHOCKED & SAID THAT WAS A DECADENT HIPPIE SONG.
HMM... I DON'T THINK HE'S A CREEP... HE SEEMS HARMLESS.
WELL, WOULD YOU LIKE TO HEAR THEM ON RECORDS? COME & I'LL TEACH YOU THE WORDS.
OH! YES! YES!
SO WHERE ARE YOU FROM?
MONGOLIA...
WHAT BROUGHT YOU HERE?
Yellow Submarine
MY FATHER IS THE MONGOLIAN EMBASSADOR TO CUBA.
IN THE END, HE THANKED ME PROFUSELY. HE SAID THIS DAY WOULD STAY WITH HIM FOREVER & THEN HE WAS GONE.

BY DAY I STUDIED FOR MY ART HISTORY COURSES, DETERMINED TO FINISH & GRADUATE. BY NIGHT, THERE WERE VISITORS, MUSIC, COFFEE, RUM & CIGARETTES AT "CONNIE'S *TERTULIAS.*"

"THEY CALL ME MELLOW YELLOW!"
LONG BEFORE MARTUGENIA'S YOUNGER COUSIN SARA PERFORMED IN CUBA & TRAVELED THE WORLD AS ONE OF THE VOICES OF LA NUEVA TROVA, SHE OFTEN VISITED, TOO.

IN THE THIRD YEAR OF OUR ART HISTORY PROGRAM, HERNÁN & I SHARED GUT-WRENCHING MARATHONS OF SERIOUS CRAMMING, AIDED BY FREELY AVAILABLE AMPHETAMINES FROM THE LOCAL PHARMACY. MEANWHILE, HIS COUSIN EDDY DRANK IN EVERY BEATLES & DONOVAN RECORD I POSSESSED.

THIS IS GIVING ME A NERVOUS BREAKDOWN!
THANK GOD THEY'VE GIVEN US A REPRIEVE UNTIL MONDAY. HERE, TAKE ONE OF THESE.
BORROMINI
EL BARROCO

AT LAST, MARTUGENIA CAME HOME FOR GOOD. THEN, ONE STEAMY, HOT NIGHT, AS I STUDIED & MARTUGENIA GRADED PAPERS, THERE WAS A SUDDEN BANGING ON THE DOOR. BECAUSE OF THE WEATHER, WE WORE AS LITTLE AS POSSIBLE...
MARTICA!!!!
MARTICA!!!!
MARTICA!!!!
¡PUTA! ¡PERVERTIDA! WHAT ARE YOU DOING IN THERE???
OH, MY GOD, IT'S ROMELIA!
HOW DID SHE FIND OUT THIS ADDRESS?
SHE HAS HER CONTACTS...
¡DEGENERADA!
OPEN THIS DOOR BEFORE I BREAK IT DOWN!
WE CAN'T LET HER IN; SHE'LL SEE I'M PRACTICALLY LIVING HERE.
SHIT! IF SHE KEEPS UP THIS SCREAMING, SHE'LL WAKE THE NEIGHBORS; THEY'LL CALL THE POLICE & WE'RE DOOMED.

FINALLY THE NOISE STOPPED. FIFTEEN MINUTES PASSED...
WHEW! THANK GOD SHE'S GONE.
NO... I KNOW HER. SHE'S OUT THERE SOMEWHERE ON THE STREET, WAITING FOR ME TO LEAVE. WE'VE GOT TO GET RID OF HER SOMEHOW!

THERE'S ONLY ONE WAY. I'LL TAKE SOME BOOKS & CLIMB OVER THE WALL FROM THE INSIDE PATIO.
I'LL COME OUT ON 45TH ST. & CIRCLE BACK UP ON MY STREET AS IF I JUST GOT OFF THE BUS. SHE DOESN'T KNOW THE GEOGRAPHY HERE.
GOOD!!! HURRY!!!
AY! ROMELIA!?! WHAT ARE YOU DOING HERE? WHAT'S WRONG?
I WAS AT YOUR DOOR. MARTICA IS IN THERE... WITH YOU...
I SAW SHADOWS MOVING UNDER THE DOOR...
ARE YOU CRAZY? I JUST GOT BACK FROM THE LIBRARY! I DON'T KNOW WHERE MARTUGENIA IS.
POR DIÓS, ROMELIA! THAT WAS MY CAT. YOU PROBABLY SCARED HIM TO DEATH.
PLEASE GO HOME, ROMELIA. I HAVE TO STUDY FOR AN EXAM.
MARTUGENIA SHOULD BE FINE. SHE'S AN ADULT, YOU KNOW.

ROMELIA SLOWLY BACKED AWAY & TRUDGED DOWN THE HILL TO 26TH AVENUE. I WAITED UNTIL I SAW HER DISAPPEAR ROUND THE CORNER DOWN TO THE BUS STOP.

THE WEDDING

NOW THAT MARTUGENIA WAS BACK AT WORK IN HAVANA AT THE UNIVERSITY, WE CAME UP WITH A PLAN FOR OUR PERSONAL FREEDOM. THIS WOULD ALLOW MARTUGENIA TO BREAK AWAY FROM HER PARENTS, SO HER PRIVATE LIFE WOULD BE HER OWN BUSINESS. IT WOULD BE A USEFUL COVER FOR ALL OF US, OUT IN THE WORLD.

AMORES! I HAVE A GENIUS IDEA! LET'S GET MARRIED, JUAN & I. WE'LL TELL THE WORLD & LATER WE CAN DISCREETLY GET DIVORCED.
¡COÑO, BRILLANTE! THEN WE'LL GET THE MARRIAGE QUOTA!
WHAT IS IT THESE DAYS? TWO CASES OF BEER & WHAT ELSE?
I THINK YOU GET TWO CASES OF BEER, TWO BOTTLES OF RUM, A WHOLE TIN OF SODA CRACKERS & THREE CASES OF SOFT DRINKS. WE'LL HAVE A FANTASTIC PARTY!
EVERYBODY'S DOING IT. THE ONLY WAY TO GET PARTY SUPPLIES.
MAMÁ! ¡PAPÁ! JUANITO & I ARE GETTING MARRIED!
OH, MY GOD, I CAN'T BELIEVE IT! I'M SO EXCITED!
I'LL HAVE TO MAKE YOU A NEW DRESS!
HUMPH... TO THAT LITTLE GUY?

THE CEREMONY
...AND NOW YOU MAY KISS THE BRIDE.
SUCH A LOVELY COUPLE!

THE PARTY
¡ARRIBA! ¡CARLOS GARDEL!

THE HONEYMOON
AS PART OF THE MARRIAGE PACKAGE, MARTUGENIA & JUAN WERE ENTITLED TO A NUMBER OF DAYS AT A FIRST-CLASS HARD-CURRENCY HOTEL & COULD PAY IN NATIONAL CURRENCY. THEY GOT A MARRIAGE SUITE AT THE HABANA LIBRE, WHERE THE REST OF US WERE ALLOWED INTO THE POOL AREA (BUT NEVER THE ROOM) AS THEIR GUESTS. THERE WE SPENT BLISSFUL DAYS & GORGED ON THE MUCH-COVETED GRILLED CHEESE SANDWICHES AVAILABLE ONLY TO GUESTS.

CHAPTER 6

A Family Visit

BY THE END OF '69, WHEN THE SUGARCANE SEASON BEGAN, THE WHOLE COUNTRY WAS MOBILIZED TO MEET FIDEL'S GOAL OF A HARVEST OF 10 MILLION TONS, THE LARGEST IN CUBAN HISTORY. IT WAS COUNTERREVOLUTIONARY TO EXPRESS ANY DOUBT THAT THIS REALLY COULD BE DONE.
BUT I MISSED THE WHOLE DEBACLE. MY MOTHER HAD LOBBIED FOR MONTHS THAT I VISIT & HAD SENT ME THE MONEY FOR A ONE-WAY TICKET TO MONTREAL ON A SOVIET FREIGHTER.
I HAVE TO GO VISIT MY FAMILY. LENORE'S SENT ME THE MONEY. IT'S BEEN ALMOST TWO YEARS...
YOU'RE COMING BACK?
OF COURSE. ¡BOBA! HOW COULD I NOT?
PART OF YOU IS HOMESICK FOR THE STATES...
THAT'LL HAPPEN WHEREVER I LIVE. I'LL NEVER BE COMPLETE ANYWHERE. THERE'S NO HELPING THAT.

WE WERE JUST IN TIME FOR ROMELIA'S FRESH COFFEE.
WHY JUST A ONE-WAY TICKET?
SHE DIDN'T HAVE THE MONEY TO SEND ME MORE. SHE SAID NOT TO WORRY.
HEY GRINGA! I HEAR YOU'RE LEAVING US?
I KNOW, GRINGA. YOU'RE A GOOD *REVOLUCIONARIA*...
NO, NO ROMELIA. I HAVE ANOTHER WHOLE YEAR OF SCHOOL, & THEN I HAVE MY THESIS TO PRESENT. I HAVE TO COME BACK.
CARIÑO, YOU'RE LIKE THE SEAFARING RAT IN "THE WIND IN THE WILLOWS"...
LISTEN...

Wayfarers All

"YOU ARE NOT ONE OF US," SAID THE WATER RAT... "RIGHT," REPLIED THE STRANGER. "I'M A SEAFARING RAT"... AND THE PORT I ORIGINALLY HAIL FROM IS CONSTANTINOPLE, THOUGH I'M SORT OF A FOREIGNER THERE TOO! ..."

"AND NOW," HE WAS SOFTLY SAYING, "I TAKE TO THE ROAD AGAIN, HOLDING ON SOUTH-WESTWARDS FOR MANY A LONG AND DUSTY DAY... THERE, SOONER OR LATER, THE SHIPS OF ALL SEAFARING NATIONS ARRIVE; AND THERE, AT ITS DESTINED HOUR, THE SHIP OF MY CHOICE WILL LET GO ITS ANCHOR..."

GRADUALLY THE RAT SANK INTO A TROUBLED DOZE, BROKEN BY STARTS AND CONFUSED MURMURINGS OF THINGS STRANGE AND WILD AND FOREIGN TO THE UNENLIGHTENED MOLE...

I WADED THROUGH THE BUREAUCRACY —GOT MY REENTRY PERMIT, SECURED A BERTH ON A SOVIET MERCHANT SHIP & MADE SURE ROBIN WOULD BE LOOKED AFTER.

THE RUSSIAN OFFICERS ALL WANTED TO PRACTICE THEIR ENGLISH.

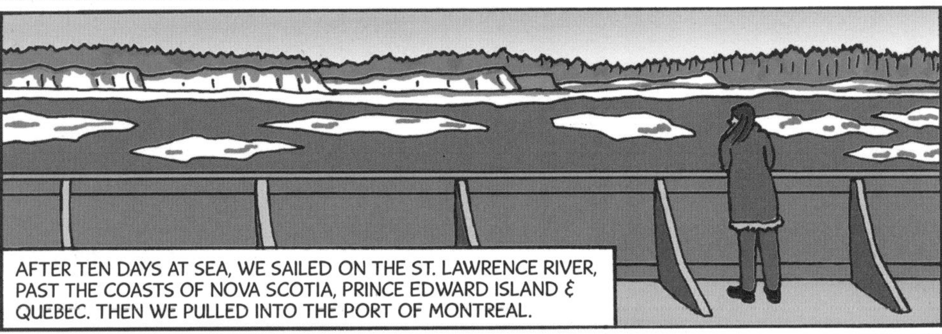
AFTER TEN DAYS AT SEA, WE SAILED ON THE ST. LAWRENCE RIVER, PAST THE COASTS OF NOVA SCOTIA, PRINCE EDWARD ISLAND & QUEBEC. THEN WE PULLED INTO THE PORT OF MONTREAL.

YOUR PAPERS AREN'T IN ORDER. ENTRY DENIED!
WHAT ARE YOU TALKING ABOUT?! I HAVE ALL MY PAPERS! THIS SHIP LEAVES TOMORROW FOR LENINGRAD! I HAVE TO GET OFF HERE. MY FAMILY IS WAITING FOR ME!
IT WAS CHRISTMAS EVE & THE CANADIAN IMMIGRATION OFFICER WAS DRUNK AS A SKUNK.

BOOOHOOO!!!
WHAT'S THE MATTER???
HE WON'T LET ME OFF THE SHIP! HE'S SENDING ME TO LENINGRAD!!!
THE FOURTH MATE WAS MY SAVIOR. HE SEARCHED EVERYWHERE FOR THE PORT MASTER —FOUND HIM BY A MIRACLE— & BROUGHT HIM TO OUR SHIP.
HMM... ALL RIGHT. THEY'RE IN ORDER. YOU MAY ENTER CANADA.

FORTUNATELY, I HAD AN OLD FRIEND WHO LIVED IN MONTREAL. I FERVENTLY HOPED HE WAS HOME.

MERRY CHRISTMAS! GOODBYE, COMRADE!
ROB! IT'S CONNIE. MY SHIP CAME IN! I MADE IT! COULD YOU PICK ME UP? I'M ON THE DOCK...

ROBERT SCOOPED ME UP AT THE FREEZING DOCK, GAVE ME SHELTER & THE NEXT DAY DROVE ME TO THE TRAIN STATION. I RODE ACROSS THE BORDER TO CROTON-ON-HUDSON, WHERE TED PICKED ME UP. IT FELT LIKE INTERPLANETARY TRAVEL.
LENORECHEN'S IN BED WITH A MIGRAINE. SHE GOT A LITTLE OVER EXCITED ABOUT YOUR VISIT.
OH, NO!!!
BRR!!! THIS MUST BE WHAT WINTER IS LIKE IN SIBERIA...
OH MY CONNIE! YOU ARE SO SKINNY! YOU HAVEN'T BEEN EATING!
OH, MY SWEETIES...
FOR TWO YEARS THERE HAD BEEN NO PHONE CALLS, ONLY LETTERS ONCE EVERY FEW MONTHS. OUR WORLDS SEEMED SEPARATED BY CENTURIES, NOT JUST BY GEOGRAPHY & THE COLD WAR.
THEN A FEW DAYS LATER...
CONNIE, I'M SORRY TO TELL YOU THIS, BUT MONEY'S VERY TIGHT...
YOU'LL HAVE TO FIND A JOB IF YOU WANT TO BUY THINGS TO TAKE BACK, ... & FOR YOUR RETURN TICKET, TOO.
OK, SO THAT'S THREE DOZEN PLUSH BLUE BUNNIES, FOUR DOZEN PINK TEDDY BEARS...
!!!
I FOUND ONE ON FIFTH AVE AS A RECEPTIONIST FOR A TOY MANUFACTURER'S SHOWROOM.
SIGH... & NOW I'M HOMESICK FOR HAVANA...
FOR A MONTH I COMMUTED FROM CROTON TO MANHATTAN TO A 9-5 JOB & WAS GRATEFUL TO BE ABLE TO MAKE SOME MONEY.

ON THE WEEKENDS I SPENT TIME WITH THE KIDS. NIKKI & I BECAME CLOSER THAN WE'D EVER BE AGAIN.
I DON'T WANT YOU TO GO BACK. STAY WITH ME.
OH, NICKAROO, BUT I DON'T HAVE A LIFE HERE. I'M STILL IN SCHOOL IN HAVANA. ANYWAY, I CAN'T LIVE WITH TED & LENORE ANYMORE.
POP MUSIC FESTIVAL PRESENTS:
TELL'EM GROUCHO SENT YA
ZAPPA THE MOTHERS OF INVENTION
VANILLA FUDGE
ISLAND AUDITORIUM
BY THE ROAD
WHAT A NICE BOX!
WELL, TAKE IT. IT'S A PRESENT.
TED'S OLD COLLEGE FRIEND & NOW HIS BOSS HAD A DAUGHTER WHO WAS A FOUNDING MEMBER OF RED STOCKINGS, A RADICAL WOMEN'S LIBERATION ORGANIZATION VERY ACTIVE IN NEW YORK AT THE TIME...
COME TO A MEETING! YOU'LL MEET A LOT OF EXCITING WOMEN & YOU CAN TELL THEM ABOUT THE REVOLUTION!
OH, THANKS. I'D LIKE THAT.
BUT... WHAT DO THEY DO IN MEETINGS?
HOW INTERESTING TO MEET SOMEONE LIVING IN CUBA! I'M WITH "RAT SUBTERRANEAN NEWS." I'D LIKE TO INTERVIEW YOU, HEAR ABOUT WOMEN IN CUBA.
HERE'S MY ADDRESS & PHONE NUMBER. WE CAN MEET THERE. CAN YOU COME TOMORROW AT 6?
FANTASTIC, I CAN GET AWAY FROM TED & LENORE!
ONE DOOR SOON OPENED ANOTHER & I MET OTHER MOVEMENT WOMEN WHO WENT TO PROTEST RALLIES & CONSCIOUSNESS-RAISING MEETINGS, WHO RAISED HELL IN THE STREETS & CREATED ALTERNATE MEDIA.
YES, BUT, UM... I'M NOT SURE I CAN EXPLAIN.

THE WEATHER UNDERGROUND, A MILITANT ULTRA-LEFT GROUP OF REVOLUTIONARIES, OR TERRORISTS —DEPENDING ON WHO'S TALKING— HAD BEEN CREDITED WITH A STRING OF URBAN BOMBINGS AGAINST "THE ESTABLISHMENT," IN PROTEST AGAINST THE VIETNAM WAR & AMERICAN IMPERIALISM.

HAVE YOU HEARD? SOME WEATHER PEOPLE BLEW THEMSELVES UP IN A BUILDING ON WEST 11TH STREET!
OH, NO! DO THEY KNOW WHO THEY WERE?
KATHY BOUDIN'S ONE. I HEARD SHE SURVIVED & ESCAPED.
YOU MEAN THE DAUGHTER OF LEONARD BOUDIN?!?
HOLY SHIT, THAT'S BOUDIN OF BOUDIN & RABINOWITZ — THE LAWYERS LENORE CONSULTED IN HAVANA..!
CONNIE, MEET SOME MEMBERS OF THE GLF, THE GAY LIBERATION FRONT.
CAN IT BE? THEY'RE REALLY TELLING THE WORLD THEY'RE QUEER? AMAZING!
3B
RAT
THESE AMERICAN "REVOLUTIONARIES" SEEMED LIKE AMATEURS TO ME, BUT IT WAS ALL VERY INTERESTING, ESPECIALLY WHEN I FIRST ENCOUNTERED MILITANT LESBIANS. I WAS INTRODUCED TO THEM AT THE APARTMENT OF BARBARA, THE "RAT" CORRESPONDENT.

TELL US ABOUT THE LIFE OF GAY PEOPLE IN HAVANA. WE HEAR THERE ARE PROBLEMS...
WHY DOES THE REVOLUTION OPPRESS GAY PEOPLE?
RAT
"10 million young people will free us!"
UM, WELL, CUBA ISN'T MONOLITHIC. THE COUNTRY'S REALLY A COLLECTION OF FIEFDOMS— SOME MORE TOLERANT, SOME MORE REPRESSIVE.
IF YOU'RE GAY, HOW YOU'RE TREATED ALSO DEPENDS ON HOW VISIBLE YOU ARE.
JESUS... THEY HAVE NO IDEA... THERE'S NO WAY TO BEGIN.

WHAT ORGANIZATIONS DO GAY PEOPLE HAVE TO FIGHT FOR THEIR RIGHTS? HOW DO PEOPLE PROTEST OPPRESSION IN HAVANA?
WHAT? WE DON'T PROTEST OUR OPRESSION! THAT'S UNTHINKABLE THERE!
OH, YOU'RE GAY? WHY DIDN'T YOU SAY SO?
ME? DON'T SAY THAT SO LOUD... I DON'T... THE WRONG PEOPLE MIGHT HEAR IT.
HOW CAN YOU LIVE IN A COUNTRY THAT SENDS GAY PEOPLE TO LABOR CAMPS?
HMM, MAYBE YOU NEED SOME LIBERATING YOURSELF. HAVE YOU BEEN TO A LESBIAN BAR YET?
A WHAT? WHY NO...
COME ON, LET'S GO FOR A DRINK...
THESE BARS ARE THE ONLY PLACE DYKES HAVE TO SOCIALIZE, BUT THEY'RE ALL CONTROLLED BY THE MAFIA, WHICH MAKES THEM VERY EXPENSIVE.
WE'RE GOING TO HAVE A BIG WOMEN'S DANCE NEXT FRIDAY, TRYING TO CREATE AN ALTERNATIVE TO THE MAFIA BAR SCENE. WHY DON'T YOU COME?
OH, I'D LOVE TO... BUT I'M LEAVING THE COUNTRY THE NEXT MORNING, BACK TO CUBA. I DON'T SEE HOW...

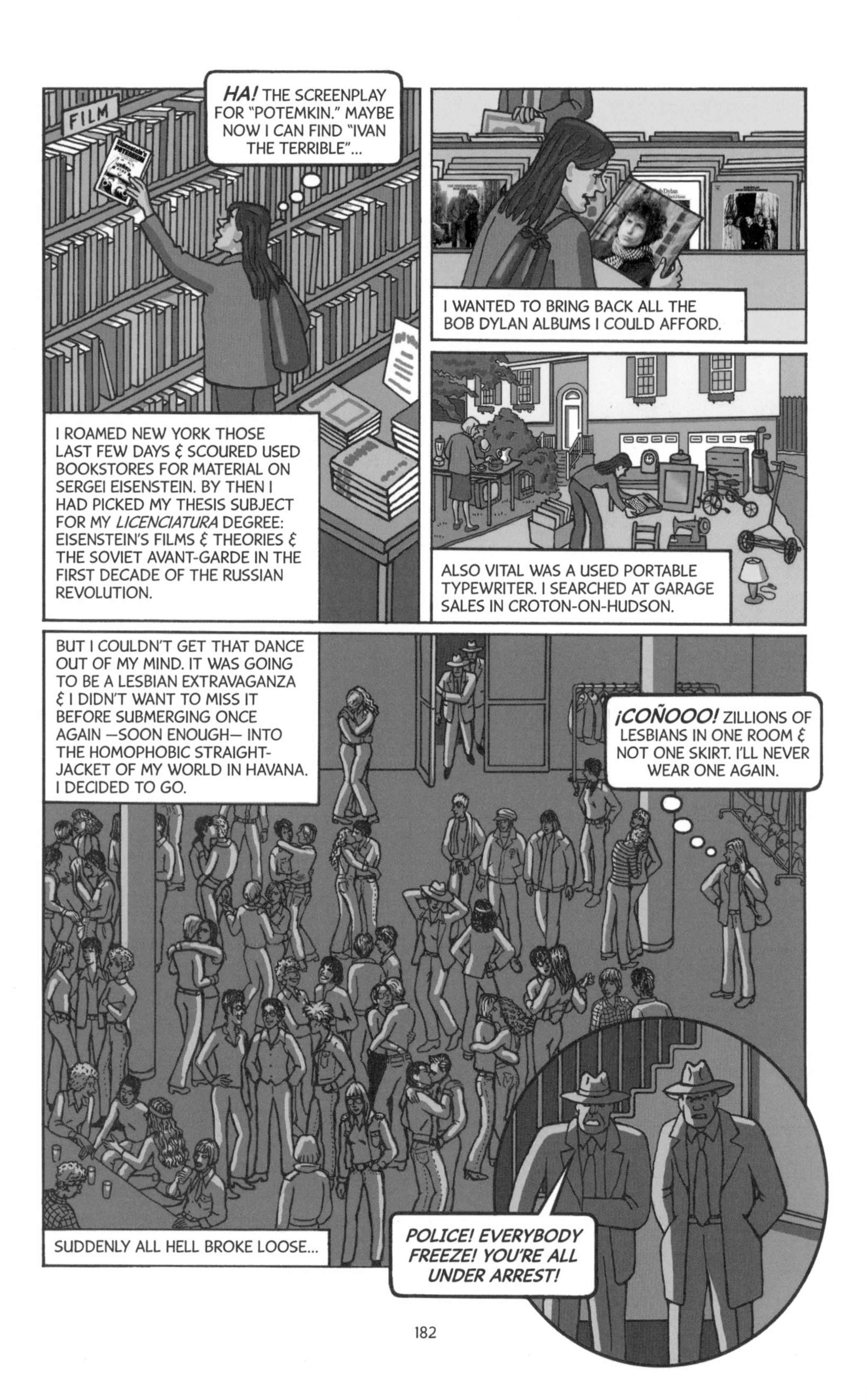
FILM
HA! THE SCREENPLAY FOR "POTEMKIN." MAYBE NOW I CAN FIND "IVAN THE TERRIBLE"...
I ROAMED NEW YORK THOSE LAST FEW DAYS & SCOURED USED BOOKSTORES FOR MATERIAL ON SERGEI EISENSTEIN. BY THEN I HAD PICKED MY THESIS SUBJECT FOR MY *LICENCIATURA* DEGREE: EISENSTEIN'S FILMS & THEORIES & THE SOVIET AVANT-GARDE IN THE FIRST DECADE OF THE RUSSIAN REVOLUTION.
I WANTED TO BRING BACK ALL THE BOB DYLAN ALBUMS I COULD AFFORD.
ALSO VITAL WAS A USED PORTABLE TYPEWRITER. I SEARCHED AT GARAGE SALES IN CROTON-ON-HUDSON.
BUT I COULDN'T GET THAT DANCE OUT OF MY MIND. IT WAS GOING TO BE A LESBIAN EXTRAVAGANZA & I DIDN'T WANT TO MISS IT BEFORE SUBMERGING ONCE AGAIN —SOON ENOUGH— INTO THE HOMOPHOBIC STRAIGHT-JACKET OF MY WORLD IN HAVANA. I DECIDED TO GO.
¡COÑOOO! ZILLIONS OF LESBIANS IN ONE ROOM & NOT ONE SKIRT. I'LL NEVER WEAR ONE AGAIN.
SUDDENLY ALL HELL BROKE LOOSE...
POLICE! EVERYBODY FREEZE! YOU'RE ALL UNDER ARREST!

WE'RE SHUTTING THIS PLACE DOWN!
I CAN'T GET ARRESTED! I'M LEAVING FOR CUBA TOMORROW!
EXIT
DANCE
THOSE AREN'T COPS! THOSE ARE MAFIA GOONS!
QUICK! COME WITH ME, WE'LL GET YOU OUT THE BACK WAY!

I RUSHED BACK TO CROTON AT DAWN. I HAD A FEW HOURS BEFORE I BOARDED MY TRAIN TO MONTREAL THAT AFTERNOON. LUCKILY I HAD PACKED IN ADVANCE.
I DON'T KNOW HOW I'LL STAND IT. COME BACK SOON.
I'LL TRY... REMEMBER THIS ONE?
"PASSING THROUGH, PASSING THROUGH, SOMETIMES HAPPY, SOMETIMES BLUE, GLAD THAT I RAN INTO YOU, TELL THE PEOPLE THAT YOU SAW ME PASSING THROUGH."
THAT WAS THE LAST TIME LITTLE NIKKI COULD OPEN HER HEART TO ME. WE SAID GOODBYE AT HOME. SHE DIDN'T WANT TO CRY AT THE STATION.

GOODBYE! GOODBYE!!! I LOVE YOU!
GOODBYE, MY CONNIE!
BYE! BYE!
HAVE A JOLLY GOOD TIME! SO LONG!
GARE WINDSOR
WINDSOR STATION
ONCE AGAIN MY FRIEND ROB TOOK ME UNDER HIS WING & GAVE ME SHELTER, WHILE I APPLIED & WAITED FOR A SOVIET SHIP WITH PASSAGE TO CUBA, PREFERABLY TO THE PORT OF HAVANA.
TWO DAYS LATER ROB INVITED ME TO THE MOVIES TO SEE "M*A*S*H" WITH A COUPLE OF FRIENDS.
I HAVE TO GO TO THE OFFICE FOR A WHILE. I'LL PICK YOU UP LATER FOR THE MOVIE.
Cheerios
I MADE SOME BROWNIES. HELP YOURSELF. I THINK YOU'LL LIKE 'EM. THEY'RE SPECIAL.
HMM... WHY NOT? SOON I'LL BE BACK IN MY OTHER LIFE. I'M IN CANADA NOW & NO ONE WILL EVER KNOW.
OF COURSE I KNEW THAT MEANT POT, AN ALLURING TRANSGRESSION.
MMMM! THAT WAS DELICIOUS. BUT I DON'T FEEL A THING. THINK I'LL HAVE ANOTHER.
PHOOEY! ROB MUST HAVE FORGOTTEN THE POT. THESE BROWNIES ARE DUDS.
...BUT VERY TASTY. I'VE GOT TO HAVE JUST ONE MORE. MMM..!
HI! I'M BACK. LET'S GO! WE HAVE TO STAND IN LINE FOR TICKETS. WE'LL MEET THE OTHERS AT THE THEATER.

ROB... I THINK... I'M... GOING... TO ... FALL ... DOWN...
SHIT! WHAT'S WRONG!?!
AS WE WAITED IN LINE... THE BROWNIES HIT ME.
TOO... MANY... BROWNIES...
MY GOD, HOW MANY DID YOU EAT?
OH, FUCK! HERE COMES A COP! NOT A WORD!
HEY... WHAT'S WRONG HERE?
OH... I'M FINE... OFFICER... JUST BAD CRAMPS.
I DON'T KNOW. I THINK I'D BETTER TAKE YOU IN TO THE EMERGENCY ROOM.
NO! NO! THAT WON'T BE NECESSARY. I FEEL MUCH BETTER.
THROUGH THE FOG I REMEMBERED THE LAST TIME I'D BEEN IN AN EMERGENCY ROOM... I SUMMONED THE STRENGTH TO CONVINCE THE COP I WAS OK.
ROB, TAKE ME HOME. I NEED A HOT WATER BOTTLE.
OH... YES... GOODBYE, OFFICER!
I STAGGERED TO MY FEET & WITH AS MUCH DIGNITY AS I COULD MUSTER, TOOK MY LEAVE AS I HELD ONTO ROB WITH EVERYTHING I HAD.
WELL, LET'S TRY AGAIN! IT'S REALLY SUPPOSED TO BE A FUN FILM.
I WAS UP & RUNNING THE NEXT DAY.

THAT WEEK I MADE THE MOST IMPORTANT PURCHASE OF THE TRIP, BESIDES ALL THE BOOKS: A TINY CUBE REFRIGERATOR. LIVING IN THE TROPICS WITHOUT ONE HAD BEEN HARD.
¡QUÉ FELICIDAD! IT EVEN MAKES ICE CUBES!
HBC 123
GULP! I HOPE THIS SHIP STOPS IN HAVANA.
BYE! SEE YOU IN CUBA SOMETIME! THANKS FOR EVERYTHING!
YEAH! TAKE CARE OF YOURSELF!
AT LAST, I HAD A BERTH ON A FREIGHTER, "THE VOLKOV," GOING TO CUBA, PORT UNKNOWN.
HMM, NOT A BAD CABIN. I'D BETTER INSPECT IT FOR PEEPHOLES...
DOBRIY VYECHER!
GOOD EVENING!
UGH!!! LARD SOUP!
NOW I HAVE TO WORRY ABOUT GETTING ALL MY STUFF INTO THE COUNTRY.
I CAN'T BELIEVE I HAVE TO TYPE UP A LIST OF EXACTLY EACH & EVERY ITEM I'M BRINGING— PANTIES, TAMPAX, EVERYTHING...
DAMN LUCKY I BROUGHT THIS MACHINE.

AT FIRST THE CREW & OFFICERS SEEMED COLD & REMOTE, ESPECIALLY THE CAPTAIN. NO ONE TALKED TO ME FOR THE FIRST WEEK OF THIS ELEVEN-DAY JOURNEY. BUT FINALLY THE ICE WAS BROKEN— ONE OF THE CREW MEMBERS, TATIANA, WANTED TO PRACTICE HER ENGLISH WITH ME.

COME TO ROOM! YOU MEET MY FRIEND!
??? YEAH, SURE...
MY BEST FRIEND!
YOU LIVE THERE?
OH, WONDERFUL! I ONCE HAD A PARROT IN HAVANA...
YES & I LOVED HIM, BUT HE ATE MY FATHER'S SCIENCE FICTION COLLECTION. I HAD TO GIVE HIM AWAY.
SO! YOU LOVE PARROT? WE HAVE 20 PARROT ON SHIP!
WE HAVE PARTY TONIGHT. COME! WE CELEBRATE LENIN'S BIRTHDAY WITH GOOD COGNAC!
SURE! THAT SOUNDS LIKE FUN!
WE DANCED HALF THE NIGHT & CONSUMED MASSIVE QUANTITIES OF COGNAC. THIS TIME THE FOOD WAS GREAT— TASTY SAUSAGES, SARDINES, BREAD & CHEESE.
MAY I HAVE THIS DANCE?

AS WE APPROACHED THE TROPICS, & THE WEATHER TURNED WARMER, THE CAPTAIN, THE FOURTH MATE, THE SHIP'S DOCTOR, & THE POLITICAL COMMISSAR ALL WANTED TO PRACTICE THEIR ENGLISH, TOO.

OH, HI, CAPTAIN.
A PRESENT FOR YOU, PICTURES OF THE KREMLIN!
AND SOME FINE WINE!
TELL US, WHAT IS THIS NONSENSE IN AMERICA ABOUT WOMEN'S LIBERATION?

I HAD PLENTY TO THINK ABOUT. WHAT WOULD I DO WITH MY LIFE AFTER I GRADUATED?
MAYBE I CAN GET A JOB AT ICAIC & BECOME A FILM EDITOR.
NOT AN ARTS BUREAUCRAT, NOT AN ACADEMIC. I WANT TO MAKE ART SOMEHOW, NOT TALK ABOUT IT.
HOW COULD I LIVE WITHOUT CUBA, WITHOUT MARTUGENIA?
I'LL ALWAYS BE A FOREIGNER IN CUBA... BUT I'M A FOREIGNER IN THE U.S., TOO...
THOSE WOMEN IN NEW YORK, SO FREE, BUT THEY SEEMED SO COLD. I COULDN'T READ THEIR BODY LANGUAGE AT ALL...
...DIDN'T GET THEIR JOKES...
HOW AM I GOING TO STAND BEING QUEER WHERE IT'S A CRIME... AFTER WHAT I'VE SEEN IN NY?
AND HOW COULD I LIVE IN A CAPITALIST COUNTRY NOW? I GOT NERVOUS JUST GOING INTO A SUPERMARKET... *25 TYPES OF TOOTHPASTE!*
HAPPINESS! CHIVIRICO MUST BE SOMEWHERE RIGHT ABOUT THERE!
WE REACHED CUBA'S COAST & CAME AROUND THE SOUTH-EAST END OF THE ISLAND. THERE WERE THE GLORIOUS SIERRA MAESTRA MOUNTAINS.

WE'LL DOCK FOR A FEW DAYS IN CIENFUEGOS. YOU CAN GET OFF THERE, BUT WE CONTINUE ON TO HAVANA. WHY DON'T YOU STAY WITH US UNTIL THEN?
THANK YOU SO MUCH, BUT I'M EAGER TO TO GET HOME. LET'S SEE IF THEY LET ME ENTER IN CIENFUEGOS.

WE ARRIVED THE NEXT DAY & I SWEATED BULLETS AS THE CUSTOMS OFFICER SET UP SHOP IN MY CABIN. HE WENT OVER EVERY SINGLE ITEM IN MY BAGS & BOXES; HE COVERED MY THREE-PAGE LIST WITH STAMPS & SEALS. FINALLY I WAS FREE TO ENTER THE COUNTRY.

COMPAÑERO, CAN YOU TELL ME HOW TO GET TO THE TRAIN STATION? IS THERE ANYONE HERE WHO CAN HELP ME GET MY THINGS THERE?
YEAH, ASK ONE OF THE MEN ON THE DOCKS WITH A TRUCK. THEY MIGHT HELP YOU.
GOOD LUCK, COMPAÑERA! WELCOME BACK TO REVOLUTIONARY CUBA!

I'M IN CIENFUEGOS!!!! FIND A BIG CAR TO BRING TO THE TRAIN STATION. I'M COMING ON THE MILK TRAIN TONIGHT!
WITH A REFRIGERATOR!!!

I MANAGED TO FIND A WORKING TELEPHONE THAT ALLOWED LONG-DISTANCE CALLS.

AT LAST I WAS HOME.
¡GRINGA!!!
LOOK! IT MAKES ICE!

CHAPTER 7

The Last Ship

AFTER MY RETURN, THE ATMOSPHERE IN THE COUNTRY HAD CHANGED. BY MAY 1970 IT BECAME OFFICIAL: THE 10-MILLION-TON SUGAR HARVEST WAS A FAILURE, DESPITE THE MOBILIZATION OF THE ENTIRE COUNTRY, TO THE EXCLUSION OF EVERYTHING ELSE, INCLUDING CHRISTMAS, ABOLISHED BY FIDEL LAST DECEMBER.
I WONDER WHAT'S GOING TO HAPPEN?
YOU'LL SEE. THE BOLOS WILL BE BACK MORE THAN EVER, NOW. IT'LL BECOME LIKE THE SOVIET UNION.
DAN MITRIONE
BULLSHIT. IT CAN'T HAPPEN HERE.
WANNA MAKE A BET?
MY LAST YEAR OF SCHOOL & MY THESIS ARE COMING UP. I'LL HAVE TO FIND A JOB SOON.
WHERE WILL YOU LOOK?
I REALLY WANT TO BECOME A FILM EDITOR. I'LL TRY TO GET AN INTERVIEW AT ICAIC.
GOOD! OK, TELL ME MORE LATER. BOLA'S ABOUT TO START.
LIFE IN MY CAVE WAS NOW MUCH IMPROVED BY THE BLESSED REFRIGERATOR. BUT DURING MY ABSENCE GOYO & JUAN HAD BROKEN UP. JUAN CAME LESS OFTEN & GOYO RETREATED INTO SOLITARY MELANCHOLY IN SANTA FE. HERNÁN'S COUSIN EDDY FILLED THE VOID.
MLN
GUESS WHAT! ÁNGEL'S INVITED ME TO A RECEPTION AT THE NORTH KOREAN EMBASSY, TO GO AS HIS GIRLFRIEND. HE'S SO PERVERSE.
WONDERFUL! BRING BACK GOODIES IF THEY SERVE ANYTHING EDIBLE!
THE MEDIA WAS FILLED WITH ADMIRING STORIES ABOUT THE TUPAMAROS GUERRILLAS IN URUGUAY. THEY HAD KIDNAPPED DAN MITRIONE, AN AMERICAN FBI AGENT, ALLEGEDLY SENT BY THE U.S. GOVERNMENT AS AN INSTRUCTOR IN COUNTERINSURGENCY TECHNIQUES—TORTURE METHODOLOGY—TO BRAZIL & URUGUAY. ON AUGUST 10 HE WAS FOUND SHOT DEAD IN HIS CAR IN MONTEVIDEO.

ÁNGEL LUIS WORKED AS A TRANSLATOR IN A STATE PUBLISHING HOUSE. ONE DAY HE WAS ASSIGNED TO WORK WITH A NORTH KOREAN EDITOR ON A SPANISH TRANSLATION OF THE COMPLETE WORKS OF KIM IL SUNG, A DEADLY TASK. HIS COUNTERPART WOULD TRANSLATE FROM KOREAN INTO LAME SPANISH & ÁNGEL WOULD TRANSFORM IT INTO ACCEPTABLE SPANISH.
COMANDANTE EN JEFE ¡ORDENE!
ÁNGEL LUIS, YOU'LL BE WORKING WITH *COMPAÑERO* RI FOR THE NEXT YEAR. ***I'M SURE YOU'LL DO A GREAT JOB!***
THE JOB WAS UNBEARABLY BORING, SO ÁNGEL DEVISED A WAY TO ENTERTAIN HIMSELF DURING THIS TRYING TIME..
I'M GOING TO TRY TO SEDUCE COMRADE RI BEFORE THE BOOKS ARE FINISHED. THIS'LL BE MY TOUGHEST CHALLENGE YET.
MMM!!! YOU MUST TELL US EVERYTHING!
YOU HAVE SUCH NICE HANDS, RI. HAS ANYONE EVER TOLD YOU THAT?
DO YOU HAVE A GIRLFRIEND? TELL ME ABOUT SEX IN KOREA.
MY GRACIOUS, RI. YOU'RE SO WELL ENDOWED!
HE HASN'T DENOUNCED ME SO FAR... HE'S COMPLETELY TITILLATED & HE DOESN'T KNOW WHAT TO DO WITH HIMSELF.
WELL, IF ANYONE CAN GET INTO HIS PANTS, YOU CAN. DIDN'T YOU MAKE IT WITH A SOVIET KOMSOMOL DELEGATE?

THE NORTH KOREANS WERE PLEASED WITH ÁNGEL'S WORK. THEY INVITED HIM TO NUMEROUS RECEPTIONS AT THE EMBASSY & I WENT AS HIS DATE.

COMPAÑERO RI! I'D LIKE YOU TO MEET MY FRIEND CONNIE.
OH! I'M PLEASED TO MEET YOU.
OH GOD. THEY'RE NOT SHOWING ANOTHER AWFUL KIM IL SUNG FLICK TONIGHT, ARE THEY? I CAN'T TAKE ONE MORE.
JUST SMILE & LET'S FIND THE FREE FOOD, GRINGA...
THE TIME CAME TO FIND A JOB.
I GOT AN INTERVIEW AT ICAIC WITH JULIO GARCIA ESPINOSA! HALLELUJAH!
I HAVE TO FIT IN SOMEWHERE IF I'M GOING TO LIVE HERE AFTER COLLEGE.
COMITE DE DEFENSA DE LA REVOLUCIÓN
TU DEBER
ES TENER TU CUADRA SIEMPRE LIMPIA

THE BIG INTERVIEW WAS IN THE ICAIC BUILDING ON THE CORNER OF 23RD & 12TH STREET. I HAD SEEN EVERY EISENSTEIN FILM SHOWN IN CUBA IN THIS BUILDING—AS WELL AS ALL THE OTHER SOVIET AVANT-GARDE FILMS THAT ICAIC OFFERED.

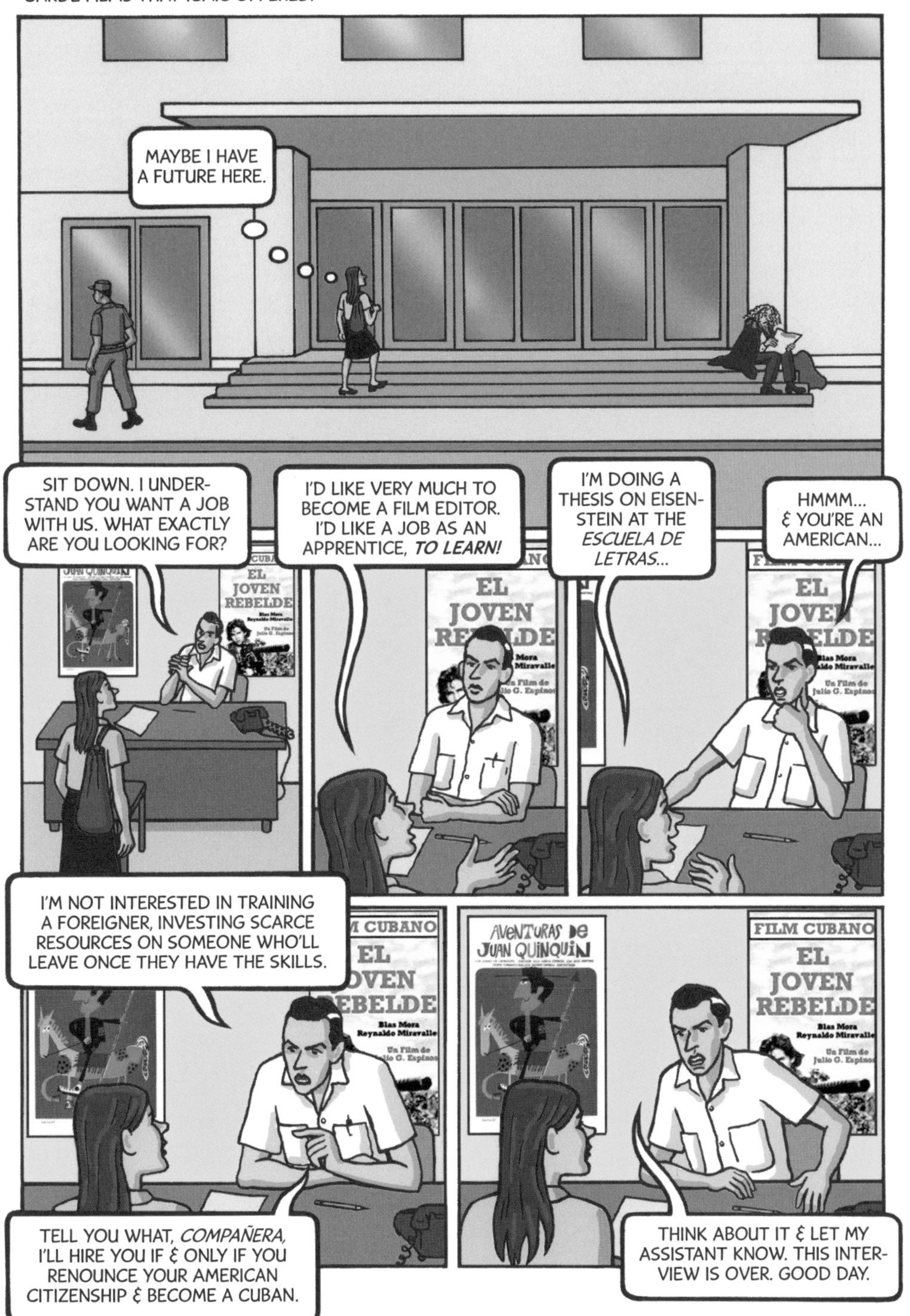

MAYBE I HAVE A FUTURE HERE.
SIT DOWN. I UNDERSTAND YOU WANT A JOB WITH US. WHAT EXACTLY ARE YOU LOOKING FOR?
I'D LIKE VERY MUCH TO BECOME A FILM EDITOR. I'D LIKE A JOB AS AN APPRENTICE, *TO LEARN!*
I'M DOING A THESIS ON EISENSTEIN AT THE *ESCUELA DE LETRAS*...
HMMM... & YOU'RE AN AMERICAN...
EL JOVEN REBELDE
I'M NOT INTERESTED IN TRAINING A FOREIGNER, INVESTING SCARCE RESOURCES ON SOMEONE WHO'LL LEAVE ONCE THEY HAVE THE SKILLS.
TELL YOU WHAT, *COMPAÑERA,* I'LL HIRE YOU IF & ONLY IF YOU RENOUNCE YOUR AMERICAN CITIZENSHIP & BECOME A CUBAN.
AVENTURAS DE JUAN QUINQUIN
FILM CUBANO
EL JOVEN REBELDE
THINK ABOUT IT & LET MY ASSISTANT KNOW. THIS INTERVIEW IS OVER. GOOD DAY.

THEY WON'T GIVE ME A JOB. I'M NOT GIVING UP MY AMERICAN CITIZENSHIP FOR ANYTHING.
NO, THAT WOULD BE CRAZY. BUT WE CAN STILL LIVE ON MY SALARY FOR NOW.
YEAH... TODAY. BUT WHAT ABOUT TOMORROW?
MAYBE THERE'S NO PLACE FOR ME IN CUBA. BUT THEN, WHERE ELSE?

MY THESIS PROPOSAL WAS ACCEPTED. JOSÉ ANTONIO PORTUONDO WAS TO HEAD THE PANEL, JOINED BY MIRTA AGUIRRE, ISABEL MONAL & THE DIRECTOR OF THE SCHOOL OF LETTERS, VICENTINA ANTUÑA. MY DEADLINE WAS IN JANUARY 1972.

ABOUT THIS TIME A MIRACLE HAPPENED. MARTUGENIA WAS OFFERED A SCHOLARSHIP BY THE BRITISH COUNCIL FOR A SUMMER PROGRAM IN LONDON.
JUST THINK! A ONCE-IN-A-LIFETIME CHANCE TO SEE SOMETHING OF THE WORLD!
AND... IT OPENS OTHER UNSPEAKABLE POSSIBILITIES... WHAT IF..?
YOU MEAN... NOT COME BACK... FROM ENGLAND?
BUT ... I'M A REVOLUTIONARY... & HOW COULD I LEAVE MY MOTHER?
I KNOW. LET'S SEE WHAT HAPPENS. WHO KNOWS IF THEY'LL EVEN LET YOU ACCEPT THE SCHOLARSHIP... AFTER THE '67 DISASTER.

"...YO HE COMETIDO MUCHÍSIMOS ERRORES, ERRORES REALMENTE IMPERDONABLES... YO, BAJO EL DISFRAZ DEL ESCRITOR REBELDE, LO ÚNICO QUE HACÍA ERA OCULTAR MI DESAFECTO A LA REVOLUCIÓN... YO HE DIFAMADO, HE INJURIADO LA REVOLUCIÓN CON CUBANOS Y CON EXTRANJEROS. YO HE LLEGADO SUMAMENTE LEJOS EN MIS ERRORES, EN MIS ACTIVIDADES CONTRARREVOLUCIONARIAS...
EN EL AÑO 1966, CUANDO YO REGRESÉ DE EUROPA A CUBA... LO PRIMERO QUE HICE FUE DEFENDER A GUILLERMITO, QUE ES UN AGENTE DECLARADO, UN ENEMIGO DECLARADO DE LA REVOLUCIÓN, UN AGENTE DE LA CIA... YO SÉ... QUE ESTA INTERVENCIEON DE ESTA NOCHE ES UNA GENEROSIDAD DE LA REVOLUCIÓN, QUE YO ESTA INTERVENCIÓN NO ME LA MERECÍA, QUE YO NO MERECÍA ESTAR LIBRE..."

ON MARCH 22, 1971, THE POET HEBERTO PADILLA WAS ARRESTED & JAILED. ON APRIL 27 HE SUDDENLY REAPPEARED AT A STAGED CEREMONY AT THE UNEAC, THE WRITERS & ARTISTS UNION, PRESENTED BY JOSÉ ANTONIO PORTUONDO, MY PROFESSOR OF ESTHETICS & THESIS JUDGE. PADILLA PERFORMED A TRANSPARENTLY-COERCED AUTO-DA-FE AS A TRAITOR, A DISGRACE TO SOCIALISM & A REPENTANT SINNER.

REMEMBER THAT AMERICAN WHO WAS HERE LAST YEAR & WE TALKED ABOUT EISENSTEIN? HE RUNS TRI CONTINENTAL FILMS. THEY DISTRIBUTE LEFTIST DOCUMENTARIES. HE OFFERED ME A JOB IF I RETURNED TO THE STATES... MAYBE WE COULD BOTH HAVE A FUTURE THERE.

PADILLA'S APPEARANCE OCCURRED IN THE SAME WEEK AS THE "FIRST CONGRESS OF EDUCATION & CULTURE," HELD IN HAVANA, APRIL 23-30, 1971. WITH THIS EVENT, THE PARAMETERS OF THE CURRENT CULTURAL & EDUCATIONAL POLICIES OF THE REVOLUTION WERE DECLARED:

WELL, LIKE SARTRE SAID, WE'RE THE JEWS OF CUBA.

FASHION— DIRECT CONFRONTATION IS NECESSARY TO ELIMINATE EXTRAVAGANT ABERRATIONS.

RELIGION— JEHOVAH'S WITNESSES & THE SEVENTH-DAY ADVENTISTS ARE COUNTERREVOLUTIONARY. CATHOLICS & THE CATHOLIC CHURCH ARE TO BE TOLERATED BUT NEVER PROMOTED.

JUVENILE DELINCUENCY— WE MUST BE CONCERNED ABOUT THE INFLUENCE OF THE ABAKUÁ ON OUR YOUTH (AN AFRO-CUBAN RELIGIOUS SECRET SOCIETY SINCE THE DAYS OF SLAVERY).

SEXUALITY— WE MUST IMPLEMENT CO-EDUCATION WHEREVER POSSIBLE. HOMOSEXUALITY IS A "SOCIAL PATHOLOGY," A "PROBLEM" FOUND IN OUR CULTURAL INSTITUTIONS. HOMOSEXUALS MUST BE FORBIDDEN TO PLAY ANY ROLE IN THE EDUCATION OF YOUNG PEOPLE & MUST NOT REPRESENT THE REVOLUTION ABROAD.

PAVÓN, SERGUERA, QUESADA
& THE CULTURAL PURGES OF 1971
THE CNC (CONSEJO NACIONAL DE CULTURA), THE NATIONAL CULTURE COUNCIL, MUCH LATER RENAMED THE MINISTRY OF CULTURE, WAS PUT UNDER THE COMMAND OF LIEUTENANT LUIS PAVÓN TAMAYO, AN ARMY OFFICER & FORMER DIRECTOR OF "VERDE OLIVO," THE OFFICIAL MAGAZINE OF THE ARMED FORCES. PAVÓN & HIS TWO ASSOCIATES, PAPITO SERGUERA & ARMANDO QUESADA, CONDUCTED A FEROCIOUS CAMPAIGN OF CENSORSHIP & REPRESSION AGAINST ORGANIZATIONS & INDIVIDUALS IN ALL CULTURAL SPHERES.
(antes Cine Foxa)
NACIONAL DE GUIÑOL
MAJOR JORGE SERGUERA WAS A LAWYER BY TRAINING. AS A MEMBER OF FIDEL'S REBEL ARMY HE HAD PLAYED THE ROLE OF PROSECUTOR IN THE SUMMARY TRIALS OF 1959; HE SENT DOZENS TO FACE FIRING SQUADS. NOW AS HEAD OF THE ICRT, HE WAS IN CHARGE OF ALL RADIO & TELEVISION BROADCASTING. HE BANNED THE BEATLES & PURGED HUNDREDS OF EMPLOYEES, ANYONE SUSPECTED OF BEING QUEER OR NOT TOEING THE PARTY LINE.
ARMANDO QUESADA WAS THE OFFICIAL WHO RULED OVER THE THEATER, & HE TOOK UP HIS TASK WITH A VENGENCE. THEATER GROUPS WERE DECIMATED. ONE WAS THE REVERED CAMEJO PUPPET THEATER. THROUGHOUT THE THEATER WORLD, PEOPLE WERE SUMMONED, FIRED, HUMILIATED, & MARGINALIZED. HIS NICKNAME WAS "TORQUESADA," IN HONOR OF TORQUEMADA, INQUISITOR GENERAL OF THE SPANISH INQUISITION.
THOSE PURGED IN LA PARAMETRACIÓN WERE ORDERED TO WORK IN FACTORIES OR FARMS, SHUT OUT OF NATIONAL INTELLECTUAL LIFE.
¡PIRULÍ! ¡PIRULÍ!

OUR FRIEND EMILIO, FROM THE SCHOOL OF LETTERS, WAS PURGED & SPENT YEARS IN A FACTORY SORTING MATCHES. LATER, TO MAKE ENDS MEET, HE SOLD CANDY OUT OF A BASKET ON THE STREET. TWENTY-FIVE YEARS LATER, HE WAS FINALLY ALLOWED TO WORK AS AN EDITOR AGAIN.

IT BECAME CLEAR THERE WAS NO FUTURE FOR ME IN CUBA. I HAD NO JOB PROSPECTS, & THE DAY OF MY THESIS DEFENSE WAS APPROACHING. MARTUGENIA'S SCHOLARSHIP FOR THE SUMMER OF '72 STILL HELD.
WHAT ARE WE GOING TO DO? I CAN'T GO ON FOREVER THIS WAY AFTER I GRADUATE.
IT'S MY MOTHER I WORRY ABOUT. I'D NEVER BE ABLE TO SEE HER AGAIN...
HOW CAN IT BE IMMORAL FOR YOU, AS A CUBAN, TO CHOOSE TO LEAVE, YET PERFECTLY FINE FOR ME, AS A FOREIGNER? HOW DOES IT CHANGE THE ETHICS?
IF YOU LEAVE, WHAT WOULD HAPPEN TO US? MAYBE THE SCHOLARSHIP IS THE ONLY WAY...
IF WE DO THIS, THE TIMING HAS TO BE PERFECT.
YEAH. I SHOULD LEAVE A COUPLE OF MONTHS BEFORE YOU & APPLY TO LEAVE RIGHT AFTER I GRADUATE.
SO I MEET YOU IN ENGLAND. BUT WITH WHAT RESOURCES? WE HAVE NOTHING.
MY MOTHER'S CHILDHOOD FRIEND ANN HILB LIVES IN LONDON. SHE ESCAPED FROM GERMANY AS A YOUNG GIRL, ON THE LAST BOAT TO ENGLAND. MY GRANDPARENTS HELPED HER FAMILY BEFORE THE NAZIS MURDERED THEM ALL. ANN WOULD HELP US. WE COULD TRUST HER.
I'LL HAVE TO TAKE THE CAVE APART.
WHAT IF THEY SUDDENLY DENY ME THE SCHOLARSHIP AFTER YOU'VE DONE THAT?
WE'LL HAVE TO CHANCE IT. HOW ELSE?
WILL YOU DO IT?
YES... WE HAVE TO.
MY MOTHER WILL BE OK... SHE'LL HAVE MY FATHER.
CAN WE STILL BE REVOLUTIONARIES?
YES... THEY CAN'T TAKE THAT AWAY FROM US.

WHEN THE DAY DID COME FOR MY THESIS DEFENSE IN EARLY JANUARY 1972, I WAS WELL PREPARED. I WANTED A HAPPY PANEL, SO I SACRIFICED PRECIOUS HARD CURRENCY DOLLARS AT THE DIPLO STORE & BOUGHT COOKIES. THEN I FILLED A LARGE THERMOS BOTTLE WITH FRESH DIPLO COFFEE & FACED MY JUDGES AT THE SCHOOL OF LETTERS.

¡DOCTORAS! GOOD AFTERNOON. ¡DOCTOR! ANYTIME YOU SAY.
PLEASE PROCEED, CONNIE! WE ARE ALL EARS!
I SPOKE FOR HOURS ABOUT SERGEI EISENSTEIN & ARGUED EARNESTLY THAT HIS TECHNIQUE & PHILOSOPHY OF MONTAGE COULD BE CONSIDERED A SOPHISTICATED HIGHER FORM OF SOCIALIST REALISM, WORTHY OF PRAISE—MULTI-LAYERED REALISM WITH A SOCIAL CONSCIENCE.
AND NOW, A SMALL COFFEE BREAK. MAY I OFFER YOU A CUP?
WELL DONE! WELL DONE! YOU SHOULD PUT IT ALL IN WRITING, GET IT PUBLISHED!
THE PANEL WAS PLEASED BY THE COFFEE & THE THESIS. I WAS ACTUALLY GOING TO GRADUATE.

SOON I HAD THE PARCHMENT IN MY HANDS. THE FOLLOWING DAY I APPLIED AT IMMIGRATION TO LEAVE THE COUNTRY. THE PAPERWORK TOOK FOREVER. IT WAS DAUNTING TO FIND AN AVAILABLE SHIP THAT COINCIDED WITH THE TIME FRAME OF THE EXIT PERMIT. BUT AT LAST I HAD ALL MY DUCKS LINED UP & BOUGHT A TICKET FROM THE SOVIET BLACK SEA STEAMSHIP LINE.

I DID IT! SO FAR, SO GOOD. NOW ALL THIS HAS TO BE TAKEN APART. I'LL NEED TO MAKE BOXES FOR ALL THE BOOKS, EVERYTHING WE TAKE.
GOYO CAN HELP WITH THAT. WE HAVE TO LOCATE HIM RIGHT AWAY.
I'VE BROUGHT THE FIRST BATCH OF MY BOOKS. WE'LL MIX THEM IN REALLY WELL WITH YOURS.
MARCH 3-28
HE SAID HE WOULD TAKE ROBIN WITH HIM TO SANTA FE. THAT'S A RELIEF.
~leo-brouwer~
BOLA CANTA BOLA
YES, PERFECT. I'LL BRING THE BOOKS LITTLE BY LITTLE, VERY CAREFULLY.
¡AY, GRINGA! I COULDN'T GET A HOLD OF ANY LUMBER AT ALL. THANK GOD I LOCATED THESE NAILS...
WE'LL HAVE TO USE THE BED & THE BOOKCASES. THOSE ARE ALL GOOD BOARDS.
THESE WILL WORK JUST FINE.
¡COÑO! I CAN'T BELIEVE EVERY SINGLE, FUCKING BOOK & MAGAZINE HAS TO BE ACCOUNTED FOR & DECLARED!

A FEW DAYS LATER...
¡UFF!!! THERE! I THINK WE'RE DONE. I KNOW A GUY YOU CAN PAY TO TAKE THE TRUCK FROM HIS WORK & PICK UP THE BOXES.
GOOD. NOW WE HAVE TO SEE HOW WE SNEAK THE REFRIGERATOR OUT FAST & BRING IT TO MARTUGENIA'S HOUSE.
THE CDR MAN CAME AROUND YESTERDAY & SAID THEY WERE GOING TO IMPOUND ALL THE FURNITURE & ELECTRICAL APPLIANCES THAT DON'T GO WITH ME...
LET'S WRAP IT UP AS IF IT WERE GOING WITH YOU ON THE SHIP, BUT WE DROP IT OFF AT ÁNIMAS ON THE WAY.
GOOD PLAN! WE CAN DO THAT WITH ALL THE OTHER STUFF TO GIVE AWAY.

SUCCESS! WE GOT AN OLD FLATBED TRUCK, & WE ALL CLIMBED UP THE BACK & DELIVERED THE BOXES TO CUSTOMS AT THE DOCK A FEW DAYS BEFORE THE SHIP WAS TO LEAVE.

NOW LET'S SEE THIS BOX. WHAT HAVE YOU GOT HERE? HMM. BOOKS, MAGAZINES, MORE BOOKS...
BIEN, COMPAÑERA, THEY ALL SEEM IN ORDER. THEY'LL BE SEALED & STORED RIGHT HERE UNTIL THEY'RE LOADED ONTO YOUR SHIP.

IT WAS TIME FOR MANY GOODBYES, FOR A GOING AWAY PARTY & LOTS OF TEARS.
DE OTRO MODO
SI EN VEZ DE SER ASÍ,
SI LAS COSAS DE ESPALDAS (FIJAS
DESDE LOS SIGLOS)
SE VOLVIESEN DE FRENTE
Y LAS COSAS DE FRENTE (INMUTABLES)
VOLVIESEN LAS ESPALDAS,
Y LO DIESTRO VINIESE A SER SINIESTRO
Y LO IZQUIERDO DERECHO...
NO SÉ CÓMO DECIRLO!

I'M VERY SCARED.
I KNOW. ME TOO. BUT WE'LL MEET UP IN LONDON & MY FRIEND ANN WILL HELP US. YOU HAVE HER ADDRESS & NUMBER.
WE'LL LEAVE AS SOON AS GOYO GETS HERE.
REMEMBER... NOT A WORD TO ANYONE.

OK, LET'S GO. WHEN WE GET THERE, IT'S BETTER THAT WE DON'T GO IN WITH YOU. WE'LL SAY GOODBYE OUTSIDE THE BUILDING.
TAXI

ADUANA
¡ADIÓS, AMORES! I LOVE YOU SO MUCH.

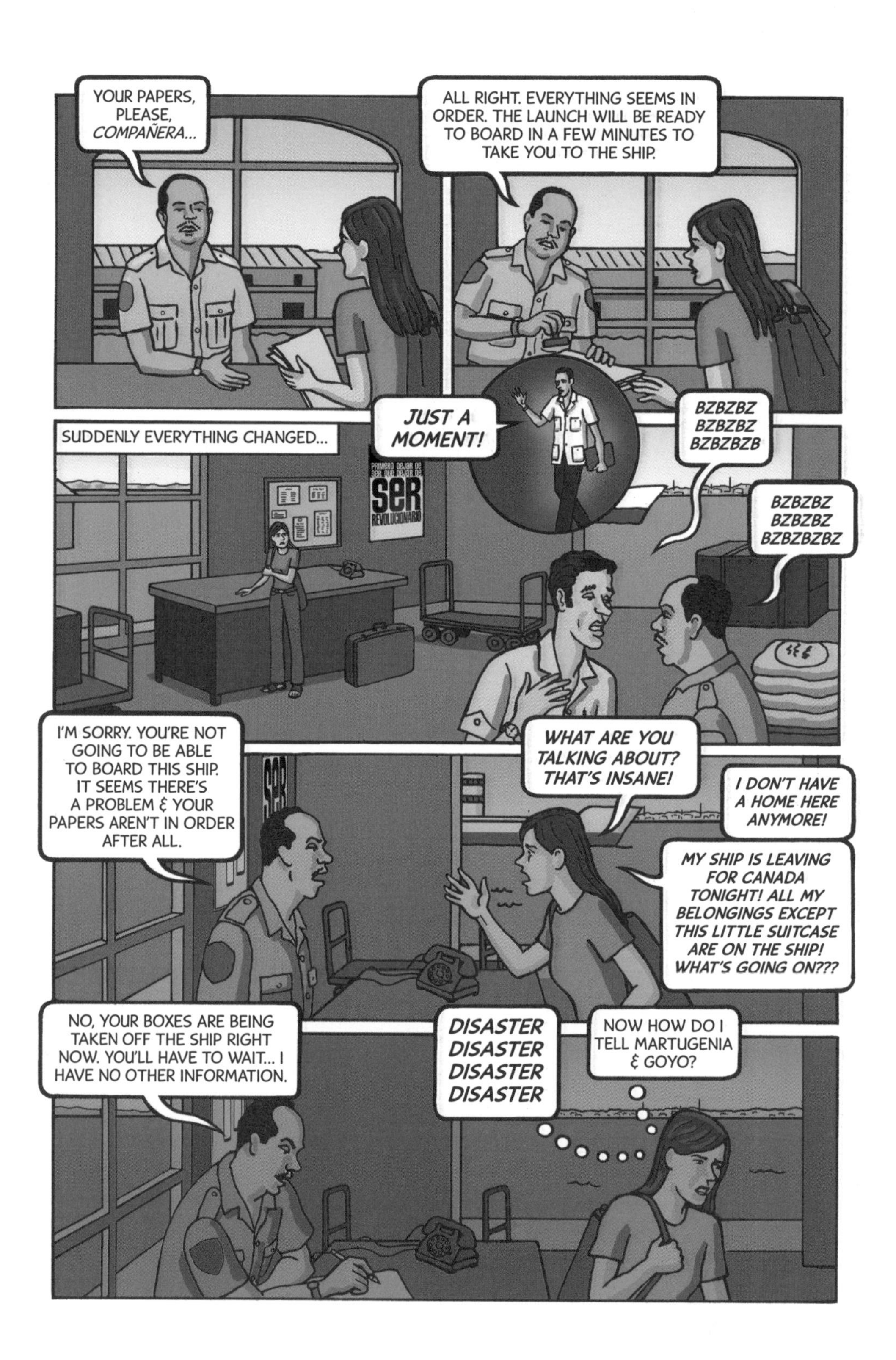
YOUR PAPERS, PLEASE, *COMPAÑERA*...
ALL RIGHT. EVERYTHING SEEMS IN ORDER. THE LAUNCH WILL BE READY TO BOARD IN A FEW MINUTES TO TAKE YOU TO THE SHIP.
SUDDENLY EVERYTHING CHANGED...
JUST A MOMENT!
PRIMERO DEJAR DE SER QUE DEJAR DE SER REVOLUCIONARIO
BZBZBZ BZBZBZ BZBZBZB
BZBZBZ BZBZBZ BZBZBZBZ
I'M SORRY. YOU'RE NOT GOING TO BE ABLE TO BOARD THIS SHIP. IT SEEMS THERE'S A PROBLEM & YOUR PAPERS AREN'T IN ORDER AFTER ALL.
WHAT ARE YOU TALKING ABOUT? THAT'S INSANE!
I DON'T HAVE A HOME HERE ANYMORE!
MY SHIP IS LEAVING FOR CANADA TONIGHT! ALL MY BELONGINGS EXCEPT THIS LITTLE SUITCASE ARE ON THE SHIP! WHAT'S GOING ON???
NO, YOUR BOXES ARE BEING TAKEN OFF THE SHIP RIGHT NOW. YOU'LL HAVE TO WAIT... I HAVE NO OTHER INFORMATION.
DISASTER DISASTER DISASTER DISASTER
NOW HOW DO I TELL MARTUGENIA & GOYO?

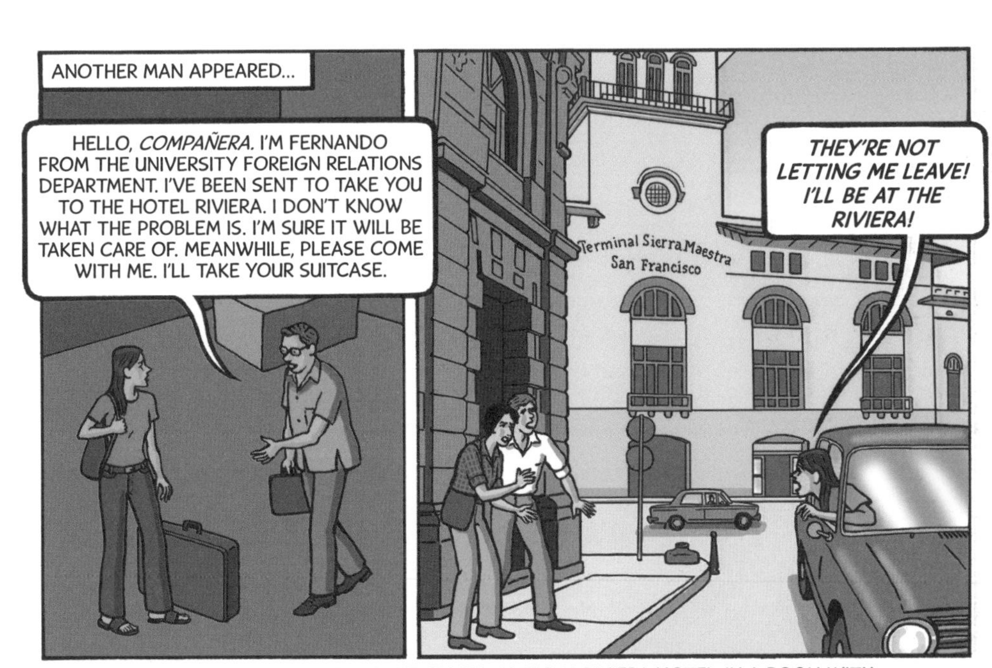
ANOTHER MAN APPEARED...
HELLO, *COMPAÑERA*. I'M FERNANDO FROM THE UNIVERSITY FOREIGN RELATIONS DEPARTMENT. I'VE BEEN SENT TO TAKE YOU TO THE HOTEL RIVIERA. I DON'T KNOW WHAT THE PROBLEM IS. I'M SURE IT WILL BE TAKEN CARE OF. MEANWHILE, PLEASE COME WITH ME. I'LL TAKE YOUR SUITCASE.
Terminal Sierra Maestra
San Francisco
THEY'RE NOT LETTING ME LEAVE! I'LL BE AT THE RIVIERA!

IN TOTAL SHOCK, I WAS INSTALLED IN THE ONCE LUXURIOUS RIVIERA HOTEL, IN A ROOM WITH A MAGNIFICENT VIEW OF THE SEA.

I PAID FOR MY PASSAGE ON THAT SHIP! YOU'D BETTER GET ME ON THE NEXT AVAILABLE FREIGHTER! THIS IS OUTRAGEOUS!
I'M SORRY. I DON'T KNOW ANYTHING ABOUT IT. YOU'LL BE NOTIFIED. MEANWHILE, YOU CAN SIGN FOR ALL YOUR MEALS & THE UNIVERSITY FOREIGN RELATIONS DEPARTMENT WILL TAKE CARE OF IT.
Habana Riviera
GOODBYE, COMPAÑERA!
OH, JESUS! I HOPE THEY'RE WAITING OUTSIDE!

YOU'RE THERE!
TELL US WHAT HAPPENED!
SHIT! WHAT DOES THIS MEAN?
I'M NOT ALLOWED TO LEAVE ON THAT SHIP. THEY SAID IT WOULD BE A FEW DAYS. I'LL HAVE TO GET THE NEXT AVAILABLE ONE.
COME ON. I'LL GO WITH YOU TWO TO ÁNIMAS, THEN I'M OFF TO SANTA FE.

WE WAITED WITH OUR TEETH CLENCHED, HOLED UP AT ÁNIMAS. I SPENT LITTLE TIME AT THE HOTEL. AFTER ALL THE GOODBYES, I COULDN'T BEAR TO SEE ANYONE ELSE.

AMOR, IF THE SCHOLARSHIP COMES THROUGH & YOU'RE STILL HERE... I'LL HAVE TO LEAVE & NOT KNOW...
I CAN'T DO IT ALONE. WHERE WOULD I GO? WITH NO MONEY, NO ONE...
YEAH... THEN WAIT FOR ME IN LONDON. THEY'LL HAVE TO LET ME GO AT SOME POINT.
ANN... MY MOTHER'S FRIEND..?
THERE'S NO GUARANTEE. WHO KNOW'S IF SHE'D HELP?
IF I HAVEN'T HEARD FROM YOU, WHILE I'M STILL IN LONDON, THAT YOU'RE OUT OF THE COUNTRY BY THE TIME MY SCHOLARSHIP IS OVER... I'LL HAVE TO COME BACK. I DON'T HAVE A CHOICE.
THEY MAY NOT LET YOU LEAVE UNTIL I'M BACK. YOU KNOW THEY'RE CAPABLE.
TOGETHER IN LONDON!
YES!
A COUPLE OF WEEKS LATER, THE SCHOLARSHIP CAME THROUGH. ROMELIA WORKED TIRELESSLY SEWING OUTFITS TO WEAR ABROAD. THEN THE DAY CAME & MARTUGENIA LEFT FOR THE AIRPORT.

I RETREATED TO THE HOTEL. THE DAYS TURNED INTO WEEKS & THEN INTO MONTHS. I TANNED MYSELF ON THE SUNROOF OF THE PENTHOUSE SPA, ALONG WITH THE CABARET DANCERS WHO GOT THEIR BEAUTY TREATMENTS THERE.

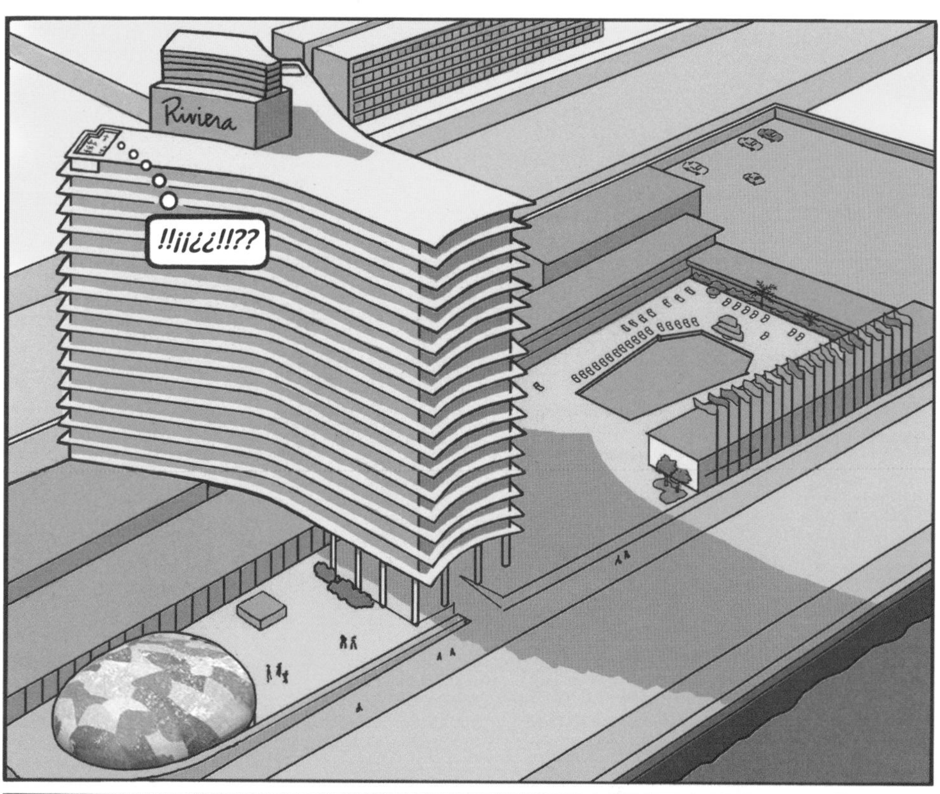
Riviera
!!¡¡¿¿!!??

FINALLY, THE TIME WAS UP. NO PAPERS, NO SHIP & MARTUGENIA CAME HOME.
I KNEW YOU'D COME BACK!
TU DEBER

THREE DAYS LATER, A MAN FROM THE UNIVERSITY'S FOREIGN RELATIONS DEPARTMENT CALLED & TOLD ME TO PACK UP. MY PAPERS WERE APPROVED FOR DEPARTURE, A SHIP WAS AVAILABLE & HE WOULD TAKE ME TO THE DOCK IN THE MORNING.

I RACED TO ÁNIMAS, I DIDN'T DARE USE THE PHONE.

THEY'RE PUTTING ME ON A SHIP TOMORROW.
WHAT CAN WE DO?
970
NOTHING. THEY'VE TRICKED US. THERE'S NO WAY OUT OF THIS.
IF I CAN'T STAND IT & I TELL YOU, WILL YOU COME BACK?
IF I CAN...

I RETURNED TO THE HOTEL AT DAWN & ONCE AGAIN WE MET AT THE DOCK, NOW WITH ÁNGEL LUIS FOR COVER. THERE WAS NO DELAY. ÁNGEL WAS ALLOWED ON THE SMALL BOAT THAT FERRIED ME TO A CUBAN FREIGHTER, THE "LUIS ARCOS BERGNES," MOORED OFFSHORE IN THE BAY.

SOMEHOW... SOMEDAY...
GOODBYE, MY SEAFARING RAT...

GOODBYE, GRINGA!
GOODBYE, MY HAVANA...
THE SHIP GLIDED BETWEEN EL CASTILLO DE SAN SALVADOR DE LA PUNTA & EL CASTILLO DE LOS TRES REYES DEL MORRO. MY YOUTH DREW TO A CLOSE & I HEADED NORTH.

Fin

EPILOGUE

It took several years for me to sort out what had happened. Why had the Cuban authorities bothered to retain me and put me up in a hotel until Martugenia returned from England that summer of 1972? Why such attention to an unimportant foreign student and a Cuban university instructor? It slowly dawned on me that there was one person who had been completely invested in Martugenia's return and who had always suspected me of being a threat—Romelia, Martugenia's mother. She couldn't understand the English we spoke as we urgently schemed to run away together to England, but she watched as Martugenia slowly removed, one by one, her most precious belongings, her books, and spirited them out of her house to my little room in Nuevo Vedado. Romelia, as president of her local Comité de Defensa de la Revolución, was well versed in surveillance and had contacts with officials in high places in the district offices of the CDR of Centro Habana. A request, a demand, for my retention was well within her powers. Decades later, in 2000, I visited Havana and Romelia gave me a poem she had written as a kind of apology for having judged me as a bad influence on her daughter.

Martugenia continued to teach at the University of Havana. She became a popular and controversial professor of English literature, specializing in Shakespeare. From a distance, we watched over each other's lives, divided by the Cuban-American Cold War. For over 40 years, we kept up a warm friendship and correspondence, often via trusted travelers, sometimes the unreliable mail. In 1990 she moved to Mexico, where she met the partner whom she lived with until she died of advanced lung cancer and emphysema in September 2015.

After a few tense months in Croton-on-Hudson with my parents and my brother and sister, I settled in New York City in 1972. My degree in history of art from the University of Havana was useless, so I found a job at a women's health clinic for a year while I studied commercial art at night at Parson's School of Design. Then I got a job in an advertising firm in the art and production department. Later I became a freelance designer and illustrator for the rest of my working years.

My mother Lenore and my stepfather Ted, upon their return in 1968, rejoined the Communist Party USA and quickly put Ted's firing in Havana behind them. Ted got a job as an electronics engineer at Mount Sinai Hospital in Manhattan through his connections from his days at Swarthmore. He retired after 10 years and moved with Lenore back to California, where they lived on a generous pension for over 30 years. Despite the good life they had there, they were very bitter that the Soviet bloc had collapsed instead of American capitalism. But as a veteran of the Abraham Lincoln Brigade in the Spanish Civil War, Ted kept his fist in the air, defiant to the end, with his death in 2008.

After Cuba, Kevin and Nikki had a difficult time adjusting to life in Croton-on Hudson—especially Nikki. After high school, easygoing and gregarious Kevin made his way to California, worked his way through college, got a law degree, and became the chief operating officer of a motorcycle parts company. He lives and thrives in California with his wife and their beautiful twins.

Nikki had a more difficult time. She experimented with LSD in high school and became seriously estranged from Lenore. She fought with our parents about where to go to college and ultimately succeeded, attending MIT as an engineering student. While a graduate student there, about to receive her master's degree, she committed suicide at the age of 28, heartbroken from a bad romance.

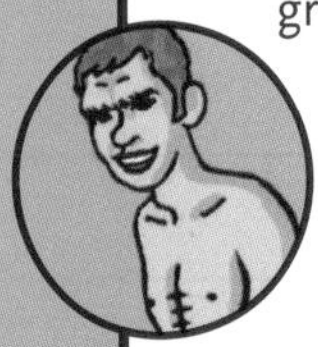

Goyo, more formally known as Pedro, died the same way Martugenia had, one year later, in San Sebastian, Spain. Juan continues his life in Cuba.

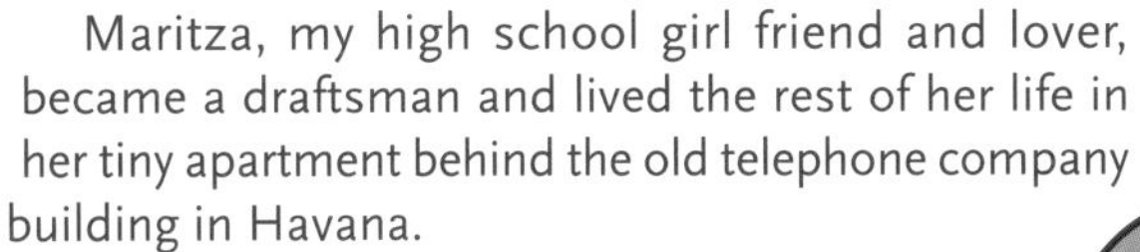

Maritza, my high school girl friend and lover, became a draftsman and lived the rest of her life in her tiny apartment behind the old telephone company building in Havana.

Monica, Bruno, his boyfriend, and the rest of their group all left the country and went into exile, like so many other gay people who had been mercilessly persecuted for the sin of not conforming to the revolutionary social norms.

My love for Cuba, for my friends there, and for the aching beauty of Havana, never wavered, despite the decay and disillusionment of the ensuing years. I was lucky to find a new life in New York, where I have lived, for thirty years and counting, with my partner Stacy and numerous mellow cats. Our beautiful daughter Sophia visits often.

ACKNOWLEDGMENTS

Many times since I left Cuba in 1972 friends and acquaintances have suggested that I write about my life there during the 1960s revolution. At last, in 2008 I decided to do it. I dedicated almost ten years to this project. From beginning to end, my friends and family helped me with valuable suggestions and moral support. I want to express my infinite gratitude to them now.

Stacy Pies, my beloved spouse of over thirty years, made it possible for me to dedicate years of work to create this book. Her generosity and belief in the project gave me the space and courage to carry this project through to the end. Sophia, our daughter, a young writer and editor, helped me from the beginning with her wise and constructive ideas and criticisms. I also want to thank Joshua Macey, Sophia's husband, who with a sharp eye and big heart gave me his impressions from the start.

The writer Dorothy Allison, our great friend, was the first person who made me believe that I could and should write this book, which until then was only a distant dream. I will be forever grateful to Barbara Jones, a friend from the publishing world, for her enthusiasm and for generously sharing her time and knowledge about how to navigate the U.S. publishing waters. Professors Yolanda Martínez-San Miguel of the University of Miami and Frances Negrón-Muntaner of Columbia University interviewed me in 2004 for an article about Lourdes Casal and the origin of her poem "Para Ana Veltfort." Their interest, friendship, and support helped me revisit my Cuban past and contributed to my decision to embark on an account of those years in Cuba. My friends Karin and Davis Thomas have, since the 1970s, tried to convince me to record my memories.

They read a draft with great care and offered me their generous comments. I also owe a special thank-you to Laura Slatkin and Alejandro Velasco for their support and faith in this project.

Alysa Nahmias—filmmaker, director, and producer of the celebrated documentary *Unfinished Spaces*—has supported this project with singular focus and vision from the very start and made it possible for this book to find a home at Redwood Press. I want to give a very big thank-you to John Loomis—architect, educator, and author of *Revolution of Forms: Cuba's Forgotten Art Schools*, published by Princeton Architectural Press (2011). John Loomis learned of my book through Alysa and was essential in finding a venue for the U.S. edition. I am so very grateful for his successful effort!

My Cuban friends in Havana, Lourdes Cairo and Josefina de Diego, helped me enormously with the photos that I needed as background references, and I am grateful always for their unwavering support. Marta Eugenia Rodríguez, Martugenia in the book, allowed me full use of the material in her detailed diary and official report from our time in the Sierra Maestra mountains with the University of Havana in 1967. She always supported this project with great interest and read drafts to confirm or correct various anecdotes and history until shortly before her death in 2015. Minerva Salado—Cuban poet, journalist, and educator and a close friend and veteran of those years at the University of Havana—gave the book her blessing after a generous critical reading, as did Rita Abreu, the Mexican television and radio journalist.

Without Pio Serrano—poet, translator, founder of Editorial Verbum, and friend since our days in the 1960s as students at the School of Letters at the University of Havana—the original Spanish edition of this book would not exist. I showed him the initial illustrated manuscript in 2016, and he took on the project of editing and revising my adequate Spanish into fluid and elegant prose. We worked together tirelessly until the successful publication of *Adiós mi Habana* by Editorial Verbum in Madrid in 2017.

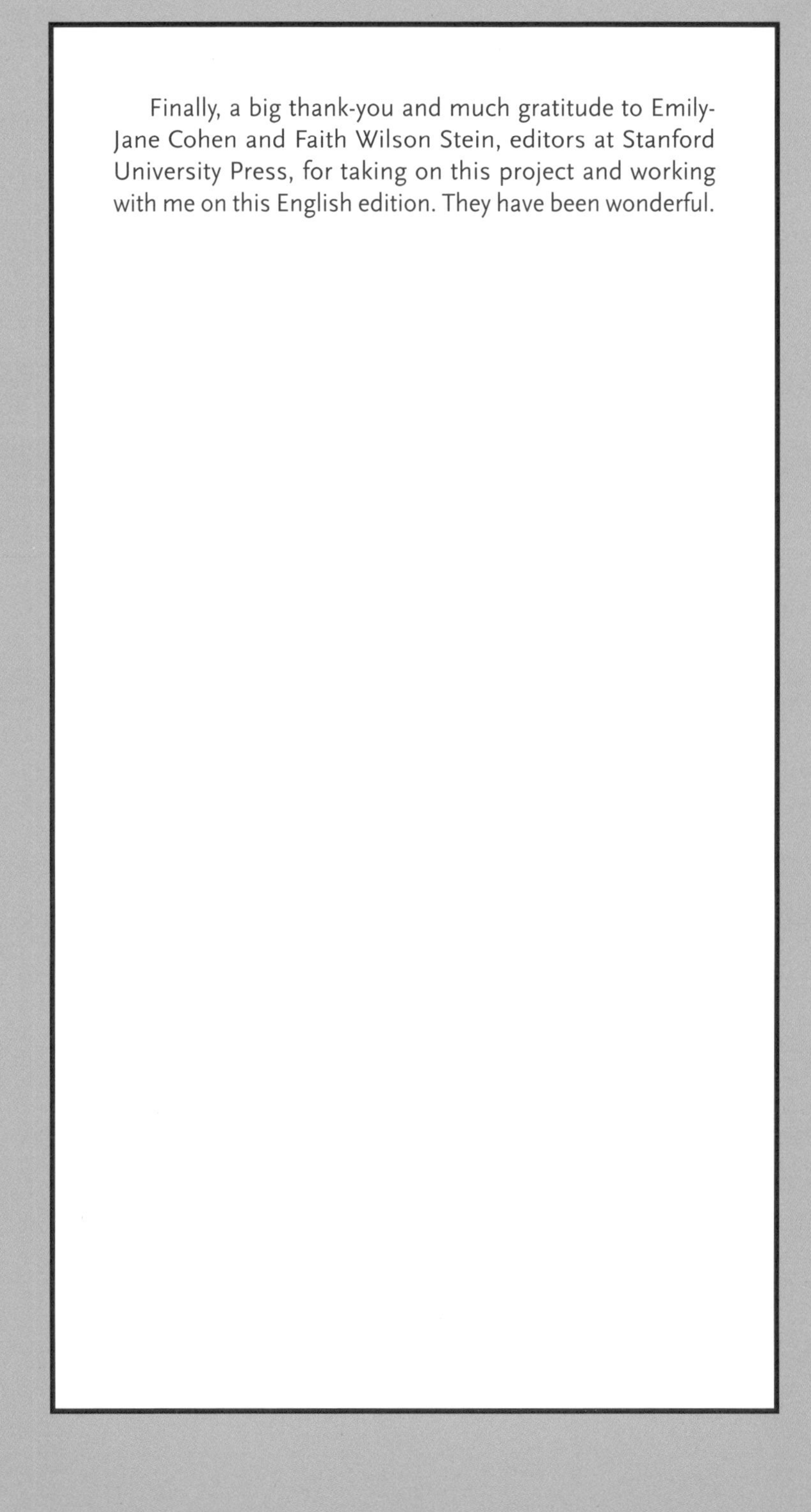

Finally, a big thank-you and much gratitude to Emily-Jane Cohen and Faith Wilson Stein, editors at Stanford University Press, for taking on this project and working with me on this English edition. They have been wonderful.

NOTES & SOURCES

1. HAVANA BAY

9 Front page of *The Daily Worker*, April 28, 1937.

11 J. Edgar Hoover, Joseph McCarthy, Chairman Mao Zedong, and Ethel and Julius Rosenberg (clockwise, starting top left).

16 "Powell Trial Opens," *San Francisco Chronicle*, January 27, 1959.

17 Fidel Castro with *New York Times* journalist Herbert L. Matthews, Fidel and Raul Castro, Che Guevara, Camilo Cienfuegos (clockwise, starting top right).

19
- "Battle of City Hall," *San Francisco Chronicle*, May 14, 1960.
- Front page of the *Huntsville Times*, April 12, 1961.

26 Groups associated with the overthrow of Fulgencio Batista in January 1959:
- El Partido Socialista Popular (PSP), the Communist Party prior to 1959.
- El Directorio Estudiantil Revolucionario (Student Revolutionary Directorate), an urban revolutionary organization.
- El Movimiento 26 de Julio (M-26-7, the 26th of July Movement), Fidel Castro's guerrilla forces.

28–29 Castro's speech on May Day, 1962, at the Plaza de la Revolución.

30 Print of *The Last Supper* by Leonardo da Vinci.

31 Film stills from *Modern Times* (1936), written and directed by Charlie Chaplin.

32 Cover of *The Well of Loneliness* (1928), by Radclyffe Hall.

39 The San Cristobal missile site, based on an aerial photograph taken on October 14, 1962, by U.S. reconnaissance aircraft.

40
- "Muerte al Invasor" ("Death to the Invader"), poster issued in 1960 by El Ministerio de la Fuerzas Armadas Revolucionarias (MINFAR, the Ministry of the Revolutionary Armed Forces).

- Adlai Stevenson at the UN Security Council in October 25, 1962, showing aerial photos of Soviet nuclear weapons in Cuba.
- "We Blockade Cuba Arms," *New York Daily News*, October 23, 1962.

42 "Reds Agree to Scrap Bases in Cuba," *Washington Post*, October 29, 1962.

47
- *Materialismo Histórico, la Comprensión Materialista de la Historia* (Dirección de Educación General, La Habana, 1962), translated from the Russian original of O. W. Kuusinen et al.'s *Fundamentals of Marxism–Leninism*.
- *Materialismo Dialectico,* (Dirección de Educación General, La Habana, 1962), translated from the Russian original of O. W. Kuusinen et al.'s *Fundamentals of Marxism–Leninism*.

49 The Marquitos Trial.

2. THE UNIVERSITY OF HAVANA

59 Soviet postcards sent in October 1964 from Moscow to Havana.

64 Film posters for *Ivan the Terrible* (1944) and *Battleship Potemkin* (1925), directed by Sergei Eisenstein, and *The Forty-First* (1956), directed by Grigori Chukhrai.

65
- Che Guevara, *Socialism and Man in Cuba* (New York: Pathfinder Press, 1978), pp. 18, 20.
- Quote from Che Guevara's speech in Algeria on February 24, 1965.

68 Press photo of a group of foreigners at the School of Letters taken in 1965.

69 Film still from *Vivre sa Vie* (1962), directed by Jean-Luc Godard.

70 Cover of *Mella* magazine, May 31, 1965

71 "La Gran Batalla del Estudiantado," *Mella*, May 31, 1965, pp. 2, 3. Signed by the UJC (Union of Young Communists) and the UES (Union of Secondary Students).

72 Cartoons by Luis Wilson Varela, "El Flautista de Hamelin," and Aristide Pumariega, "No sé que tiene de malo esa gente," *Mella*, May 31, 1965, p. 4.

73 Virgilio Martinez, "Vida y Milagros de Florito Volandero," *Mella*, May 24, 1965, pp. 20, 21.

74
- "Alerta," poster by Jesus Forjans issued by the Comisión de Orientación Revolucionaria in 1962.
- "26 de Julio Fidel Castro," poster (1959).
- Cover of Bob Dylan album, *The Times They Are a-Changin'* (1964).

75–76 Jose Mario, "Allen Ginsberg en La Habana," *Mundo Nuevo* (April 1969), pp. 48–54.

77 • "Nuestra Opinión," editorial, *Alma Mater*, June 5, 1965, p. 2.
• Vietnamese postage stamps and media images of the Vietnam War.

78 Fidel Castro's speech on the Escalinata at the University of Havana, March 13, 1963.

79 "10 de Mayo todos con Fidel a la Plaza de la Revolución," poster issued by the Confederación de Trabajadores de Cuba in 1965.

81 Virgilio Martinez, "Las Caperucitas se Cosechan en Primavera," *Mella*, c. June 1965, p. 20, and "Hay que Hervirlos," *Mella*, June 7, 1965, p. 20.

83 • "UMAP: Forja de Ciudadanos," *El Mundo* April 14, 1966.
• A UMAP camp in the upper left corner based on a sketch by "el pintor Anibal," an inmate, as shown in the film *Improper Conduct* (1984), a documentary by Néstor Almendros and Orlando Jiménez Leal.

84 Birth of the Communist Party newspaper *Granma*, which merged *Hoy*, the official newspaper of the PSP, and *Revolución*, the official newspaper of the M-26-7.

85 • Posters for the Tricontinental Conference issued by the Organización de Solidaridad de los Pueblos de Africa, Asia y América Latina (OSPAAAP): "Vietnam Vencerá," "Laos," "Jornada de Solidaridad con Angola."
• Tricontinental commemorative stamp.

86 "Comandante en Jefe Ordene!" poster issued by the Organizacíon Continental Latinoamericana y Caribeña de Estudiantes (OCLAE) in 1966.

87 "Carta de Pablo Neruda a los Cubanos," *Política*, August 15, 1966.

88 Virgilio Martinez, "Pucho," *Mella*, October 4, 1965. Pucho, representing the Cuban "common man," pees on modern art.

3. THE SIERRA MAESTRA

This chapter is based on Martugenia's detailed field report, which she preserved and kindly shared with me for this book, as well as on my own field notes. All of us were required to write reports and hand them in to the school authorities after our return to Havana.

92 Carlos Amat, "Sociología e Investigación Social, Cuba: Un Laboratorio para la Investigación Social," *Universidad de La Habana*, no. 190 (April–June 1968), p. 74.

93 • Posters issued by the Consejo Nacional de Cultura: *Las Preciosas Ridículas de Moliere*, Teatro Nacional de Guiñol, 1963; *Las Cebollas Mágicas*, Elenco Nacional de Guiñol, 1963; *El Canto de la Cigarra*, Teatro Nacional de Guiñol, 1963; *La Caperucita Roja*, Teatro Nacional de Guiñol, 1964; *El Maleficio de la Mariposa*, Teatro Nacional de Guiñol, 1963.
• A print of Vincent van Gogh, *The Starry Night*.

94 Carlos Amat, "Sociología e Investigación Social, Cuba" *Universidad de La Habana*, no. 190 (Comisión de Extensión Universitaria, April–June 1968), p. 75.

99 From the poem "Dame la Mano," by Gabriela Mistral, set to music by Teresita Fernandez, who often sang it at El Coctel and other Cuban nightspots in the 1960s.

103 From *La Margarita Blanca* (n.d.), by the dramatist Luis Interián.

108
- "Hay golpes en la vida. . .": César Vallejo, *Los Heraldos Negros: Antología Poética de Cesar Vallejo* (La Habana: Biblioteca del Pueblo, 1962), p. 15
- "Puedo Escribir los Versos más Tristes. . .": Pablo Neruda, "Sonnet 20," *20 Poemas de Amor y una Canción Desesperada* (Buenos Aires: Editorial Losada, Buenos Aires, 1975).

120 The Salon de Mayo, an art exhibition that took place in the summer of 1967. On July 17, a hundred painters, cartoonists, sculptors, writers, and critics, both foreign and Cuban, began to paint a 10- by 5.5-meter collective mural for the event, a piece of which is depicted here.
- Pages from the Salon de Mayo exhibition catalog (Edición de los Talleres de Granma, 1967), cover, pp. 5, 7.
- Postage stamp reproductions of the paintings of Salon participants, including Joan Miró, Serge Poliakoff, Roberto Matta, and René Magritte.
- Cover of the wildly popular album *Orquesta Cubana de Música Moderna* (1967), with Chucho Valdés, Paquito de Rivera, Carlos Emilio Morales, Pucho Escalante, Oscar Valdés, and Guillermo Barreto. The group was soon marginalized for being "too American."

123 "Despidió Fidel a los Estudiantes Universitarios que van al Agro," *Granma*, August 5, 1967.

4. "MORGAN!" & THE MALECÓN

126 Film still from the movie *Morgan!*, a British film directed by Karel Reisz, 1966.

134 One of many court summonses issued by the Juzgado Correcional Sección 8va.

140 "If I ever find out you are actually a homosexual, you two will have fooled me like *un chino*." This expression used by Carlos Amat, "engañado como un chino," is a reference to nineteenth-century Chinese who were falsely lured to Cuba and were practically enslaved as indentured servants.

5. THE REVOLUTIONARY OFFENSIVE

146
- José Antonio Portuondo, "Significación del Congreso Cultural de La Habana," Revista Universidad de La Habana, no. 189 (1968), p. 16.

- President Osvaldo Dorticós's speech at the Preparatory Seminar, October 1967.
- *Discurso en la Clausura del Seminario Preparatorio al Congreso Cultural de La Habana, RC-Revolución y Cultura*, November 30, 1967, no. 3 (Instituto del Libro), p. 16.
- Che Guevara in Bolivia.

147 Raul Castro's report to the Central Committee of the Communist Party, broadcast on national television, June 24, 1968.

150–51 "En Paz Descansen Cabarets, Cabaretuchos y Similares," Ofensiva-Suplemento especial, *Alma Mater*, March 1968, p. 4.

152 "Más Revolución," *Vida Universitaria*, no. 210 (March–April, 1968), a bimonthly published by the University of Havana.

155
- Front page of *Granma*, August 24, 1968.
- Fidel Castro's speech on national television, August 23, 1968.
- Media images of the Soviet invasion.

156 Fidel Castro's speech, October 29, 1968, on the eighth anniversary of the Comités de Defensa de La Revolución.

159
- Three articles by Leopoldo Ávila: "Las Provocaciones de Padilla," *Verde Olivo*, November 10, 1968; "Sobre Algunas Corrientes de la Crítica y la Literatura en Cuba," November 24, 1968; "El Pueblo es el Forjador, Defensor y Sostén de la Cultura," December 1, 1968. *Verde Olivo* was the official magazine of Las Fuerzas Armadas de la Revolución (FAR, the Revolutionary Armed Forces).
- Cover of Heberto Padilla, *Fuera del juego* (La Unión de Escritores y Artistas de Cuba, 1968).
- Cover of Anton Arrufat, *Los Siete Contra Tebas* (La Unión de Escritores y Artistas de Cuba, 1968).

160
- Film still from *P.M.* (1961), directed by Sabá Cabrera Infante and Orlando Jiménez Leal.
- "Cinemateca de Cuba," poster by Rafael Morante (1961).
- Cover of *Verde Olivo*, November 10, 1968.

162 The poem 390 from *El Libro de las Mil Noches y una Noche: Traducción Directa y Literal del Arabe por J. C. Mardrus*, trans. Vicente Blasco Ibáñez (Valencia: Prometeo, 1899).

This is my literal translation (with no poetic pretensions) of how we read the Spanish version of this poem in *The Thousand and One Nights* as an ode to our forbidden private lives:

> Free houris and virgins,
> We laugh at all suspicious thoughts,
> We are the untouchable gazelles of Mecca!
> The cretins accuse us of vices
> because our eyes are languid
> and our words so enchanting!
> We flaunt indecent gestures
> that lure pious gentlemen into deviate perversions!

6. A FAMILY VISIT

175 Kenneth Grahame, *The Wind in the Willows*, illustrated by Ernest H. Shepard (New York: Charles Scribner's Sons, 1954), pp. 174, 176, 183, 184, 186.

176 Portraits of Vladimir Lenin and Leonid Brezhnev.

178
- "Peace Is a Human Right," print by Emmy Lou Packard.
- Images of Paul Robeson and Ho Chi Minh.

179 "Pro Music Festival Presents: 'Tell 'em Groucho sent ya,' " featuring Zappa, The Mothers of Invention, Vanilla Fudge, and Beacon Street Union, at Rhode Island Auditorium, produced by Vik Armen & Alberta Productions. Poster created by Mad Peck Studios for show on August 8, 1969.

180–81 Covers of the underground newspaper *Rat Subterranean News*, October 8, 1969; June 1, 1968; March 9, 1970.

182 Covers of Bob Dylan albums *The Freewheelin' Bob Dylan* (1963), *Bringing It All Back Home* (1965), *Blonde on Blonde* (1966), and *John Wesley Harding* (1967).

183 Dick Blakeslee, "Passing Through" (1948).

185 Poster for *M*A*S*H** (1970), directed by Robert Altman.

186 Poster of Vladimir Lenin.

187 N. V. Gordeev, *Bolshoi Kremlevskii dvorets* (Moscow: Sovetskaia Rossiia, 1967).

7. THE LAST SHIP

192 Media images of the murder of Dan Mitrione, the torture of a *tupamaro*, and Cuban sugarcane fields during the 1970 harvest.

193 Portrait of Kim Il Sung.

194
- Media image of the young Kim Il Sung.
- "Tu Deber es Tener tu Cuadra Siempre Limpia," poster issued by the Comisión de Ornato Regional.

195 ICAIC posters for *Aventuras de Juan Quinquín* (1967) and *El Joven Rebelde* (1961), both directed by Julio Garcia Espinoza.

197
- Heberto Padilla, quoted in Lourdes Casal, *El Caso Padilla: Literatura y Revolución en Cuba; Documentos* (New York: Ediciones Nueva Atlantida, 1971), pp. 79–82.
- Cover of *Casa de las Americas*, no. 65–66 (1971), the issue dedicated to the First National Congress of Education and Culture.
- Quote from the Declaration of the Congress.